COLLABORATION
UNCOVERED

COLLABORATION UNCOVERED

The Forgotten, the Assumed, and the Unexamined in Collaborative Education

*Edited by Merle Richards, Anne Elliott,
Vera Woloshyn and Coral Mitchell*

BERGIN & GARVEY
Westport, Connecticut • London

Library of Congress Cataloging-in-Publication Data

Collaboration uncovered : the forgotten, the assumed, and the unexamined in collaborative education / edited by Merle Richards . . . [et al.].
    p. cm.
   Includes bibliographical references and index.
   ISBN 0–89789–784–6 (alk. paper)
   1. Education—Research. 2. Group work in education. 3. University cooperation.
  4. College-school cooperation. I. Richards, Merle, 1941–
  LB1028.C57214   2001
  378.1'04—dc21   00–065992

British Library Cataloguing in Publication Data is available.

Library of Congress Catalog Card Number: 00–065992
ISBN: 0–89789–784–6

First published in 2001

Bergin & Garvey, 88 Post Road West, Westport, CT 06881
An imprint of Greenwood Publishing Group, Inc.
www.greenwood.com

Printed in the United States of America

The paper used in this book complies with the Permanent Paper Standard issued by the National Information Standards Organization (Z39.48–1984).

10 9 8 7 6 5 4 3 2 1

Contents

Acknowledgments

It probably goes without saying that any book on collaboration is a collaborative effort. That is certainly true of this one, and we would like to acknowledge the contributions that have been made to the completion of this project. We first want to thank the authors of the chapters for sharing their experiences and insights with us. Without their willingness to write about their work and their ability to meet some rather tight deadlines, this book would not have happened. We want also to acknowledge the contributions made by all the school and university people who have served as collaborative partners with the authors of the chapters. Their stories have brought each of us to deeper insights about the contested terrain that we call collaboration. Our deep appreciation goes to each individual who is represented in the stories told in these pages.

The Centre on Collaborative Research at Brock University represents the research heart and academic home for the editors of this book as well as for many of the chapter contributors. In addition to the four editors, the following individuals have been members of the Centre over the years: Sharon Abbey, Joyce Castle, Susan Drake, Ellen Foster, Brigitte Harris, Bev Haskins, Janet Killins, Karen Krug, Norah Morgan, Nancy Murray, Cecilia Reynolds, Ruth Scott, Alice Shutz, Helen Stewart, Susan Sydor, Adele Thomas, Andrea Toepell, and Arja Vainio-Mattila. Additionally, several graduate students have served the Centre as administrative and research assistants over the years. To each of these individuals we extend our gratitude and appreciation for the insights, encouragement, assistance, and support they have provided.

Technical assistance for the completion of the manuscript has been provided by Leigh Golden. We are grateful for her expertise with word processing, APA formatting, and conventional writing. The book has also benefited from the efforts of Jane Garry, from the Greenwood Publishing Group, who oversaw the publishing aspects of the project and helped us bring the book to completion.

Finally, we wish to note the contribution made by Brock University, the institution at which the Centre on Collaborative Research is located. Through the allocation of space and the provision of research assistant funds, the university has provided financial support to the Centre as well as to this project.

Introduction

Anne Elliott

A climate of change and reform, marked by the entry into the twenty-first century, has demanded that educators and researchers establish strong collaborative connections so that theory and practice can inform each other and ultimately improve educational practices (Clark & Clark, 1996; Fullan, 1999; Leiberman, 1995; Schecter & Parkhurst, 1993). No longer can either teachers or researchers operate effectively in isolation (Hargreaves, 1994). Rather, through the process of collaboration, people with a variety of strengths and backgrounds can collectively address substantive issues in education and ensure that the results are disseminated over diverse educational cultures. For the past 50 years, this orientation toward collaboration has increased academic debate about how to promote collegiality among educators to establish a truly collaborative educational community. This vision of a collaborative community has also given rise to much reflective discussion and research (Bickel & Hattrup, 1995; Castle & Giblin, 1992; Elliott & Woloshyn, 1997; Mitchell & Boak, 1997). Often, this discussion has focused on how to create authentic collaborative processes. Less often, but just as valuably, the conversation has included the inherent pitfalls of such processes.

DEFINITION OF COLLABORATION

Perhaps not surprisingly, a precise definition for collaboration has been difficult to achieve. This confusion has sometimes led to a superficial use of the term, particularly when it is applied to any project in which people work together. Some have suggested that collaboration is synonymous with "partnership" or "cooperation" (Clift & Say, 1988). Others have suggested that the collaborative phenomenon occurs when people from different settings work together to solve problems or to create a product (Clift, Veal, Holland, & McCarthy, 1995). Still others have emphasized equity, declaring that collaboration involves partners working equitably on an ongoing basis to achieve mutually beneficial goals (Frymier, Flynn, & Flynn, 1992; Glickman, 1985). For instance, Tchombe (1997) states that collaborative partnerships are joint efforts that involve the pooling and sharing of expertise for the attainment of a common set of goals. Nevertheless, a precise and mutually agreed-upon term remains elusive. Even after decades of study, the term "collaboration" remains somewhat tentative in nature, with its definition often being dependent upon the context of a particular experience.

ESTABLISHING A CENTER TO STUDY COLLABORATION

Many of the authors of this book are members of the Centre on Collaborative Research (CCR), and, as such, have extensive experience researching the collaborative process. The CCR was formed in the early 1990s by a group of 11 female university researchers at Brock University's Faculty of Education, located in St. Catharines, Ontario, Canada. The primary purpose of this group was to study the phenomenon of collaboration. Specifically, the group set out to investigate and examine examples of collaborative research in multiple and diverse educational contexts. They were also determined to develop a deeper understanding of the collaborative process and to develop models or frameworks that would exemplify this process. A secondary purpose of the CCR was to facilitate the sharing of information and ideas by breaking traditional patterns of isolation and competitiveness in the university culture and by building strong school–university partnerships. Finally, the CCR decided to observe its own growth in order to increase understandings about how such a collaborative group develops an identity (Richards & Schutz, 1997).

From the beginning, the group was encouraged to identify joint purposes and establish a method of sharing values and understandings. Metaphor was one vehicle used to help create this vision (Stewart, 1997). One such metaphor, which is discussed at length in the final chapter of this book, is of a sailboat. On this sailboat, everyone is able to take a turn serving as captain as the vessel sails through rough water with all hands working in harmony to ensure a safe voyage. Many of the chapters included in the book reflect the work done in the CCR, with the final chapter using and extending the sailing metaphor.

WHAT IS KNOWN ABOUT COLLABORATION

Over the past decade, researchers have identified several characteristics of successful collaborative partnerships. For many collaborative endeavors, caring human relationships have been perceived as central for success (Elliott & Woloshyn, 1997). Building rapport among partners has been identified as an essential element for creating mutual understanding and sensitivity to the diverse cultures of coresearchers. As people make meaningful interpersonal connections, an ethic of care rooted in receptivity, relatedness, and responsiveness is created, which serves as a solid foundation for working together (Noddings, 1984). Several researchers have pointed out that building such rapport takes time, energy, and commitment if it is to be accomplished in a meaningful way (Bickel & Hattrup, 1995; Mitchell & Boak, 1997). Hollingsworth (1992) believes that the relational aspect of collaboration is best achieved by the sharing of prior experiences, particularly as they relate to the project. Schratz (1993) agrees, stating that early conversations should focus on "collective self-reflection" in order to create a space for the expression of fears, misunderstandings, and inferential assumptions. At this time, language can be negotiated and clarified, so that a shared language will emerge naturally in the context of meaningful conversation that provides the basis for ongoing dialogue that will continue throughout the project (Crowe, Levine, & Nager, 1992). One successful project fraction reported that a period of 1½ years was necessary to discuss beliefs, share visions, and determine methods before the project was actually launched (Elliott & Woloshyn, 1997). In other cases, the process of establishing rapport occurred throughout the project, with the ongoing dialogue constituting a central component of its success (Clark et al., 1996). This dialogue is especially essential when school-based educators, who hold an ethic of action, form collaborative partnerships with university-based researchers, who predominantly hold an ethic of inquiry with publication as an essential outcome (Anderson & Herr, 1999).

Without attention to building rapport, there is a distinct risk that some partners, particularly practitioners, may feel marginalized and remain both silent and uninvolved (Hargreaves, 1996). Although they may appear to participate by contributing their time, any sense of ownership is absent, and subtle resentments and resistance may affect the project negatively (Mitchell & Boak, 1997). This is a critical issue with respect to collaborative action research (Drake & Haskins, 1995), where the gap between theory and practice is narrowed through positive interactions between practitioners and university researchers. When the bridge is solid, it provides a place for inquiry and critical interpretation that enables all parties to share in realistic informed construction or professional knowledge (Bickel & Hattrup, 1995; Trubowitz & Longo, 1997). All partners need to recognize and accept that there is no single way of knowing and that multiple perspectives exist and are valued (Hollingsworth & Sockett, 1994).

Voluntary participation and the maintenance of practitioner autonomy may alleviate some of these problems, as long as there is a clear understanding that any partner can choose to leave a project at any time, without recrimination (Buerk, 1998; Elliott & Drake, 1995). Not surprisingly, Cooper (1997) believes that international collaboration has its own set of difficulties that often prevent the outcomes of a research project from being realized as conceptualized. However, she contends that although some goals may be met, others partially met, and still others ignored, the relationships that emerge as a function of collective study are important because they build bridges based on friendship and curiosity among people who would otherwise not come to know one another at all.

Another important step in the collaborative process is the determining of project goals in a democratic manner, so that each partner perceives equity in terms of rewards. Although it is not necessary for all partners to hold the same goals, their goals must be compatible, stated clearly, and accepted by all partners (Elliott & Drake, 1995; Elliott & Woloshyn, 1997). The goals must also be subsumed under the umbrella of commitment to the overall success of the project (Elliott & Drake, 1995). Thus, authentic collaborative ventures with common and complementary goals will extend the knowledge base of all participants (Chodzinski, 1997). Sinclair and Woodward (1997) concur by pointing out the need for balance in collaborative partnerships, where both theory and practice are valued in the project and where learning is reciprocal for all partners.

Commitment is also central to the collaborative process. First, partners must be committed to the idea and value of working with others. This commitment assumes a certain humility as partners acknowledge that they cannot as effectively complete the project alone. Second, after initial stages of negotiation, they must be committed to both the project goals and their collaborative partners. Davis (1999) asserts that although partners may not hold the same goals for the project, they must honor and respect one another's goals. It often appears that commitment to the partners overrides all other senses of commitment (Elliott & Woloshyn, 1997).

Even if human relations appear strong and project goals are mutually compatible, the constraints associated with the research partners' cultures may clash. For example, the cultures of school-based teachers and university-based researchers tend to be very different, with the institutional constraints on each being substantial. These differences need to be articulated and valued in a sensitive manner (Hattrup & Bickel, 1993). When differences are not discussed adequately, some practitioners may not confront their deep-seated beliefs about the irrelevance of research for their own practice (Graham, 1988). With this in mind, Tambo (1997) suggests that collaborative partners should come to a project with realistic expectations that acknowledge the time and resource constraints of all those involved when determining tasks. Failing to acknowledge the partners' cultural and institutional differences may cause a lack of awareness of the importance of structuring projects in particular ways and at particular times. Although conflict in collaborative projects is often viewed as negative, Davis (1999) suggests realistically that some of these problems may never be resolved. On the other hand, Richards and Schutz (1997) state that, by confronting and discussing issues of conflict, insights can be acquired that enrich the understandings of all collaborators, even when no solutions are found. For school–university relationships to be successful, partners need to break out of the tradition that defines the relationships and responsibilities within their own institutional culture. Additionally, Tambo (1997) cautions that it is imperative for collaborators to stay out of each other's internal politics. Such comments and observations, however, are few, as the overwhelming majority of the collaborative literature draws conclusions based on examples of successful projects and partnerships (Cornbleth & Ellsworth, 1994; Drake & Basaraba, 1997; Elliott & Drake, 1995; Hollingsworth, 1992; Nias, 1987).

In most cases, decisions about project tasks are mutually agreed upon according to individual areas of expertise. This suggests that partners must agree that leadership is revolving and shared according to their strengths and weaknesses and the current demands of the project (Bickel & Hattrup, 1995; Drake & Haskins, 1995; Elliott & Drake, 1995; Leiberman, 1992). For instance, Drake and Haskins (1995) found that a key element that related to the success of their collaborative action research project was the ability to shift roles according to the immediate needs of the project. Thus, sometimes they facilitated and provided materials, at other times they functioned as participant researchers and, on still other occasions, they wrote grants to secure funding for the project.

It is generally accepted that collaborative research extends and enhances networks and relationships, thus building a foundation for the mutual understanding of educational issues (Mitchell & Boak, 1997). Collaborative reflection on the results and outcomes of projects has been found repeatedly to deepen and extend the insights and understandings of both the researcher and the researched (Castle, Abbey, & Reynolds, 1998; Castle, Drake, & Boak, 1995; Drake, Elliott, & Castle, 1993).

Recently, it has become the vogue in many disciplines to describe all working relationships as "collaborative," regardless of the nature of the project, the method of negotiating partners' roles and responsibilities, or the perceived success of the project. In reality, many projects fail to meet the needs of all partners, with teachers in particular often feeling violated and used by researchers who blithely claim they have been collaborating. This kind of rhetoric is problematic, as the complexities and subtleties inherent in any collective human endeavor prohibit easy or pat solutions to the perennial issues of hierarchy, power, leadership, coercion, resistance to change, ownership, negotiation, and resistance.

The editors of this book believe that working collaboratively is challenging in any context, especially in the school–university context. Furthermore, they believe that the negotiation of the collaborative process is not only the key to successful outcomes but is also often difficult to accomplish. We also suspect that much can be learned from examining collaborative projects that have neither produced a satisfactory product nor met the individual needs of the collaborators. Finally, we point out that merely working together does not necessarily constitute an authentic collaborative project, and that many so-called collaborators would benefit from a more considered approach to what it means to work together.

This book, therefore, is designed to deepen and extend the dialogue about the collaborative processes in education. How are these issues playing out in the new millennium? What assumptions have strayed into our thinking about collaboration? What can we learn about collaboration from examples where collaboration has been unsuccessful from the perspectives of some or all of the participants? What have we begun to take for granted? These are the kinds of questions that the editors and authors have sought to address in this book. Each chapter in this collection addresses some aspect of these questions. The authors also raise other issues that will enhance our understanding of how collaborative processes can be best accomplished so that the vision of improving teaching and learning can be pushed forward.

EXTENDING THE DIALOGUE

The Forgotten: Negotiation as an Essential Process

We have titled this section of the book "The Forgotten," as much of the literature to date has either minimized or given scant attention to negotiation among partners. Collaboration requires that partners negotiate project goals, methodologies, tasks, conclusions, and dissemination of results. Perhaps when partnerships spontaneously establish good will and cohesive personal relationships, decisions are made more easily, and negotiation appears minimal. In other cases, however, we believe that partnerships flounder on the basis of a rushed, ignored, or dictatorial notion of negotiation. We believe any discussion of the collaborative process will benefit from a thoughtful look at the process of negotiation that is essential to the building of successful collaborative partnerships.

This four-chapter section, therefore, begins with a consideration of the term "negotiation" as it is used in the business community and examines the consequences of an uncritical application of the concept to educational contexts. The second chapter in this section considers negotiation in educational contexts and examines potential pitfalls before recommending how it can be accomplished most effectively. Finally, the last two chapters provide examples of projects that floundered because of failed negotiation. In these projects, the assumptions by granting agencies, the universities, and the researchers made negotiation virtually impossible. The frustration and lack of perceived success in these projects are painfully described.

In the chapter titled, "What Is This Thing Called Negotiation? Exploring the Concept in Education," Joyce B. Castle and Susan Sydor examine the business literature related to the use of the term "negotiation," and find it translates poorly from that context to an educational one. Using the common example of a researcher "negotiating" entrance into a classroom, they demonstrate how each partner can believe that fruitful and clear negotiation has occurred, when in reality the negotiation process has been interpreted differently by each partner. Thus, a power hierarchy combined with social expectations can create a situation where one party is uncomfortable with the negotiated results. This example provides evidence that "power hierarchies" are alive and well in education and need to be carefully considered when "negotiating" any collaborative process. Ethical considerations are raised that are related to the negotiation of tasks when one party has more to gain than the other. This chapter raises more questions than it answers, but it serves to challenge the complacent view of the term "negotiation" as a panacea for resolving differences in educational settings.

Coral Mitchell, in "Negotiating Agendas in Collaborative Research," picks up this issue, stressing the complex nature of negotiation and examining it critically as it pertains to school–university partnerships. The negotiation of agendas among partners is acknowledged as a complicated process and is explored through substantive, ethical, and procedural lenses. Mitchell then moves from theoretical considerations to some practical strategies for negotiating agendas. She states that partners need to accept responsibility and commit to meeting frequently so that goals and activities can be established. These suggestions support existing knowledge about relationship building but define it in practical, workable terms.

Much has been written about reflection and collaborative reflection. Previous researchers have identified the value of collaborative reflection as it pertains to goals, methods, values, and ongoing action in the project. Mitchell agrees, but points out that self-reflection, conducted before and after collaborative reflection among partners, will help identify and dispel inaccurate assumptions. She asserts that self-reflection is an essential process if individuals are to truly come to new and mutual understandings. In fact, she suggests that without self-reflection, nothing new may be learned by some collaborators.

Finally, Mitchell suggests that collaborators challenge themselves by pushing the boundaries of problems with their partners in order to enrich their thinking. Learning to trust intuition, to discuss political agendas, and to confront any conflict that may impede the project are all strategies notably missing from the existing literature.

The final two authors in this section provide detailed examples of collaborative projects that were begun with good intentions, but that floundered because negotiation became impossible. Each author acknowledges her particular lens on the project and, as readers, we are not privy to alternative lenses that undoubtedly exist. The openness and honesty with which each author describes her experiences reflect a kind of courage not often found in the academic literature. In "Negotiating across Cultures," Merle Richards describes an experience shaped by cultural differences that undermined her intention to negotiate for shared understanding. As a result, resistance, misunderstanding, and eventually the complete breakdown of interpersonal relations plagued the implementation of the project. Richards finally compromised her own goals and rewards to achieve some results and closure. This chapter serves as a good example of the self-reflection that Mitchell advocates.

Andrea Toepell's self-reflection in "Cooperative versus Collaborative Research: Assessing the Difference" is evaluative, as she compares two projects that to date have not met her personal goals. She raises ethical and power issues in her first example, pointing out her own helplessness in the context of a "cooperative" venture where the team leader wielded the majority of the power. She painfully describes how negotiation proved impossible. Her second example she terms "collaborative," largely because of the strength of the relationships established. This experience clearly illustrates the fallacy of believing that building strong relationships is sufficient to ensure positive outcomes to collaborative partnerships. The example does, however, point out that such relationships can be satisfying outcomes. Collectively, the four chapters address, explore, and extend our understanding of the theoretical and practical issues related to the key issue of negotiation among collaborative partners.

The Assumed: Collaboration as a Tool for Professional Development

This section includes four chapters that continue the dialogue about the central importance of negotiation in the collaborative process, but also extend it to how collaborative partnerships have the potential to foster professional development for all participants. It is generally accepted that educators today need to grow and hone professional knowledge and skills throughout their careers. Conventional wisdom also holds that educators learn best with and from each other. In this vein, the four chapters in this section all address situations where educators from diverse but interrelated contexts learn together while accomplishing a particular project or program. All four chapters acknowledge explicitly that collaborative relationships can present frustrating challenges. Why then do people keep collaborating? Why do they seek to complete complex projects together? One reason implied by the authors is that educators recognize the value of the energy generated by working with collaborative partners, which adds to the satisfaction of completing a worthy project. In collaborative conversations, worldviews can be shared, deepened, and expanded and collaborators are both professionally and personally enriched.

In Chapter 5, titled "Collaboration as the Foundation for Negotiating New Models of Education," Susan M. Drake's context reflects a unique period of time in Ontario, Canada. Educators were being required to adapt not only to a changing society, but also to a changing interdisciplinary curriculum and to changing expectations for students. Quick responses were demanded, but teachers were given no blueprint for how to accomplish the rapid programmatic and curriculum changes. Drake illustrates how the power of collaboration helped teachers respond to the mandate for change during these turbulent times in Ontario. She documents how the schools that worked most effectively created collaborative networks where teachers and others could learn from each other. Teachers had to find partners who were interested in collaborating and then find the time to share philosophical backgrounds and practical applications of the curriculum. To do this, they formed "learning organizations," which held collaboration as the way of promoting professional learning at its core. By the end of three years, Drake noted that as a result of their collaborative relationships with colleagues, the teachers involved described themselves primarily as "learners" The need to survive and function in a changing workplace created an imperative for collaborative professional development.

Karen Krug picks up the theme in "Is Collaboration in the Classroom Possible?" by describing her experience of including collaborative learning tasks in her university classes. She outlines a strong case for not only helping students learn course content, but also providing them with an opportunity to develop the life-skill of working collaboratively. She finds that, as a result of previous school experiences, students are programmed to place primary value on individual learning derived from a teacher who holds all the knowledge. Krug's frustrations are evident as she describes trying to create a collaborative climate among her students, who are resistant because they are more familiar and comfortable with a competitive climate. Such difficulties point out that not only do elementary and high schools not effectively teach students to collaborate, but that collaboration is a skill, like any other, that needs to be developed over time. Additionally, the power dynamics present in the university classroom can inhibit the development of authentic collaborative relationships. Krug acknowledges her position of power as instructor, and also points to the growing body of literature about how gender, race, and the ability to speak frequently and well create perceived power inequities among students. She suggests methods for instructors to reduce power differentials by sculpting the collaborative task to include a variety of skills and by providing the freedom for students to learn effectively from each other. She also cautions that instructors need to be cognizant of the role they play in shaping the collaborative learning task, so that reflection is part of the process and individual learning also occurs. Krug's reflections on her own experiences indicate a strong commitment to creating a collaborative culture in an alien environment so that her students can learn a skill that will enable them to work with and learn from others throughout their careers.

The third chapter in this section, "Searching for Collaborative Balance: Negotiating Roles in School–University Partner Research," authored by Linda L. Lang, also focuses on professional growth and learning, but this time for participants in a school–university partnership. Lang stresses that commitment to shared educational goals and the opportunity to learn together more than compensate for the challenges created by partnerships from two distinct institutional cultures. She suggests that to overcome obstacles, all partners need to be flexible and prepared to compromise. Lang's description of the project illustrates how her skills of negotiation and compromise enabled her to adjust her expectations as researcher to include unexpected roles. This shift allowed her to maintain her research goals while responding to the emerging needs of her collaborative partners. The fostering of creativity and the integration of theory and practice are central in this story of teacher change arising from a situation of developing new teaching skills through a collaborative partnership.

The final chapter in this section, "A Committee with Commitment," by Jessie Lees and Vianne Timmons, describes a collaborative process among members of a committee formed to implement a province-wide teacher induction program for beginning teachers in Prince Edward Island. This initial professional development was designed to help retain young teachers, who often leave the profession because of the demanding and isolating early stage of their teaching careers. The collaborative process discussed in the chapter, however, involves a number of committee members from diverse educational backgrounds who worked together to create handbooks, workshops, and a mentoring program for beginning teachers. The authors believe that the thoughtful and inclusive selection of a collaborative committee from a comprehensive group of stakeholders including the Department of Education, federations, university, school districts, and retired teachers was a critical first step to the success of the project. Each of these groups recognized the problem and was committed to the professional growth of beginning teachers. A significant component of this chapter is that all members also recognized their own need for professional growth as a condition of being a member of this committee. For instance, they attended workshops to hone new skills for conveying professional knowledge to newcomers. They also developed skills for mentoring, designing and facilitating workshops, and goal setting. Equally important was the fact that through these experiences they began to learn more about each other. They learned about the diverse views and beliefs about education held by committee members in various educational roles throughout the province. Thus, although professional development for beginning teachers was the purpose of the committee, the professional development of committee members as they achieved these goals was also substantial.

Finally, the authors raise some unexpected questions. Are successful collaborative groups eventually vulnerable to self-destruction as key individuals leave? When a group is dynamic and functional, do members eventually become complacent? Can new members join tightly knit and effective collaborative groups and achieve the same results? These authors take a highly positive collaborative experience and pose questions that challenge complacency about the ongoing effectiveness of collaborative principles. Thus, these four chapters all describe the richness of learning together and illustrate the collaborative principles in distinctly different educational contexts.

The Unexamined: The Role of Collaboration in Personal Development

While continuing to support the previous themes, the chapters in this section also explain how the professional intertwines with the personal. All these chapters describe growth, but in a personal sense. Alice Schutz and Sharon Abbey begin the section by drawing parallels between the principles of collaboration and mentoring and showing how they overlap and spin together to allow the individual strengths of one collaborator to serve as a guide for another. Anne Elliott and Vera Woloshyn describe their experiences of learning from each other as a result of collaborating together. Their experiences underline that when professional development is deemed important to the recipient, it becomes intertwined with personal growth.

Schutz and Abbey connect collaboration and mentoring in "Collaborative Mentoring: Insights from a University Research Center" by deconstructing both terms and finding connections with the way learning has occurred in the Centre for Collaborative Research (CCR). Most CCR members have intuitively experienced such connections, but Schutz and Abbey have surveyed the relevant literature on each practice and found points of agreement between them. For instance, they explain that the act of mentoring, traditionally one-way, can be reciprocal, reflexive, and self-critical, and that good mentoring, like collaboration, can imply learning in both directions. Therefore, they contend that the traditional differences between mentoring and collaboration are no longer significant, and that the best features of both can be combined. One facet of this change may be the emergence of self-reflection as a key to working together, regardless of the expertise and authority held by any one individual. Another may be the emphasis on equality in both mentoring and collaborative relationships and the downplaying of power and status distinctions. In either collaborative or mentoring relationships, both parties are currently acknowledging that personal lives are enriched as professional knowledge grows.

In "Collaboration: A Vehicle for Professional Development," Elliott and Woloshyn describe their personal experiences of the professional growth that occurred as a result of working with a group of teachers over four years. Their project began as a school–university undertaking to enable teachers to use explicit strategy instruction in their classrooms and to determine how that could best be accomplished. But it also created an unexpected forum for individual and diverse learning for each author. This learning, although arguably professional in the strictest sense of the word, is described in personal terms, which illustrates once again the strong relationship between the personal and the professional. This chapter shows that the authors' professional growth, embedded in the context of the personal social relationship, was both satisfying and enriching. In the spirit of collaboration, each author brought different but complementary strengths and experiential backgrounds to the project. Over time, a trusting and respectful personal relationship provided an environment where each partner gained knowledge in the domain of the other's strength. Specifically, Elliott identifies how Woloshyn served as a collaborative mentor for honing research skills. On the other hand, Woloshyn explicitly consulted with Elliott to develop new teaching skills. This reciprocal learning, a by-product of a school–university project, resulted largely from the collaborative partnership that made the project successful.

In "Mentoring Graduate Students through Involvement in Faculty Research," Susan Gibson, Dianne Oberg, Rosemarie Pelz, and Doug Zook illustrate the reciprocal nature of learning when seasoned researchers mentor graduate students by collaborating on a project that requires the expertise of all partners. As with the previous chapter, the lens shifts back and forth among participants, illuminating the experiences of each one in highly personal terms. The supportive, respectful, and open relationships that developed are clear from the reflections of the mentees, Pelz and Zook. Collectively, the researchers identify four factors that define the aspects of mentoring that produced the professional and personal development. These are mutual support, professional development, research, and psychosocial support. Psychosocial support involved assisting mentees to understand and adapt to their new roles as researchers. The authors agree that all participants benefited from the project: The graduate students gained valuable knowledge and experience in conducting research, and the researchers received the help needed to accomplish their research. Academic and personal lives of all participants were enhanced in the process.

The final chapter in this section, "University Researchers' Collaborative

Experiences: A Gender Analysis," by Merle Richards and Nancy Murray, shifts the focus yet again, to university professors collaborating with peers or other professionals. First, the authors employ metaphors of the symphony orchestra, the vocal quartet, and the jazz band to identify three forms of collaboration. The chapter also explicitly addresses an issue that is implicit in other chapters in this collection: the effects of gender on attitudes toward collaboration. In particular, women professors comment about the stresses of time management, about personal relationships as a goal of collaboration that sometimes hindered it from moving forward, and about collaboration as a method of mentoring colleagues.

The book concludes with the CCR's Readers' Theater production, titled "Not Just Smooth Sailing: Issues in Collaboration," in which all the themes addressed in this book converge. The Readers' Theater script shows the audience the workings of the collaborative process that inspired the production itself. It also uses a sailing metaphor to bring new life to understandings of abstract concepts of collaborative work.

REFERENCES

Anderson, G., & Herr, K. (1999). The new paradigm wars: Is there room for rigorous practitioner knowledge in universities and schools? *Educational Researcher, 28*, 12–21, 40.

Bickel, W., & Hattrup, R. (1995). Teachers and researchers in collaboration: Reflections on the process. *American Educational Research Journal, 32*(1), 35–62.

Buerk, S. (1998). In the driver's seat. *Journal of Staff Development, 19*(2), 39–42.

Castle, J. B., Abbey, S., & Reynolds, C. (1998). Mothers, daughters and education: Struggles between conformity and resistance. *Canadian Journal of Education, 23*(1), 63–78.

Castle, J. B., Drake, S., & Boak, T. (1995). Collaborative reflection as professional development. *Review of Higher Education, 18*(3), 243–263.

Castle, J. B., & Giblin, A. (1992). Reflection-for-action: A collaborative venture in preservice education. *Teaching Education, 4*(2), 21–34.

Chodzinski, R. T. (1997). Working together in a meaningful partnership: Reflective voices. *Brock Education, 7*(1), 114–123.

Clark, C., Moss, P. A., Goering, S., Herter, R. J., Lamar, B., Leonard, D., Robbins, S., Russell, M., Templin, M., & Washa, K. (1996). Collaboration as dialogue: Teachers and researchers engaged in conversation and professional development. *American Educational Research Journal, 33*(1), 193–231.

Clark, D. C., & Clark, S. N. (1996). Building collaborative environments for successful middle level school restructuring. *NASSP Bulletin, 80*(576), 1–16.

Clift, R. T., & Say, M. (1988). Teacher education: Collaboration or conflict? *Journal of Teacher Education, 39*(3), 2–7.

Clift, R. T., Veal, M. L., Holland, P., Johnson, M., & McCarthy, J. (1995). *Collaborative leadership and shared decision making: Teachers, principals and university professors.* New York: Teachers College Press.

Cooper, L. (1997). International collaboration for the improvement of teacher education. The case of the Regina-Yaounde project. *Journal of the International Society for Teacher Education, 1*(3), 34–41.

Cornbleth, C. & Ellsworth, J. (1994) Teachers in teacher education: Clinical faculty roles and relationships. *American Educational Research Journal 31*(1), 49–70.

Crowe, G., Levine, L., & Nager, N. (1992). Are three heads better than one? Reflections on doing collaborative interdisciplinary research. *American Educational Research Journal, 29*(4), 737–753.

Davis, M. D. (1999). The restructuring of an urban elementary school: Lessons learned as a professional development school liaison. *Early Childhood Research and Practice, 1*(1), 2–10.

Drake, S. M., & Basaraba, J. (1997). School–university research partnership: In search of the essence. In H. Christiansen, L. Goulet, C. Krentz, & M. Maeers (Eds.), *Recreating relationships: Collaboration and educational reform* (pp. 209–218). Albany, NY: State University of New York Press.

Drake, S. M., Elliott, A. E., & Castle, J. (1993). Collaborative reflection through story: Towards a deeper understanding of ourselves as women researchers. *Qualitative Studies in Education, 6*(4), 291–301.

Drake S. M., & Haskins, B. (1995, June). *Two facilitators in search of a collaborative action research process that works.* Paper presented at the annual conference of the Canadian Society for the Study of Education, Montreal, Quebec.

Elliott, A. E., & Drake, S. M. (1995). Moving from "two solitudes" towards a "blended" culture in school/university partnerships. *Journal of Staff, Program and Organizational Development, 13*(2), 85–95.

Elliott, A. E., & Woloshyn, V. (1997). Some female professors' perceptions of collaboration: Mapping the collaborative process through rough terrain. *Alberta Journal of Educational Research, 43*(1), 23–36.

Frymier, R., Flynn, J., & Flynn, R. (1992). *School-university collaboration.* Bloomington, IN: Phi Delta Kappa Educational Foundation.

Fullan, M. G. (1999). *Change forces: The sequel.* Philadelphia: Falmer Press.

Glickman, C. D. (1985). *Supervision of instruction: A developmental approach.* Boston: Allyn & Bacon.

Graham, G. (1988). Collaboration in physical education: A lot like marriage? *Journal of Teaching in Physical Education, 7*, 165–174.

Hargreaves, A. (1994). *Changing teachers, changing times: Teachers' work and culture in the postmodern age.* New York: Teachers College Press.

Hargreaves, A. (1996). Revisiting voice. *Educational Researcher, 25*(1), 12–19.

Hattrup, R., & Bickel, W. (1993). Teacher–researcher collaboration: Resolving the tensions. *Educational Leadership, 29*(2), 373–404.

Hollingsworth, S. (1992). Learning to teach through collaborative conversation: *American Educational Research Journal, 29*(2), 373–404.

Hollingsworth, S., & Sockett, H. (1994). Positioning teacher research in educational reform: An introduction. In S. Hollingsworth & H. Sockett (Eds.), *Teacher research and educational reform: Ninety-third yearbook of the National Society for the Study of Education* (pp. 1–20). Chicago: University of Chicago Press.

Leiberman, A. (1992). The meaning of scholarly activity and the building of community. *Educational Researcher, 21*(6), 5–12.

Leiberman, A. (1995). Restructuring schools: The dynamics of changing practice, structure and culture. In A. Leiberman (Ed.), *The work of restructuring schools: Building from the ground up* (pp. 1–17). New York: Teachers College Press.

Mitchell, C., & Boak, T. (1997). Collaborative research: The power, the perils and the possibilities. *Brock Education, 7*(1), 1–14.

Nias, J. (1987). Learning from difference: A collegial approach to change. In J. Smyth (Ed.), *Educating teachers: Changing the nature of pedagogical knowledge* (pp. 137–154). London: Falmer Press.

Noddings, N. (1984). *Caring: A feminine approach to ethics and moral education.* Los Angeles, CA: University of California Press.

Richards, M., & Schutz, A. (1997). Reflections on the collaborative experience: The CCR in review. *Brock Education, 7*(1), 76–86.

Schecter, S., & Parkhurst, S. (1993). Ideological divergencies in a teacher research group. *American Educational Research Journal, 30*(4), 771–798.

Schratz, M. (1993). From cooperative action to collective self-reflection: A sociodynamic approach to educational research. In M. Schratz (Ed.), *Qualitative voices in educational research* (pp. 56–70). London: Falmer Press.

Sinclair, C., & Woodward, H. (1997). Creating a balance. Who owns the partnership? *Journal of the International Society for Teacher Education, 1*(3), 60–69.

Stewart, H. (1997). Metaphors of interrelatedness: Principles of collaboration. In H. Christiansen, L. Goulet, C. Krentz, & M. Maeers (Eds.), *Recreating relationships: Collaboration and educational reform* (pp. 27–53). Albany, NY: State University of New York Press.

Tambo, L. I. (1997). University–school collaborations in student teaching: Issues and perspectives. *Journal of the International Society for Teacher Education, 1*(3), 24–33.

Tchombe, T. M. (1997). Partnerships and linkages for teacher empowerment as a function of the cognitive authority among partners. *Journal of the International Society for Teacher Education, 1*(3), 15–23.

Trubowitz, S. & Longo, P. (1997). *How it works—inside a school–college collaboration.* New York: Teachers College Press.

PART I

The Forgotten

CHAPTER 1

What Is This Thing Called Negotiation? Exploring the Concept in Education

Joyce B. Castle and Susan Sydor

People cannot work together without communication. As they share their thoughts, ideas, and feeling, they either have to make decisions or they have to settle disputes between themselves about their work. When they do this, people are most often said to be negotiating. While the term is commonly used, we suggest that "negotiation" not be taken for granted in its meaning and application to educational contexts. In this chapter we examine the meaning of negotiation and its use in the literature. Our interest is in the implications of an uncritical application of concepts from one area of human endeavor to another, quite different context. In particular, we question whether negotiation is an apt term for describing the communication between collaborators in educational settings.

COLLABORATION IN EDUCATIONAL CONTEXTS

What has driven the rhetoric in the reform movement of the past two decades is a belief that new and extended forms of collaboration will serve as the vehicle to make education more effective and meaningful (Christiansen, Goulet, Krentz, & Maeers, 1997; Goodlad, 1993; Smith, 1992). As part of this movement, collaborative ventures have been promoted across a range of educational settings, all calling in one way or another for individuals or groups to interact and work together. With the increased attention to collaboration has come an increased body of literature on the topic, as well as an increased awareness of the complexity of the phenomenon (Bracey, 1990; Laine, Schultz, & Smith, 1994; Petrie, 1995). Much of the research that has attempted to explain what collaboration entails has confirmed the importance of attending to the ways in which individuals in educational settings actually work together to achieve some level of reform. What has taken on increased significance is the centrality of open communication and a desire to understand the viewpoints of others.

The term that has often been used to refer to this collaborative communicative process is negotiation. For example, a decade ago, Nias, Southworth, and Yeomans (1989) reported that the teachers in schools that were moving to establish collaborative cultures were "continuously involved in negotiating their relationships in response to the forces of change acting upon them" (p. 76). In another study, in which Hookey, Neal, and Donoahue (1997) described their own collaborative study as three teachers, they highlighted the negotiating they undertook as they explored their own professional growth. Hollingsworth (1992) stressed that negotiation is a key component of collaboration and that such components change traditional patterns of working together, often making participants more vulnerable. Investigations of school–university partnerships have stressed that those involved do have to work together in new ways and that they need to negotiate understanding and respond to one another's needs if the collaborative venture is to be successful (Darling-Hammond, 1994). How individuals and groups respond to one another and negotiate understandings, then, has come to be considered by many as central to collaborative efforts in education.

Yet even with the increased attention to the significance of negotiation in education, little effort has been directed at examining the concept itself as it applies to education. Just what does it mean to negotiate in this context? And what are the implications of using the term to describe an element of collaboration in educational settings? These are the questions we address in the following sections as we explore the concept of negotiation and examine the use of the term in both social science and business and management literature.

NEGOTIATION AS PROCESS AND PRODUCT

As a specific category of the general process of communication, negotiation has been conceptualized in a number of ways. Nierenberg (1968) brought the term into a new light over three decades ago, when he wrote *The Art of Negotiation*. He held that: "whenever people exchange ideas with the intention of changing relationships, whenever they confer for agreement, they are negotiating" (p. 8). Later, Raiffa (1982) identified both an art and a science to negotiation, referring to the "art" side as the domain that includes interpersonal skills and abilities, and the "science" side as the "theory" side dealing with "systematic analysis." More recently, other views of negotiation have shifted the focus. Avruch (1998) claims that negotiation is the most fundamental form of conflict resolution and can be understood in a number of ways ranging from educative to degrees of coercion. The focus in such arguments is often on negotiation as a means of solving problems and arriving at solutions. But others propose quite different conceptualizations. Doctoroff (1998) defines negotiation as "a conversation in which parties try to influence or persuade one another" (p. 65). While parties might indeed be looking for the mutually acceptable solution, Doctoroff holds that there are also situations where "negotiators may walk away from good deals because the deals do not match the organization's articulated position" (p. 65). Bazerman and Neale (1992) also claim that in some situations no agreement may be the better outcome of discussions. The purpose of negotiation should be to maximize one's interest, they argue, and such negotiations must be conducted rationally. While these authors do not limit the applicability of their approach to business situations, it is worth noting that the language they use is combative: "information from the trenches," and "the most honed and effective tools in your arsenal," for example (pp. 4–5).

While numerous definitions of negotiation have emerged, the perspectives driving these can generally be viewed as falling into two broad categories: negotiation as a management process within formal business contexts and negotiation as a social tool in everyday life situations. In the first and largest field, that of management, the literature is further divided into three separate categories: one, that which describes negotiation as conflict resolution, especially in relation to management–employee relations; second, that which sees negotiation as resolving problems (as opposed to conflicts); and third, literature specifying negotiation behaviors and skills. Across these categories, negotiation is considered in terms of effectiveness and goal orientation, and it becomes the preferred way of solving problems of management and obtaining support for the goals of the organization (Gappmayer, 1994). The direction of much present-day thinking about negotiation in management grew from Fisher and Ury's (1981) book *Getting to Yes: Negotiating Agreement without Giving In*, which proposed a negotiating style based on principle rather than positioning. Fisher and Brown followed with *Getting Together* (1988), in which they emphasized working relationships that deal well with differences. In organizations, then, the current approach to negotiation leans toward achieving a product that pleases all parties and leaves them feeling satisfied as well as willing to continue the relationship.

Apart from the literature on negotiation in management, the second category focuses on negotiation that occurs daily during informal social interactions. In social psychological literature, negotiation is the term used to describe a particular nature of social interaction, a process that occurs "in the ordinary social interactions of everyday life" (Martin, 1976, p. 3). From a social interactionist perspective, individuals act on the basis of the meanings they derive from their daily interactions with others, and any subsequent order in social life then becomes a consequence of people playing out their roles as they interpret them. "Everywhere in social life we see bargaining, negotiation, deliberation, agreements, temporary arrangements, deliberate suspensions of the rules, and a variety of other procedures in the accomplishment of social order and coordinated activity" (Hewitt, 1976, p. 205). In this tradition, negotiation is characteristic of human approaches to problem situations, and negotiated order describes the way large, complex organizations coordinate efforts to achieve their purposes. Strauss (1978) has gone further to argue that "A social order—even the most repressive—without some forms of negotiation would be inconceivable. Even dictators find it impossible and inexpedient simply and always to order, command, demand, threaten, manipulate, or use force; about some issues and activities they must persuade and negotiate" (p. ix). According to Strauss, people go about ordering and articulating their worlds in various ways, and negotiation is one particular kind of activity that can be found in combination with other social processes such as education and coercion. As such, Strauss's perspective on negotiation is much broader than the focus of the management literature. The "negotiated order approach" sees negotiation as a universal activity with implications for the study of larger social and organizational issues.

Mulholland (1991), also operating from a social perspective, approaches the concept of negotiation generically, identifying it as a social activity set within the domain of language. To see negotiation generally, Mulholland contends, one must see it first as a subform of language. As such, it partakes of many of the conventions of conversation, but also operates within its own narrower range of speech, stricter rules of procedure, and defined goals. To Mulholland, the conversation, then, is for the purpose of producing some action or arriving at some decision that will settle the disagreement among the participants. As such, she says, negotiation only occurs when differences, whether of opinion, interest, purpose, or so on, exist among people.

De Bono (1991), known for his work on the mind as a self-organizing system and the teaching of thinking as a skill, challenges the popular acceptance of negotiation as an effective means of resolving disputes. He refers to the notion of "differences among people" as "conflict thinking" and finds it inadequate. He uses four terms—fight, negotiate, problem-solve, and design—and questions which action is best in different conflict situations. Negotiation, he suggests, is not the best choice, for he sees the term as suggesting compromise and a willingness to work within boundaries that already exist, rather than designing new ones. De Bono says that bargaining as an approach to conflict is superior to fighting and argument, but that bargaining is also flawed because it involves value trading and leads to "superfluous demands simply as trading material where appeasement is always a danger" (p. 37). In conflict situations, De Bono suggests, a "design" idiom would be preferable to a "negotiation" idiom. He proposes that design thinking is conceptually creative and superior to approaches that seek to simply effect compromise or to remove a problem, because design thinking is open-minded and not constrained by existing circumstance (working within boundaries). The significant contribution of De Bono's approach is that it moves us from "conflict thinking" to "design thinking" and in doing so helps us see conflict as only one element in the need to design process and product outcomes for particular situations and contexts.

REVISITING NEGOTIATION IN EDUCATIONAL CONTEXTS

As noted above, the term "negotiation" is a commonly used one, and it has come to be considered a key component of collaborative interaction in educational contexts. Yet the literature dealing directly with the concept of negotiation in education has been sparse. There has been considerable literature produced on collaboration in education, but little on the separate component of negotiation. Despite the increased importance accorded to understanding how individuals and groups can interact effectively, what it means to negotiate has not yet come to mean much beyond simply "working things out."

Illustrative of the need to examine the use of negotiation in collaborative settings in education is the following example of Ulichny and Schoener's (1996), which describes the events of a research project from the viewpoints of each participant. The researcher in the venture (Polly) first reports on her ethnographic practice of gaining entrance to the research site:

I had negotiated entry into a college level ESL classroom through the teacher I wanted to investigate. I explained some of my purposes to her . . . and she agreed to have me attend her classes weekly, talk informally to both her and the students as time permitted, and to tape-record interactions. I further explained to her that I had no preconceived notion of the categories I would be looking at. . . . Within three weeks, however, I sensed a growing tension that eventually resulted in my leaving the class prematurely. Although the teacher never really asked me to leave, when the discomfort with my tape-recording caused her to suggest that I might be "stealing" her method, I offered to disband my study, and she readily agreed. (p. 500)

The researcher clearly reports her feelings about following an appropriate research methodology and sensitively responding to the growing unease of the teacher. She felt she had negotiated the context with the best of intentions and information. Yet her partner in the experience (Wendy) reports a different perspective.

I had been teaching ESL at the university level for just over a year when my office-mate, Polly, asked me a favor. She was teaching graduate courses at the same school, and we knew each other, though not well, through the forced acquaintance of shared offices at the university. The favor had to do with the other part of her life—completing a research project on ESL teachers. My sincere impulse was to say "No, thank you." A whole school semester? My blood pressure rose when supervisors came in to observe for a mere twenty minutes. Nevertheless I said yes, though with misgivings. . . . My secondary motivation was to avoid disappointing the director of our center, who was always enthusiastic about teachers' involvement in research. (p. 504)

On the surface, Wendy had freely participated in the decision to collaborate with Polly. Wendy's account, however, gives no indication that she was able to state her position or concerns. She goes on later to say that she was uncomfortable with the role of the researcher and had some sense that the researcher and a former supervisor would be judgmental. She also reports that:

There was nothing Polly could have said before we worked together to dispel my fears. She had been her usual approachable self through our initial negotiation for the project, the same friendly office-mate that I had known for a semester. But her simple suggestion that we step into the roles of observer and observed was enough to make me feel more wary. (p. 504)

In an effort to understand such scenarios, selected literature over the past three decades offers perspectives that prove helpful. First, work by Martin (1976) points out nicely the kinds of negotiations that occur daily in schools as individuals arrive at common understandings around specific issues. Martin studied individuals in varied situations and compared their interactions, both teacher–teacher and teacher–pupil. What he used to guide his observation was a conceptual framework with five main elements: the preconditions for negotiation; the extent of the negotiation (content, direction of influence, and degree of change); the stages in the negotiation; the strategies used; and the outcomes of the process. Martin's findings pointed to the distinctive nature of negotiation in school settings. He found that teacher–teacher interaction differed from teacher–pupil interaction; that different strategies and stages were used in different contexts; and that different sources of conflict arose, along with different ways of handling the conflicts. Taken together, the findings contributed to the understanding of the distinctive and complex nature of negotiation in educational settings like schools.

Cook (1992) presents a different perspective on negotiation in education.

He focuses on both the process and product, and claims that negotiation in education is similar to negotiation in other traditional contexts:

Negotiating means about the same in education as it does in politics or industry. All the parties in an operation come together, bringing with them their own points of view, needs and wants, and together they work for the outcomes most satisfactory to all concerned. In educational terms, the result of negotiation may come to a meshing of minds, an interlocking of intentions, an agreement about means and ends between teacher and learners. (p. 15)

According to Cook, the key to negotiation in any context, education included, lies in the "ownership principle." This stance draws upon an analogy of capital and labor, and argues that people work hardest to obtain things they want or keep things they already have. From this perspective, education flourishes when the main stakeholders have ownership.

Boomer, in his book with coeditors Lester, Onore, and Cook (1992), raises questions about the impediments to negotiation in schools, especially as it relates to his major focus, the negotiation of the school curriculum. Boomer deals in particular with the power inequities between teachers and pupils. His concern is with how to ensure student ownership of the curriculum, when teachers traditionally own the power. The harmful effects of power are only offset, Boomer says, when those in power make quite explicit the values and assumptions directing their actions and decisions, thereby allowing others "more chance of negotiation . . ." (p. 8).

These selected works of Martin (1976), Cook (1992), and Boomer and colleagues (1992) all serve to illustrate how the predominant view of negotiation in education is that of a process by which parties deal with differences and arrive at solutions to problems. The assumptions are that there will be differences that lead to problems and that negotiation will lead to solutions. These selections from the literature also present perspectives that help pinpoint some of the issues arising from a consideration of negotiation as it applies in collaborative workings in education such as the Polly and Wendy scenario presented above. Three issues in particular appear to be paramount.

The first issue relates to the complexity associated with attempts to define negotiation. On the one hand, the concept can be isolated and viewed as a process for solving a problem and arriving at a solution. In this capacity, negotiation serves a specific purpose, operates in a specific capacity, and has a specific "life." On the other hand, negotiation can be viewed as an ongoing process that is part of the social interactions individuals engage in constantly. From this social interactionist perspective, negotiation occurs daily and is much more of an informal, ongoing process.

The first issue, then, springs from the fact that little is known about educators' perspectives on negotiation. Do educators, who work in highly social environments that promote a notion of community, view negotiation as an isolated process that addresses a specific goal and solves a specific problem? Or do they see negotiation as the daily ongoing interaction they engage in while constructing meaning? Or do both perspectives drive the use of the term in education, perhaps with different individuals or groups holding different perspectives and not being aware of how these differ? Polly and Wendy's story illustrates how the researcher in the collaborative venture felt she had successfully negotiated entry into the classes (she had solved a specific problem), while the teacher felt increasingly uncomfortable each day and felt that the relationship was not one in which she could construct ongoing meaning (negotiation was not ongoing daily). The framework the two individuals were operating under was not the same. One cannot talk of negotiation in education, then, without addressing what is being negotiated and how and for what purpose. It must be clear that those involved are setting out to "negotiate" something they both agree needs to be dealt with and then needs to be dealt with via "negotiating." Just what is it that the parties in educational settings want to achieve? It might be the case that one or both parties prefer De Bono's (1991) suggestion of "design thinking" as the method to solve any difference or problem. And if negotiation is desired, just how much ownership does each party have? Clearly, if ownership is the key to successful interaction, as Cook (1992) suggests, then many parties like Polly and Wendy who find themselves involved in educational ventures are simply not negotiating at all.

The second issue relates to the concept of power and to the intentional influence one has over another. The concept takes on particular significance in educational settings where inherent power structures are firmly established. As Johnston (1996) points out, whether the interactions involve pupils–teachers, teachers–administrators, or schools–universities, the differences in the power base, both real and perceived, are great.

The brief look at Polly and Wendy's noncollaborative experience leads us to question the part that power and role played here. Hillman (1995) points out that power is "the invisible demon that gives rise to our motivations and choices. Power stands behind our fear of loss and desire for control" (p. 2). As Wendy progresses in the project, she takes on Hillman's view that "our lives are lived inside fields of power, under the influence of others, in accord with authority, subject to tyrannies" (p. 15).

Is education a special case in the question of power relationships and collaboration? Perhaps. Kreisberg (1992) says:

Teachers occupy a paradoxical place in the web of institutional and ideological domination in schools. Although they are central figures of authority and control in the classroom, in the larger hierarchy of the educational bureaucracy they are remarkably isolated and often strikingly powerless. (p. 9)

Kreisberg proposes a form of power radically different from the more common model of domination and "power over." He calls for "power with," a concept characterized by "mutual assertiveness and reciprocity, a process in which individuals and social systems mutually create each other" (p. xi). This is the view that characterizes the rhetoric on collaborative ventures, and it has come to be a view that is easier to articulate than to play out in practice. Clearly, Wendy did not perceive that she possessed the same power that Polly did. Equally clearly, the power differential helped to inhibit any form of collaboration and effective interaction. Can negotiation in educational contexts occur, then, when power relations, whether real or perceived, are present? Bickel and Hattrup (1995) stressed the importance of dealing with power differentials; they noted in their study that "negotiating the successful working out of power among researchers and teachers became a critical and ultimately highly successful ingredient for the collaboration" (p. 47).

The third and final issue associated with the use of the term "negotiation" in educational settings revolves around the questions of which skills are needed to interact well in educational contexts, how these skills are learned and developed, and how they can be taught.

From a management perspective, negotiating skills are considered distinct skills, separate from interpersonal skills. They are also not considered to be automatically present, even in individuals with excellent interpersonal skills. Sachs (1998) cautions that "it is a mistake to assume that because a person has good communication or 'people' skills, he or she is therefore a good negotiator" (p. 70). This view has consequences for those in educational contexts because those in education are often viewed as having high-level communication skills, the kind needed to facilitate pupil learning and relate to parents and colleagues. If these are the skills that educators use when interacting with colleagues and others outside school, they are working only from a set of interpersonal characteristics, and this can leave them at a disadvantage if those they are interacting with have separate and additional negotiation skills. In fact, it may be that what is needed is even more than a separate set of negotiating skills. Bickel and Hattrup (1995) noted the difficulty they encountered in finding teachers able to participate in their collaborative venture; they found that a range of characteristics, both intellectual and interpersonal, proved essential to sustain the collaborative project.

The follow-up issue, then, is whether, how, and when to make instruction in effective interaction and "negotiation" available to educators. The materials and manuals from management do not apply automatically to the social environment of education, so some type of additional training appears to be called for. What is perhaps essential to develop first is the mind-set that communication and interpersonal interaction are inevitable in education, and that they call for dealing with differences. Beyond this, however, there are more questions than answers about the best direction to follow.

Taken together, the three issues raised here point to the difficulties arising from the use of the term "negotiation" to refer to the interaction occurring between individuals and groups working together in educational contexts. The term has continued to remain loose and largely undefined. Clearly, there is a need for new directions in thinking and a new formulation of negotiation for education. This in turn can lead to an enhanced understanding of how it is that educators can work together successfully.

REFERENCES

Avruch, K. (1998). *Conflict and conflict resolution.* Washington, DC: United States Institute of Peace Press.

Bazerman, M. H., & Neale, M. A. (1992). *Negotiating rationally.* Toronto: Macmillan.

Bracey, G. W. (1990). Rethinking school and university roles. *Educational Leadership, 49*(8), 65–66.

Bickel, W. E., & Hattrup, R. A. (1995). Teachers and researchers in collaboration: Reflections on the process. *American Educational Research Journal, 32*(1), 35–62.

Boomer, G., Lester, N., Onore, C., & Cook, J. (1992). *Negotiating the curriculum: Educating for the 21st century.* London: Falmer Press.

Christiansen, H., Goulet, L., Krentz, C., & Maeers, M. (Eds.). (1997). *Recreating relationships: Collaboration and educational reform.* Albany, NY: State University of New York Press.

Cook, J. (1992). Negotiating the curriculum: Programming for learning. In G. Boomer, N. Lester, C. Onore, & J. Cook (Eds.), *Negotiating the curriculum: Educating for the 21st century* (pp. 15–31). London: Falmer Press.

Darling-Hammond, L. (Ed.). (1994). *Professional development schools: Schools for developing a profession.* New York: Teachers College Press.

De Bono, E. (1991). *Conflicts—A better way to resolve them.* London: Penguin Books.

Doctoroff, J. (1998). Reengineering negotiations. *Sloan Management Review, 39*(3), 63–71.

Fisher, R., & Brown, W. (1998). *Getting together: Building a relationship that gets to yes.* Boston: Houghton Mifflin.

Fisher, R., & Ury, W. (1981). *Getting to yes: Negotiating agreement without giving in.* Boston: Houghton Mifflin.

Gappmayer, M. (1994). Negotiation can avert litigation. *Trustee, 47*(3), 28.

Goodlad, J. (1993). School–university partnerships and partner schools. *Educational Policy, 7*(1), 24–39.

Hewitt, J. P. (1976). *Self and society: A symbolic interactionist social psychology.* Toronto: Allyn & Bacon.

Hillman, J. (1995). *Kinds of power: A guide to its intelligent uses.* Toronto: Currency Doubleday.

Hollingsworth, S. (1992). Learning to teach through collaborative conversation: A feminist approach. *American Educational Research Journal, 29*(2), 373–404.

Hookey, M., Neal, S., & Donoahue, Z. (1997). Negotiating collaboration for professional growth: A case of consultation. In H. Christiansen, L. Goulet, C. Krentz, & M. Maeers (Eds.), *Recreating relationships: Collaboration and educational reform* (pp. 69–81). Albany, NY: State University of New York Press.

Johnston, M. (1996). Postmodern considerations of school/university collaboration. *Teaching Education, 6*(2), 99–106.

Kreisberg, S. (1992). *Transforming power: Domination, empowerment and education.* Albany, NY: State University of New York Press.

Laine, C. H., Schultz, L. M., & Smith, M. L. (1994). Interaction among school and college teachers: Toward recognizing and remaking old patterns. In K. A. Borman & N. P. Greenman (Eds.), *Changing American education: Recapturing the past or inventing the future* (pp. 381–397). Albany, NY: State University of New York Press.

Martin, W. B. W. (1976). *The negotiated order of the school.* Toronto: Macmillan.

Mulholland, J. (1991). *The language of negotiation.* London: Routledge.

Nias, J., Southworth, G., & Yeomans, R. (1989). *Staff relationships in the primary school.* London: Cassell.

Nierenberg, G. I. (1968). *The art of negotiation.* New York: Simon and Schuster.

Petrie, H. G. (Ed.). (1995). *Professionalization, partnership and power.* Albany, NY: State University of New York Press.

Raiffa, H. (1982). *The art and science of negotiation.* Cambridge, MA: Harvard University Press.

Sachs, S. (1998). Negotiation skills: A platform for success. *Risk Management, 45*(4), 70–76.

Smith, S. D. (1992). Professional partnerships and educational change: Effective collaboration over time. *Journal of Teacher Education, 43*(4), 243–256.

Strauss, A. (1978). *Negotiations: Varieties, contexts, processes, and social order.* San Francisco: Jossey-Bass.

Ulichny, P., & Schoener, W. (1996). Teacher–researcher collaboration from two perspectives. *Harvard Educational Review, 66*(3), 496–524.

CHAPTER 2

Negotiating Agendas in Collaborative Research

Coral Mitchell

Since at least the early 1990s, in almost every sector of society, collaborative partnerships have been advocated, proposed, or formed. For example, the jargon gaining ascendancy in the business sector includes such terms as "networks," "alliances," and "synergies" (Kanter, 1989). The educational research community has also joined the partnership dance, and collaborative research among a variety of stakeholder groups has become common (Hatch, 1998). But even a cursory read of the literature indicates that cross-sector collaboration is a veritable minefield. This chapter explores one potential landmine—that of agenda-setting in research collaborations between university researchers and school practitioners.

My starting premise is that agenda-setting is a complex and conflicted construct and that agendas must be explicitly negotiated at the outset and consistently throughout any collaborative research program. Agendas cannot be assumed to be monolithic. Rather, a counterpoint of institutional and personal agendas makes up the music of the dance. Ways must be found to make audible each underlying tune and to bring them all into harmony. These strategies, however, constitute only part of the score. In this chapter, the notion of agenda-setting is explored through a variety of substantive, ethical, and procedural complications. The chapter concludes with some strategies for negotiating agendas that I have, or should have, used in collaborative research projects.

THE "PROBLEM SITUATION"

Processes of collaborative research have been studied long enough now for certain "guiding principles" to be documented. At the risk of over-simplifying a deeply complex concept, sound collaborative research is characterized, at the least, by caring relationships, cultural sensitivity, shared leadership, voluntary participation, mutual benefits, intellectual flexibility, adequate time, and structured activity (Bickel & Hattrup, 1995; Drake & Haskins, 1995; Elliott & Drake, 1997; Lieberman, 1992). This certainly is not a comprehensive list of success indicators nor does the presence of all constitute a "necessary and sufficient" condition for successful collaborative research. However, many, if not all, of these characteristics appear in those projects that enjoyed at least some measure of success.

Yet in spite of all that is known about "what works," the literature abounds with examples of collaborative projects that yielded unsatisfactory, equivocal, or contested outcomes. In several cases (Bickel & Hattrup, 1995; Hatch, 1998; Roemer, 1991), the causes appear to be rooted not in bad process but in a failure to clarify purposes and positions on a continual basis. Hatch (1998) tells the story of a school reform partnership among several stakeholder groups that foundered because of differing but mostly unarticulated understandings about the fundamental purpose of the project. He notes,

Even in a case where there was considerable agreement on goals and mission—when differences in approach were viewed as simply a matter of emphasis and not direct disagreement, where good relationships existed at the highest levels, and when significant funding was provided—different approaches to three of the basic dilemmas of schooling made it extremely difficult to make decisions and to carry out the collaborative work that school improvement required. (p. 24)

In this case, the original intent and initial planning of the collaborative project were not sufficient to sustain the project over the long term, and conflict and controversy plagued the project for much of its life.

This outcome should perhaps not be surprising. From both a psychological and sociological perspective, it is probably safe to assume that the original purpose of a study or the initial collaborative planning will seldom, if ever, suffice. Speaking from a psychological perspective, Hermans, Rijks, and Kempen (1993) argue that the self is fundamentally multifaceted and that one's personal narrative changes over time, space, and events. They believe that the narrative evolves, at least in part, as a consequence of dialogue and that the personal narratives inform the subsequent relationships: "It is only when an idea or thought is endowed with a voice and expressed as emanating from a personal position in relation to others that dialogical relations emerge" (p. 213). Speaking from a sociological perspective, Schratz (1993) notes that people's social behavior is often governed by motives, desires, and forces of which they may not be consciously aware. Thus, the initial goal of a research project may change as a result of the interactions among the people involved in the project. Schratz labels this readjustment "design in action" (p. 57). These notions indicate a need for explicit attention to agenda-setting throughout a collaborative venture. But that process is decidedly complex and some interesting complications can be expected to intrude from time to time.

COMPLICATING THE PROCESS

Complications in agenda-setting can arise within substantive, ethical, or procedural arenas, or combinations of the three. In this chapter, I give specific meanings to these terms. The substantive arena is associated with professional and research action and outcomes, the ethical arena with the nature of the interactions and relationships between researcher and teacher, and the procedural arena with the prerequisites and processes of research activity. Each of these arenas represents one element of a research context.

Substantive Complications

From a substantive standpoint, complications arise from the ambiguity, complexity, and indeterminacy of the context within which professional action and educational research take place. For the most part, the puzzles with which teachers and researchers deal are multifaceted, contextualized, and personalized (Altrichter, 1993; Drake & Haskins, 1995). The ambiguity of a puzzle leads different actors to define and solve it differently, and access to these various social constructions is a considerable challenge (Diamond, 1993). Furthermore, the "correctness" of a definition or solution is dependent upon the agenda or purpose being pursued and the benefits hoped for. From a teacher's standpoint, correctness is usually a function of improved teaching and learning; while from a researcher's standpoint, it is often a function of newly constructed knowledge or insights (Drake & Haskins, 1995). Neither of these standpoints is inherently more correct than the other. Instead, each represents a different "logic of action" (Forrester, 1993) that underpins the constructions of particular actors and that needs to be admitted into research negotiations.

While it may be relatively easy to recognize differences among teachers' and researchers' constructions, it is not so easy to understand or to integrate them. For example, collaborative researchers often espouse "valuing of difference," but they have not always been successful with practicing that value. At times, individuals have reported feeling constrained by norms of collegiality or unanimity to silence their dissent and to hide their difference (Richards & Shutz, 1997). And people (including collaborative researchers) appear to be generally more oriented toward constructing similarity than to valuing diversity (Lather, 1991), that is, for most of us, the familiar is the correct.

I am not suggesting here that teachers and researchers should be homogenized. The literature is clear that differences between the two always and already exist, and attempts to reduce the differences have not been particularly successful (Roemer, 1991). Instead, successes seem to be associated with those projects where the differences have been described, debated, discussed, and directed within the project. Johnston and Kerper's (1996) insight is helpful in this regard:

We now understand the inherently political nature of our roles and the ways these must be appreciated, critiqued, and integrated into our collaborative relations. Our differences provide the framework within which we must ground our work . . . we must commit ourselves to ongoing conversations that take into account differences, construct understandings with these differences in mind, and appreciate what each individual and institution can contribute to shared as well as conflicting agendas. . . . There are many personal and public agendas in a collaborative project, and at times certain capabilities are more important for some goals than for others. (p. 21)

Instead of keeping differences in mind, initial agenda setting often appears to be undertaken in a spirit, either conscious or unconscious, of attempting to construct sameness and to overcome or to ignore difference (Hatch, 1998). In such cases, it could lead to a "false consensus" (Anderson, 1993, p. 43) that could undermine subsequent efforts and reduce the efficacy of the project, from both the practitioner's and the researcher's point of view.

Ethical Complications

From an ethical standpoint, educational research, regardless of its genesis, is an intervention in a social situation (Altrichter, 1993), and the teachers are the ones who take the greatest risks in collaborative research projects (Goodman, 1994). Within that context, then, researchers are particularly charged with the task of applying strict ethical standards to their research actions. The typical standards of anonymity, informed consent, voluntary participation, and so on, while important, are only a beginning. Altrichter (1993) points out that "Action research is considered 'ethical' if research design, interpretation and practical development produced by it have been negotiated with all parties directly concerned with the situation under research" (p. 48). Because collaborative research often aims at the heart of the teaching and learning process, researchers need to honor the autonomy of the professional context and the professional knowledge base of the teachers (Altrichter, 1993; Bickel & Hattrup, 1995). They need to enter a research venture with the understanding that both the researchers and the practitioners will be "the changer and the changed" (Lather, 1991, p. 56).

Unfortunately, however, Gitlin and Thompson (1995) argue that most collaborative and/or action research is grounded in an implicit deficit theory in which "teachers are characterized as lacking political knowledge, as lacking a problem-solving method, or as considering themselves to have a need of one sort or another" (p. 139). This assumption places researchers in the "expert" role and teachers in the "learner" role. Goodman (1994) argues that the intentions of the researchers are less important than the effects of their actions. He says, "Although external change agents armed with 'research' firmly believe that as long as they are not conscious of any ideological agenda they are neutral and objective, in fact, they are merely unconscious" (p. 127). Goodman's point here is that the interactions deriving from such role definitions, whether they are consciously or unconsciously embedded, cannot support attempts to bring parity to the research relationship or to the negotiation process.

According to Gitlin and Thompson (1995), researchers try to resolve the parity problem "by moving past the research relationship or by defining and proceeding in terms of a corrected or 'right relationship' between professional researchers and classroom practitioners" (p. 140). This is not to underplay the differences between teachers and researchers in terms of the political clout each role enjoys within the educational hierarchy. However, Nespor and Barylske (1991) frame the political distinctions between teachers and researchers in unique terms: "What separates teachers and researchers, we argue, is not a style of thinking or reflection; it is the technologies of representation we employ, the relative size of our networks, and the points of accumulation within those networks" (p. 818). Their argument suggests that, while the divide in political power may be wide, it is a function of the constituted networks within which teachers or researchers operate, not a function of deficit on the part of teachers. More appropriate, then, would be a capacity-building model, in which "all involved in the research relationship are expected to learn and benefit" (Gitlin & Thompson, 1995, p. 142).

The purposes for which collaborative research is undertaken present a particularly sticky ethical complication. At times, researchers have been conscripted to engage teachers in collaborative research that aims to "sell" a particular innovation or to "convince" teachers of a particular point of view (Gitlin & Margonis, 1995). Such projects may be driven by external change agents or by system administrators. An example of administrator-driven collaborative research is found in Roemer's (1991) story. She tells of a project that began as an exploration into teacher knowledge about student writing and ended up as an articulation of one standard of accountability for assessing student writing. Her story highlights the dangers that can emerge when researchers enter a professional context in order to implant a change initiative that has been planned, ordered, or directed from outside the school. In general, such research projects violate the standards of voluntary participation, professional autonomy, mutual change, and shared leadership, and they render futile any attempt by teachers to negotiate the research agenda. Altrichter (1993) would see such projects as inappropriate for collaborative action research. He notes, "Action research is not indicated when mandated change has to be 'sold' to practitioners and clients, when reflection and change are only allowed within very narrow margins, or generally whenever reflected professionalism is inhibited" (p. 53).

Procedural Complications

From a procedural standpoint, complications might arise in relation to the capacity of the partners for collaborative process. Altrichter (1993) argues that teachers must have the capacity for self-reflexive, inferential, and transformative thinking. Bickel and Hattrup (1995) further this discussion by saying, "teachers who were most comfortable and able to participate in the collaboration drew on a wide range of social and intellectual skills, knowledge bases, and attitudes in their interactions with researchers" (p. 49). However, the capacity of teachers is not the only procedural problem. Researchers also must bring certain competencies to the collaborative process. Of course, they need the same intellectual capacity for self-reflexive, inferential, and transformative thinking. And they also need flexibility, respect for the professional context (Drake & Haskins, 1995; Hattrup & Bickel, 1993), participatory consciousness (Heshusius, 1994), and process sensitivity. In other words, researchers need the capacity to watch the process. They are charged with ensuring that "good" process is happening, that research agendas are not being driven at the expense of the teaching agenda, and that the practitioners are not being used or manipulated. They are responsible for recognizing when the research process needs to take a different direction, when it needs clarification, when it needs a push, or when it needs to be shelved for a period of time. And they need to recognize when the time has come for another round of negotiation.

Readiness for action, which has been cited as a prerequisite condition for collaborative action research (Altrichter, 1993), is an interesting procedural complication because it can be interpreted to mean "teachers' readiness to be taught." That kind of interpretation comes directly from a deficit model (Gitlin & Thompson, 1995) and can be used to blame or to co-opt teachers. Neither of these uses is in the spirit of sound collaborative research. But the notion of readiness for action is still a useful one: It could mean recognition of problems or tensions waiting to be resolved; it could mean individual and institutional will to do things differently; it could mean the emergence of shared language and common vision; and it could mean readiness to move forward on negotiated purposes and plans. Readiness for action should not imply moving forward on prescribed paths or other-directed activity. Instead, it should signal that certain individuals have a desire or a need to engage in a research event and are ready to develop at least some common meanings and understandings, to negotiate some purposes and plans, and to move into action phase.

Practically everyone writing about collaborative research agrees that time is a problem. In most cases reported in the literature, the limited time dedicated for meetings was used to plan and direct research activities rather than to discuss purposes, beliefs, and values or to develop shared meanings and common understandings (Hatch, 1998; Roemer, 1991). Yet Bickel and Hattrup's (1995) experience suggests that time should be devoted to affective and reflective aspects as well as to cognitive and active ones. They comment:

Establishing a dialogue that integrated the research and practitioner knowledge bases was a painstakingly long process. It was not until the second summer workshop that the collaboration understood the direction that needed to be taken to promote such a dialogue. Among the things that had been missing in the collaboration's original projections was an understanding of the *meaning making* that each participant had to go through in order to be productively involved in the work. (original emphasis, pp. 50–51)

Unfortunately, teachers' work worlds are not constructed to allow time for reflection or negotiation. In most cases, teachers add research activities to already demanding work schedules, and neither system administrators nor research leaders appear willing or able to reconstruct teachers' time (Bailey & Hess, 1996–97; Gitlin & Margonis, 1995).

Each of these constellations of complications can be read as a barrier to agenda-setting or as a reason for carefully negotiating agendas. Negotiating the substantive aspects of professional and research activity can lead to better connections between theory and practice (Lieberman, 1992), can facilitate the infusion of research results within the wider community (Forrester, 1993), and can lead to synergies derived from commingling researchers' and practitioners' knowledge bases and political constituencies. Negotiating from an ethical perspective can increase the confidence that researchers and teachers place in the research relationship and process; negotiating procedural issues can generate better research processes; and, of course, negotiation can be undertaken for particularly pragmatic reasons. If agendas are clearly defined and carefully negotiated throughout the project, it is likely that any real or potential gaps between research activities and individual agendas will be reduced or closed. This kind of alignment increases the chances of sustaining the project (Altrichter, 1993; Bickel & Hattrup, 1995).

STRATEGIES FOR NEGOTIATING AGENDAS

Clearly, different reward systems, different professional concerns, different political constituencies, and different work structures separate the worlds of researchers and teachers and lead to a host of fundamentally different agendas for collaborative projects (Drake & Haskins, 1995; Johnston & Kerper, 1996; Roemer, 1991). Thus, when these partners undertake collaborative research, negotiation is likely to be a critical and necessary part of the process. The negotiation strategies that I propose in the following pages fall into three major categories: structural, reflective, and apperceptive strategies. The structural and reflective strategies outlined are consistent with the meanings usually associated with those terms. Apperceptive strategies, however, may be less familiar. I use that term to refer to strategies that aim to reveal some of the hidden influences on an individual's perceptions. That is, they provide opportunities to raise to conscious awareness some patterns in how we see, think, believe, and know.

Structural Strategies

As with any process, such as communication or conflict resolution, negotiating agendas should be an iterative procedure through which the "design in action" (Schratz, 1993) unfolds. This means that the partners need to meet often. In other words, regularly scheduled and ad hoc meetings need to be built explicitly into the research process (Shuttleworth, 1993). These two kinds of meetings can serve different but complementary ends. Regular meetings signal to individuals that the progress of the partnership is their responsibility and that the partnership requires their personal time and attention. Ad hoc meetings provide opportunities to deal with emergent issues, to change direction if necessary, or to check on current needs or perceptions. Of course, finding time for all these meetings is a definite challenge, but they are essential for supporting the collaborative relationship and for furthering the project (Bailey & Hess, 1996–97; Drake & Haskins, 1995).

What to do with, before, or during those meetings is another question. Clearly, the partners need to set goals and plan activities together. This kind of collaborative process places the responsibility for the project upon the shoulders of each individual in the partnership. Through collaborative goal-setting and planning, practitioners and researchers sort out their individual and collective agendas and develop a research path that respects the needs of each partner and honors the desires for growth in both local and public knowledge (Bickel & Hattrup, 1995; Drake & Haskins, 1995).

Research meetings should focus on underlying hopes and wishes as well as on actions and tasks. This means that participants need to engage in conversation, discussion, dialogue, or other communication strategies. Of critical importance are the depth and breadth of the talk, since the level of discourse can dictate the outcomes. If talk remains at a structural, procedural, or instrumental level, it may do little to uncover deep or hidden purposes, values, beliefs, and assumptions. And those unspoken or hidden elements have been cited as the ultimate downfall of many collaborative projects (Hatch, 1998; Roemer, 1991). Thus, the following reflective and apperceptive strategies are ones that I have used, or wish I had used, to make explicit some of the implicit "stuff" in the collaborative projects of which I have been a part.

Reflective Strategies

Self-reflexivity has been one of the most important a priori strategies for me as a researcher. In the spirit of self-reflexivity, I have considered, written, and talked about the effects of my actions and theories (as suggested by Edwards, 1992, p. 12). In one research project, I worked with a group of elementary school teachers for a period of eight months to explore the notion of organizational learning in their school (Mitchell & Sackney, 1998). I started with the assumption that this was a new concept for them and that it held great benefits for their work. During my months in the school, I gradually became aware that their lack of familiarity was not with the actual practices of organizational learning but with the ways in which I was wording the construct. In short, they were practicing organizational learning in much of their collective activity but did not attach the "appropriate" terms to what they did. Nor had I, until I began to think through the ways in which I had structured and named certain aspects of the project—and the ways in which I was evaluating "appropriateness." Once I realized that many of the practices (although not the labels) were already in place, the teachers and I were able to work out research activities that were closely tied to their school activities. From that point on, the research became more integrated into the life of the school, and our agendas began to merge.

An accompanying strategy is collective reflection. This strategy engages participants in thinking together and talking about the purposes, plans, values, and actions already articulated or undertaken, those still to be described, and those perhaps not yet considered (Schratz, 1993). It is a strategy that can help individuals to deconstruct existing processes and understandings and to reconstruct more authentic ones (Schratz, 1993), to develop shared language and common meanings (Bickel & Hattrup, 1995), and to gain a deep and respectful understanding of one another (Hatch, 1998). In my own work with the teachers on organizational learning (Mitchell & Sackney, 1998), the meetings dedicated to collective self-reflection were the most highly praised and prized research activities of the entire year. In those meetings, we began to critically evaluate what we were doing and to ask the "why" questions underlying the "what." For most of the teachers, the collective reflection meetings constituted the heart of the research project and, for some, the essence of organizational learning. It was in these meetings that the teachers, many of whom had worked together for several years, finally began to see the world through the eyes of their colleagues. As one teacher commented, "This knowledge has allowed me insights into personal beliefs that help me to understand why the individual staff members do what they do."

Apperceptive Strategies

Edwards (1992) discusses the need to reconceive a problem's boundaries in order to understand it deeply. Extending his notion yields a strategy whereby individual participants in a collaborative project describe and reconceive personal boundaries or limits. Describing the boundaries serves to articulate the points of leverage individuals believe they have and the limits they believe to be insurmountable. Reconceiving the boundaries involves contesting self- or other-imposed limits and pushing them back to open more points of leverage. My experiences, both in research and in life, have led me to understand that we can often do far more than we believe we can. For example, a boundary that I have noticed myself and some of my colleagues placing around ourselves is the assumption that we do not have sufficient knowledge or ability to do a particular job when, in fact, we are accomplishing the tasks quite nicely. Often our efforts are limited by boundaries that are held in place by our own perception or our own acquiescence. Although I have only described and reconceived boundaries privately, it is perhaps best done in public. In the public forum, our discussions of boundaries can open spaces for understanding why partners act or refuse to act as they do. It can make explicit some assumptions and agendas that may be driving the research process but that have not been spoken aloud. And seeing our boundaries through our partners' eyes can help us to recognize possibilities and directions we may have not previously considered. (I have a sense, though, that publicly describing my personal boundaries will be somewhat embarrassing, even while publicly contesting them may be freeing.)

A second apperceptive strategy, also derived from Edwards (1992), is to invite intuition. He argues that "intuition can operate where quantification cannot—and where forced quantification misleads" (p. 18). He cautions that intuition, because of its nonrational genesis, should always be tested, reconsidered, and, if appropriate, revised or replaced. But he believes that inviting intuition into private and public discourse opens a window into information and ideas not usually visible or manifest. In my collaborative work on organizational learning (Mitchell & Sackney, 1998), inviting intuition simply took the form of asking the teachers to share their instincts or "gut feelings" about an activity, idea, direction, or plan without giving any reasons for why they felt as they did. Because they often did not have reasons for some of their feelings, they had hesitated to share them with the group. At times, their concerns proved to be unfounded, and we were able to move through these unspoken concerns. At other times, a teacher's amorphous unease led us to uncover a deeply rooted problem that, if left unattended, could have undermined future research efforts—or other collaborative efforts in the school. And at times inviting intuition gave the teachers a forum for advancing insights or ideas of which they had not been consciously aware or that they had never before spoken aloud.

Because teachers and researchers work in two different worlds and because collaborative research can be appropriated for all sorts of purposes, a significant strategy is to foreground politics (Gitlin & Thompson, 1995), as many times and at many levels political sensitivities intrude on the research process. Power relationships and power dynamics do not disappear simply because we are working collaboratively. Instead, they are always and already a part of every collaborative project, even those between "equal" peers. During a multiple-partner research project in which I was a co-investigator (Mitchell & Boak, 1997), political sensitivities were particularly troublesome, primarily because the funding partners had specific research outcomes in mind from the outset of the project. Since we had not included in the design any regular or ad hoc meetings among the various partners, we had no forum to raise process questions or to address political issues. At times, the funding partner and the teaching partners made decisions about the project that jeopardized the integrity of research results. Because our place as researchers was somewhat peripheral to the overall project, we remained silent about some of our concerns (although we did raise other concerns privately with relevant individuals). Certainly, foregrounding politics is a decidedly tricky strategy and one that must be handled with great sensitivity, empathy, and care. But it is a strategy that I believe to be critical. In this project, the failure to foreground politics proved to be a stumbling block that separated the researchers from the other partners and that kept the research from being as thorough or as useful as we would have liked.

A related and equally valuable strategy is to embrace conflict (Richards & Shutz, 1997) rather than to ignore it or avoid it. Individual partners in a collaborative venture have both differences and similarities. To focus on similarity and to avoid difference is to do an injustice to both aspects. I have yet to be involved in a collaborative project where conflict is handled well. In the organizational learning research (Mitchell & Sackney, 1998), the teachers and I avoided conflict in pursuit of harmony and acceptance. However, conflict rumbled underground from time to time, the most notable and long-standing example being a difference of opinion over who should assume administrative tasks when the principal was absent from the school. Avoidance of this issue led to some troubling administrative gaps and served to undermine the level of trust among school personnel. The sensitive aspect of the issue was that the teachers and the vice-principal had different assumptions about the role of the vice-principal. If we had dared to confront the conflict, we might have been able to understand the different purposes, to clarify roles, to close the administrative gaps, and to re-build trust. At the end of the project, several teachers commented that, while they had come to appreciate the place of conflict in collective activity, they still did not know how to manage it positively. I suspect that is true in most cases. If conflict is viewed in terms of win–lose, then the tendency is to avoid it. If, on the other hand, it is viewed in terms of opportunity, then the chances of using it to further understanding and to negotiate purpose and process may be enhanced. Embracing conflict implies that it is, indeed, seen as an opportunity and not a threat.

These strategies suggest that the process of negotiating collaborative research agendas and processes is fundamentally paradoxical. Partners are faced with both difference and similarity, with affect and cognition, with reflection and action, with process and product, with relationship and purpose, with trust and conflict. We can either keep these nested oppositions distinct (and choose between them) or find ways to enfold paradox. In the organizational learning study (Mitchell & Sackney, 1998), we were surprised at the number of times that what we thought was reflection, for example, led us quietly and unexpectedly to an obvious plan of action. What we thought was conflict led, when we allowed it, to deeper trust. At the end of the study, we were only beginning to understand the paradoxical nature of the collaborative process, and we did not explore alternative ways of enfolding paradox. Roemer's (1991) experience, however, is instructive. The collaborative project in which she was a co-investigator foundered on the rocks of goals, action, purpose, and product. She laments, "we spent our time talking about policies, rules, rubrics, and logistics. We never spoke about our individual values as teachers, what we wanted to preserve, protect, or foster, or what we hoped to improve" (p. 441). I wonder if the more intuitive or affective side of the nested oppositions is more likely to lead to their counterpart than the other way around. The situated interplay of oppositional forces in collaborative ventures is inherently paradoxical, and I do not yet clearly understand the best ways of bringing them into counterpoint. I have been raised and educated by more linear, rational, dichotomous, and distinctive patterns and expectations, and paradox, as both a word and a construct, is only starting to come into focus in my mind.

CONCLUSION

The reason for negotiating agendas in collaborative research, of course, is to come to some deep agreements about the purposes and processes for the project. However, from an ethical standpoint, the agenda of the practitioners should probably always take precedence (Drake & Haskins, 1995). From time to time, this stance could place the research agenda at risk, but when researchers undertake collaborative projects with school people, they are intruding into the space of those people's lives. Edwards and Usher (1993) assert that practice-based research is not automatically or inherently emancipatory and that it "can easily become part of a discourse with oppressive consequences" (p. 20). Hence, the process of negotiating research agendas should not be a hollow, contrived, or orchestrated one. Instead, it should be an authentic exploration of possibilities that is grounded in a deep respect for the participating practitioners and for the professional context.

Negotiating agendas is not easy. Some of the strategies outlined above may be unfamiliar to some of us, and they are inherently difficult. But they are possible. A prior concern, of course, is the model within which they are embedded. If they derive from a deficit model (Gitlin & Thompson, 1995), I am not optimistic about their chances to flourish. If, on the other hand, the strategies flow from a capacity-building model, then they have the potential to bring coherence to a research project and to extend the knowledge of all participants, including researchers and practitioners. We all stand to gain when the learning of each individual is at the heart of a collaborative research agenda.

REFERENCES

Altrichter, H. (1993). The concept of quality in action research: Giving practitioners a voice in educational research. In M. Schratz (Ed.), *Qualitative voices in educational research* (pp. 40–55). London: Falmer Press.

Anderson, G. (1993, July). Group based research: Commitment or compromise? In N. Miller & D. J. Jones (Eds.), *Research: Reflecting practice* (pp. 43–46). Proceedings from the 23rd annual Standing Conference on University Teaching and Research in the Education of Adults, University of Manchester, UK.

Bailey, B., & Hess, M. L. (1996–97). The teacher as researcher: An uncharted course. *Brock Education, 6*(1–2), 1–12.

Bickel, W. E., & Hattrup, R. A. (1995). Teachers and researchers in collaboration: Reflections on the process. *American Educational Research Journal, 32*(1), 35–62.

Diamond, C. T. P. (1993). Writing to reclaim self: The use of narrative in teacher education. *Teaching and Teacher Education, 9*(5/6), 511–517.

Drake, S. M., & Haskins, B. (1995, June). *Two facilitators in search of a collaborative action research process that works.* Paper presented at the annual conference of the Canadian Society for the Study of Education, Montreal, Canada.

Edwards, D. V. (1992, June). *Ethics, efficiency, and reflexive reflective practice.* Paper presented at the second international conference on Public Service Ethics, Siena, Italy.

Edwards, R., & Usher, R. (1993). "Research: Reflecting practice?" Modern paradigms, postmodern controversies. In N. Miller & D. J. Jones (Eds.), *Research: Reflecting practice* (pp. 20–22). Proceedings from the 23rd annual Standing Conference on University Teaching and Research in the Education of Adults, University of Manchester, UK.

Elliott, A., & Drake, S. (1997). Moving from "two solitudes" toward a "blended" culture in school/university partnerships. *Journal of Staff, Program and Organization Development, 13*(2), 85–95.

Forrester, K. (1993, July). Collaborative research and the wider community: The case of the trade unions. In N. Miller & D. J. Jones (Eds.), *Research: Reflecting practice* (pp. 136–138). Proceedings from the 23rd annual Standing Conference on University Teaching and Research in the Education of Adults, University of Manchester, UK.

Gitlin, A., & Margonis, F. (1995). The political aspect of reform: Teacher resistance as good sense. *American Journal of Education, 103*, 377–405.

Gitlin, A., & Thompson, A. (1995). Foregrounding politics in action research. *McGill Journal of Education, 30*(2), 131–147.

Goodman, J. (1994). External change agents and grassroots school reform: Reflections from the field. *Journal of Curriculum and Supervision, 9*(2), 113–135.

Hatch, T. (1998). The differences in theory that matter in the practice of school improvement. *American Educational Research Journal, 35*(1), 3–31.

Hattrup, R. A., & Bickel, W. E. (1993). Teacher–researcher collaboration: Resolving the tensions. *Educational Leadership, 50*(6), 38–40.

Hermans, H. J. M., Rijks, T. I., & Kempen, H. J. G. (1993). Imaginal dialogues in self: Theory and method. *Journal of Personality, 61*(2), 207–236.

Heshusius, L. (1994). Freeing ourselves from objectivity: Managing subjectivity or turning toward a participatory mode of consciousness? *Educational Researcher, 23*(3), 15–22.

Johnston, M., & Kerper, R. M. (1996). Positioning ourselves: Parity and power in collaborative work. *Curriculum Inquiry, 26*(1), 5–24.

Kanter, R. M. (1989). *When giants learn to dance.* New York: Simon and Schuster.

Lather, P. (1991). *Getting smart: Feminist research and pedagogy with/in the postmodern.* New York: Routledge.

Lieberman, A. (1992). The meaning of scholarly activity and the building of community. *Educational Researcher, 21*(6), 5–12.

Mitchell, C., & Boak, T. (1997). Collaborative research: The power, the perils, and the possibilities. *Brock Education, 7*(1), 1–14.

Mitchell, C., & Sackney, L. (1998). Learning about organizational learning. In K. Leithwood & K. S. Louis (Eds.), *Organizational learning in schools* (pp. 177–199). Lisse, The Netherlands: Swets & Zeitlinger.

Nespor, J., & Barylske, J. (1991). Narrative discourse and teacher knowledge. *American Educational Research Journal, 28*(4), 805–823.

Richards, M., & Shutz, A. (1997). Reflections on the collaborative experience: The CCR in review. *Brock Education, 7*(1), 76–86.

Roemer, M. (1991). What we talk about when we talk about school reform. *Harvard Educational Review, 61*(4), 434–448.

Schratz, M. (1993). From cooperative action to collective self-reflection: A sociodynamic approach to educational research. In M. Schratz (Ed.), *Qualitative voices in educational research* (pp. 56–70). London: Falmer Press.

Shuttleworth, S. (1993, July). Working collaboratively on research into collaborative working: I thought I saw a palindrome. In N. Miller & D. J. Jones (Eds.), *Research: Reflecting practice* (pp. 168–173). Proceedings from the 23rd annual Standing Conference on University Teaching and Research in the Education of Adults, University of Manchester, UK.

CHAPTER 3

Negotiating across Cultures

Merle Richards

"Collaborative negotiation" has become a fashionable term in both education and business circles, where it is viewed as a way for parties with differing goals to resolve disagreements for the benefit of all participants. It implies movement from an initial stance of "our side, your side," with different values, desires, and goals, to mutual understanding. Through dialogue, each party is enabled to attain satisfactory outcomes. Sachs (1998) distinguishes between communication or "people" skills and the more complex ability required for negotiation: "successful negotiating requires a strong knowledge of techniques and a belief in the 'win–win' concept" (p. 70).

The situation applies to members of different cultures attempting to work together. Social groups develop stereotypes that act as a lens, which causes us to see ourselves and others in certain ways. Aboriginal people in Canada have been victims of racist stereotypes for centuries; they were kept separate from the mainstream and not regarded as citizens or adults for most of Canada's history (Paul, 1993). As a result, Aboriginal people are conscious of the effects of injustice and generations of colonialism (Battiste, 1998), which have left in many a legacy of bitterness and anger. Working alongside white people may activate those feelings, making cooperation difficult.

Collaborative relationships depend on trust and openness, which permit the development of shared understandings and perspectives (Stewart, 1996). But cultural traditions and stereotypes can act as screens, preventing the deep sharing essential to collaboration and mutually beneficial negotiation. A factor in ethnic identity is the semantic labels individuals use to describe themselves and their group. The labels reflect a sense of identity and membership in a group (Hecht & Ribeau, 1988). Like other language groups, Aboriginal people have distinctive ways of speaking about themselves and others; words or phrases with special meaning can become triggers to activate stereotypes and the associated emotions (Gudykunst & Schmidt, 1988). "Us and Them" categories also suggest different values and emotions, such as trust and mistrust. Calliou shows that dichotomies are extremely powerful, and that we need to learn new ways of using language "in order to speak previously silenced truths" (Kalia, 1991, p. 276, as cited in Calliou, 1998).

The literature on culture and social identity reveals the effects of stereotypes, in which assumptions about "the other," shaping our communications, may be based on false understandings that distort the relationships essential to joint efforts to attain goals. Even the customary language use of each party may heighten distrust and hostility, making the effort to collaborate a difficult process.

To be successful, negotiation depends on mutual acceptance of both goals and the process of negotiation itself. Otherwise, we may develop "the learned incapacity to hear and understand what another human being is saying and the choice to respond in dishonesty" (Jourard, 1978, p. 47). Gudykunst and Schmidt (1988) cite examples of how stereotypes constrain interactive patterns, resulting in judgments about others that lead to negative self-fulfilling prophecies. Bardovi-Harlig and Hartford (1997) describe how language learners encounter formulas and idioms, assimilating them whole and only later "unpacking" them into meaningful elements and structures. Similarly, intercultural encounters face us at first with unfamiliar behavior patterns whose connotations we may not immediately understand, and to which we may therefore assign negative meanings. Multicultural and antiracist approaches try to overcome these problems through empathy, plain language, and values clarification (McLeod, 1984). But underlying assumptions about the situation in which the negotiation is occurring may be unnoticed by the participants, and hence remain unvoiced. Their effect on communication, however, can suffice to derail efforts at collaboration.

A case in point was a project intended to develop teaching materials for an Aboriginal teacher education program and the school language program in which most of the learners expected to work. The project required collaboration between the author, an academic experienced in language teaching and curriculum, and a coordinator, a member of the Native community who would ensure that the curriculum resources produced would be culturally appropriate. Unfortunate assumptions on both sides rendered the partnership untenable but provided an object lesson in the collaborative process.

A MODEL FOR SUCCESSFUL NEGOTIATION

Sachs's (1998) model of collaborative negotiation provides a framework for discussion of the project. Sachs outlines several steps to successful negotiation:

Prepare! Prepare! Prepare!

Establish a valid mutual objective.

Identify the issues and both parties' interests.

Do not assume that you know the other side's win.

Identify and study the participants' backgrounds, behavior, and negotiating styles.

List the strengths and weaknesses of both sides.

Identify your highest goal and walk-away position.

Look for any precedents.

Identify any deadlines.

Establish your strategy and preferred alternatives.

Be prepared for the long haul.

Prepare! Prepare! Prepare!

I thought I had prepared! Having consulted widely to ascertain the need for Iroquois language curriculum and teaching materials, I wrote the proposal, which was supported by several members of the Aboriginal community. The intent was to bring together fluent speakers, writers, and curriculum developers who would collaborate to produce classroom-ready materials that could be used by student teachers in our program and by their supervising teachers. For this purpose, a native person fluent and literate in Iroquois culture was needed to coordinate the shared efforts and develop the overall curriculum plan. This coordinator would be selected by a hiring committee chosen from the university's Aboriginal Council.

What had not occurred to me was that I needed to prepare the hiring committee itself to understand the nature of the work. My assumption was that to write language curriculum, one needed teaching experience, an understanding of the nature of curriculum, and fluency in the language. But the phrase "curriculum development," a technical term for me, held little meaning for the other committee members, who assumed that anyone could write curriculum, as long as they were steeped in the culture and its values. As the non-native committee member, I felt obliged to defer to their judgement. Callie, the person hired, had impressed us as a strong, knowledgeable advocate for her culture and community, but lacked the fluency, curriculum experience, and background in language teaching that I felt were necessary for the project.

Establish a Valid Mutual Objective

The proposal explained the goals and intended outcomes of the project, and I assumed that accepting a contract to work on the project implied accepting those goals as well: to develop a curriculum outline for native second-language programs in the elementary grades, write exemplary unit plans, and produce the needed resources for those units. As a teacher, I thought in terms of learning objectives, activities to attain them, and materials to support the activities. As a linguist, I understood the need to structure the curriculum to include active learning and learner initiative.

Callie, however, was suspicious of such planning, declaring it inconsistent with her culture and evidence that I was attempting to subvert native values by using non-native structures. She held that native teachers would only use materials they had requested or chosen themselves, even though most of the materials they were currently using were inadequate and not at all representative of native culture. Callie did not view the project as related to the native teacher education programs or even to the Iroquois community beyond her reserve; she stated that "the teachers would only use a curriculum that they themselves had worked on," and that the scope and sequence could be developed only in consultation with each of the immersion teachers. My suggestion that the teachers be approached with a prepared outline that they could modify was brushed aside.

On the other hand, Callie was committed to the native-language immersion programs on her reserve, and wanted our project to support and strengthen them and hence also Iroquois language and culture. Since many of the immersion teachers were enrolled in our programs and would later become supervisors of our student teachers, I agreed that we could adjust our goals to provide classroom materials suited to the needs of the immersion program as well as of the student teachers. It appeared that we had negotiated a common purpose.

Identify the Issues and Both Parties' Interests

Again, my assumptions were wrong. I thought our mutual interest was to produce materials that would benefit language teachers and the student teachers placed in their classrooms, and thus help native teachers to strengthen their language and culture. But Callie did not feel that a university should have any role in a project involving native language and culture, stating that a native cultural center should have received the project funding. Although contracted to the university, she perceived herself to be working on behalf of the immersion teachers in her own community. This interest also made her reluctant to use examples of curriculum from other native groups, even when they provided models or frameworks for language teachers. For example, when I brought in some materials developed at another reserve, Callie dismissed them at a glance: "They don't do things our way."

Moreover, in a school community with two native languages and two immersion programs, some teachers perceived a competition between the two for resources. Callie suspected that I was favoring one group over the other, with which she herself identified. When she asked which group I was working for, I didn't at first understand her question. Only later did it become evident that she had talked with some of the teachers, who now believed the project would be used to benefit the other group. Callie's comments on several occasions showed that she expected me to have only ulterior motives, and that the project would somehow be profitable to me or to my university. I became aware that others shared these notions when teachers I had worked with for years would not talk to me when I visited their school. I had spoken to Callie about the need to prepare our materials for publication; one of the conditions of the grant was that all materials produced would be sent to the provincial Aboriginal Education Council for distribution. But the term "publication" had dark overtones in the community, who recalled early experiences with anthropologists and others using community members as research subjects. Some fence mending was needed, in the form of a phone call and letter to the school principal.

February 29, 1996
Dear Mrs. Vale,

As you know, the Faculty of Education has been engaged in a project to develop learning materials for the use of the student teachers in the native Teacher Education programs, especially in the Onkwehonwe language courses. We much appreciate the participation of your teachers in this effort. Our intent was that the teachers should benefit by gaining needed materials while also providing them for prospective teachers.

There seems to be some misunderstanding about the project and publication of the materials. Because they are to be used in the teacher education courses, all the materials developed will be copied and made available to the native student teachers and others. A full set will be kept for . . . [the language] teachers. . . . As well, the Aboriginal Education and Training Council who funded the project requests a set of materials, which they may circulate to other teachers. No other publication is planned, and the materials are not to be sold.

We are grateful for any materials that your teachers are willing to share with student teachers. Collaboration among Onkwehonwe teachers to produce culturally sound materials will help to ensure that future pupils learn and retain their culture and values.

I hope you will share this letter with your staff, and thank you for supporting our programs.

Sincerely,

But the issues remained unspoken. Without face-to-face discussion, grievances and suspicions grew and festered.

Do Not Assume That You Know the Other Side's Win

This is perhaps the crux of the matter. Assuming from the first that we were partners, I had thought the "win" was the same for us both: achieving the goals of the proposal. But Callie saw me as an adversary to be defeated, perhaps because I was an outsider getting involved in a culture where I didn't belong, because I might be exploiting the culture, or simply because I was a "white" person upon whom to vent old angers.

Identify and Study the Participants' Backgrounds, Behavior, and Negotiating Styles

Neither partner did this accurately. Callie knew several people whom I had worked with in the past, and had taken a Cayuga language course that I had organized at the reserve, but we had never met. She was aware that I was myself taking Mohawk courses taught by an instructor from another reserve and was in charge of a native teacher education program offered in her community. Perhaps this was cause enough for Callie to treat me, from our first meeting, with hostility and suspicion, not taking my words at face value, implying that I had hidden agendas.

I knew Callie by reputation as a strong member of the traditional community, steeped in the culture. But I also knew from the language class that she was a beginner in language study, with little background in teaching or curriculum. The Aboriginal members of the hiring team, however, saw her as a person able to promote the needs of the community.

Not realizing at first that we did not share goals and commitment to the task, I adopted the multicultural approach of trying to understand, empathize, and clarify my perspectives. My first act as project leader was to try to schedule regular meetings to develop and monitor a work plan. But Callie would only agree to meet on Fridays, when I was in class. Her tactic was silence: she seldom responded to phone calls or faxes, arrived late or not at all at scheduled meetings, and refused to answer queries about her work.

Five months passed with no sign of any accomplishment before Callie finally agreed to meet in the library of the local native center, which I hoped would be neutral territory. We began by sitting at a table, Callie not looking at me but addressing asides to the librarian about "white people" and "special rules for Indians." When we finally got on task, I said we needed a work plan and a budget, that is, a list of priorities for spending the project funds. She astounded me by saying, "You said we had no budget"—and I suddenly realized she had interpreted that phrase as meaning we had no money. I pointed out that we had a project grant from which she was being paid; she replied that she had not been shown the account and should be in charge of it. It became very clear that we had different ideas about the duties of a coordinator. Callie saw herself as responsible not to me or the university but only to the Aboriginal Council that had originally approved the project, and therefore resented the fact that she did not have signing power over the funds. Realizing that we would not be able to discuss the project face-to-face, I resorted to letters (slightly edited for confidentiality):

Dear Callie,

Our meeting made it obvious that we have not been communicating. Until today, every meeting we have scheduled has been postponed, cancelled, or cut short; it appeared that you hadn't the time to sit down to discuss the project in detail. From the beginning, I had expected to do so in order to draw up a work plan and organize projected expenditures, that is, a "budget" within the grant guidelines.

I am . . . concerned about . . . the time it took to discover the misunderstanding. Clearly, we have been operating at cross-purposes; productive meetings would have corrected this situation right from the start. Since I don't respond well when under attack, I shall attempt to answer your questions now that I've had time to think about them.

Assuming that we are allies and not adversaries, we need to agree on the purposes of the project. I don't believe our intent is simply to help the [local] immersion teachers, but that is a good place to start. Here is how I see our objectives at this stage:

Project Objectives

1. Assist teachers to develop teaching objectives and sequence them into an order they can use as a guide to instructional planning.

2. When teachers have stated their wishes and decided the teaching themes or units for their long-term plans, assist them to construct units with clear aims and evaluation devices they will need. If possible, also provide teaching resources such as pictures, grammar outlines, wordless books, and English materials suitable for translation.

3. Provide language teachers with a general outline of objectives for language learners.

4. Supervise translation of student materials.

5. Maintain safe copies of all materials developed.

6. Find fluent speakers to tell stories or reminisce. Record them in quiet, comfortable settings. Transcribe the recordings.

7. Develop native scripts and/or recordings to accompany slide shows and filmstrips, possibly videotapes.

8. Maintain curriculum materials on the hard disk of the computer so that they may be updated and adapted as needed upon teachers' requests.

Problems That Have Arisen

The main difficulty is one of communication. Without regular productive meetings, it is impossible for me to know what is being accomplished, and where we need more help. It's also impossible to coordinate the various aspects of the project without knowing what curriculum is being developed.

Possible Solutions

1. If DIA concurs, move the project to #1 school, where many curriculum resources are available. This would provide a suitable meeting place where I won't feel like an interloper when I need to keep track of the work being done.

2. Exchange your computer for one you are more comfortable with. We need all curricula and materials in progress on the hard disk, with backups safely kept in a different location (the safe at Brock is relatively fireproof).

3. It is important to understand that all the books, resources, hardware, and software bought with project funds belong to the University, but they are accessible to Six Nations teachers and others. At present, some of these materials are at #1 school, where the Mohawk curriculum team is working.

I hope this clarifies my sense of the project and its objectives. I am to be away from the 14th till the end of the month. However, I am willing to meet with you this Friday, Saturday, or Sunday. If that is impossible, we should meet early in September.

Please answer by phone or by fax. I await your response.

Sincerely,

The response was a change of tactics on Callie's part. From this point, she did not simply fail to talk with me, but also used Aboriginal Council members as her voice. A letter to the Council using my comments about "publication" of the materials to be developed in the project implied that I would claim as my own the work of others and publish culturally sensitive materials belonging to the teachers. Although the accusations had no substance, they put me on the defensive and removed me even farther from the project. My strategy was to look for other ways to accomplish the project goals without depending on Callie; I turned to some fluent speakers who were interested in developing curriculum materials and with whom I could work.

List the Strengths and Weaknesses of Both Sides

In this project, my strengths were academic but my weakness was social. The converse was true for Callie. Not only did I naively assume mutual respect as the basis of partnership, but also I was extremely concerned lest I or the university be seen as racist. Callie, on the other hand, did not hesitate to ascribe to me motives of personal benefit, exploitation of native culture, and irregularities in using the project funds. She brought several such complaints to the university's Aboriginal Council, which permitted her to hire family members and friends to work on the project. She was thus surrounded by helpers who did not know the objectives of the project and communicated only with her. In this way, Callie succeeded in locking me out of project activities.

It is an interesting phenomenon to see someone hold a meeting for the purpose of not communicating. Each time I asked for a meeting of the project staff, Callie would arrange one, but each time, some members were unavailable. The native people present would greet one another and chat in a friendly fashion, then the meeting would begin and silence would fall. I would ask for a progress report, request paper copies and backups of all the materials, and be told they were unavailable. Callie would then describe the ongoing work without actually showing any samples or outlines.

Identify Your Highest Goal and Walk-Away Position

The highest goal, of course, was to accomplish the aims of the original proposal. But it became obvious that knowledge of language teaching methods and curriculum design were essential to attain this. Since I could not communicate with Callie, my expertise was useless. A walk-away position must at least produce some resources that could be used in the target programs; Callie would develop a scope and sequence chart, the picture collection, and a resource kit for elementary "native studies" classes, while I would work with fluent speakers to write down stories in the two immersion-program languages, which my artist son would illustrate without payment.

Again, silence ensued. The project termination date was approaching, a report must be written, and I had seen no products.

February 28

Dear Callie,

I went to the school on February 7 and again on February 12 to pick up the picture files and scope and sequence you worked on. However, they were not there, and I was assured that nothing had been brought into or removed from the school.

Please send the materials in promptly. They are part of the project and needed for summer school.

I also look forward to seeing the kit.

No response. It transpired that the picture collection was growing, but without any original work designed to reinforce cultural values or support the teaching units that had been promised. The assistants were spending much of their time preparing classroom materials for immediate use in one school, cutting out and collecting magazine pictures and copying commercial blackline masters. As a result, the collection could not be further duplicated without infringing copyrights, so it was unavailable even to the other immersion teachers on the reserve.

Communication worsened. Now even my answering machine received no messages. Unable to contact Callie herself, I attempted to reach her through others, enlisting the aid of the Chair of the Aboriginal Council, with whom Callie stayed in contact. After a year, still not having seen any output from her team, I asked the Chair to arrange a meeting with Callie's team at their workplace. When we arrived, Callie said she could not access the computer, but would fetch her brother to show us the unit he was completing. Eventually he arrived and showed us a title page. Delivery of the kit was promised and a date set. More letters followed.

Dear George,
    Not having heard from you, I am writing to inquire whether you have received the completed kit Callie was working on. I understood from the letter you circulated at the last Council meeting that the finishing date was February 19. Acting on that information, I closed the petty cash account at the end of February, only to find that the work was still in progress. On March 6, Joseph was still making final copies of the text, which he expected to finish that week. However, I have not received from him any requests for payment, so I am assuming that he was working out his hours that had been missed during the Longhouse days. I have received no communications from Callie, and have still not seen any output from her team.
    Please let me know if you have the kit or any other of the project materials. I will be glad to come and pick them up.
    Sincerely,

After several months and renewed funding, the kit was finally delivered. The scope and sequence did not exist: I designed one myself with the help of a fluent speaker. The picture collection could not be sent to the sponsors, but the kit itself included some excellent pictures that satisfied them.

Ironically, although the finished products did not reflect the original proposal, the products did attain some of the goals and were praised as the best of all those submitted to the funding agency.

Look For Any Precedents

Precedents abound for such incidents. An old tradition, inherited from colonial and paternalistic governments, of writing proposals to get funding for particular projects and then using the funds for other community purposes, still exists. The proposal is not necessarily viewed as the goal statement, simply as a means to obtain funds for the community. In hindsight, I believe Callie, loyal to her community, felt she was acting in their interests by using the project moneys to benefit the language teachers. But I, shaped by the culture of academe, regarded the accepted proposal as a binding contract.

Identify Any Deadlines

The project lasted three years. The deadlines set by the sponsors were flexible, in that funding could be carried over to the next year and further funding applied for. Our own deadlines, however, were imposed by the project goals; we wanted the student teachers in our summer program to become familiar with the materials before their practice teaching placements. This was not accomplished.

Establish Your Strategy and Preferred Alternatives

It became clear early on that Callie did not consider me to be either in charge of the project or her supervisor; I was merely the liaison—or the obstacle—to the project funds. She considered herself to be contracted to the University Aboriginal Council, and therefore not obliged to communicate with me. My strategy was to keep the channels open, but also to talk with others in the hope of getting some messages heard. Dureault (1987) discusses the results of avoidance, the most common way of dealing with conflict. "Invariably, suppressed conflict leads to anger . . . [while] confrontation means that conflict is accepted. The conflict is examined and the elements in opposition are described and analyzed" (p. 17). This was the medicine needed: an open discussion of perceptions and disagreements that would allow us to plan some actions that would satisfy both our goals.

Callie's assistants believed that the aim of the project was to provide the native immersion teachers with classroom materials for their immediate use. When I pointed out that the funding was to support the Native Teacher Education Program, they were clearly confused, having had no idea of such a connection. However, because they were working for the immersion teachers, they were unconcerned that most of their time was spent reproducing commercial materials rather than developing new materials, as was intended. As a result, the picture file consists almost entirely of photocopies of easily available commercial materials. They saved the teachers much time and energy, but did not actually increase the store of culturally sound materials for native pupils.

It was through one of the project assistants that I first realized Callie was working on a music unit rather than one the Council and I had originally requested. However, since it was within her area of expertise, I made no objection, expecting that in her own field, she would do good work—an expectation that was borne out.

Be Prepared For the Long Haul

It was a long haul, but persistence and endurance finally brought the project to a conclusion. Recently, a colleague asked me, "Why didn't you just quit?" The question was startling, because I hadn't ever thought of such a possibility. Reflecting, I have come to believe that my own personal stereotype had come into play: having undertaken a task, I would complete it. I would not see myself as a "quitter"—even a sensible one.

LESSONS LEARNED

Bruner (1962/1967) commented that "Man lives in a symbolic world of his own creation, a symbolic world that has as one of its principal functions the ordering and explication of experience. A change in one's conception of the world involves not simply a change in what one encounters but also in how one translates it" (p. 159). Collaborative experiences can have such a transformative effect (Stewart, 1996), but in this case, lack of collaboration was equally powerful. This was not a "clash between cultures," but a contest between two people shaped by different backgrounds and experiences. Neither party, although influenced by its values, is typical of her ethnic group, and either might have communicated successfully with another person. Somehow, the cues and stereotypes that I aroused in Callie made it impossible for her to try to breach the communication barriers.

The strongest lesson is that collaborative negotiation requires more than good will. Different cultures may emphasize values that differ at a deep level and cannot be glossed over in a partnership; if they are not discussed, true collaboration cannot be established. Transparency and equality can only be attained when both parties reveal their perceptions of the task, the situation, and the collaborative process itself. Liberal values of acceptance and tolerance mask but do not resolve conflict; if parties "agree to disagree," they must leave sensitive issues out of the working relationship.

For me, a basic cultural value is *tikun olam* ("repair of the world"): one who sees an injustice is obliged to do what is possible to correct it. When I began the project, working to help restore languages that have been damaged by oppressive policies of the mainstream community seemed a worthy task. But Ann Pineault, a wise Micmac woman, later explained to me that for most natives, noninterference is a higher value. One must not offer advice or help until it is asked for. In this case, I was asked to help, but not by my coworker or her personal associates; she could only see me as a member of the oppressing culture interfering in her community's concerns.

Another lesson is that both sides must be willing to negotiate for a "win–win" outcome. Each must recognize that the other has a need for satisfaction and goal attainment. Collaboration is not a poker game, where players mask their intentions and feelings to preserve a position of strength; the habit of deception also leads to distorted interactions, which strengthen negative stereotypes and prevent problem solving.

PERSONAL FEELINGS AND REACTIONS

Being Jewish, I have a deep aversion to racists and racism. I also know how hard it is to deal fairly and openly with those who can be regarded as oppressors of one's people. The possibility that my university or I could be perceived as racist, together with the Aboriginal Council's approval of Callie's appointment, prevented me from giving her notice. However, to continue her contract when she was not supporting the project objectives meant that she was retained because she was Aboriginal. This was not affirmative action, because her appointment did not lead to a collaborative relationship that would have enabled me to see from her perspective and help her to build skills and develop expertise. She did not profit from my experience or help me to know her culture better. Neither of us gained significantly from the project; and we both lost out on an opportunity for growth and deepened understanding.

REFERENCES

Bardovi-Harlig, K., & Hartford, B. (Eds.). (1997). *Beyond methods: Components of second language teacher education*. New York: McGraw-Hill.

Battiste, M. (1998). Enabling the autumn seed: Toward a decolonized approach to Aboriginal knowledge, language, and education. *Canadian Journal of Native Education, 22*(1), 16–27.

Bruner, J. (1967). *On knowing: Essays for the left hand*. Cambridge, MA: Harvard University Press. (Original work published 1962)

Calliou, S. (1998). Us/them, me/you: Who? (Re)thinking the binary of First Nations and Non-First Nations. *Canadian Journal of Native Education, 22*(1), 28–52.

Dureault, G. (1987). Resolving conflict: Confrontation, negotiation are best. *Education Manitoba, 14*(4), 17.

Gudykunst, W. B., & Schmidt, K. L. (1988). Language and ethnic identity: An overview and prologue. In W. B. Gudykunst (Ed.), *Language and ethnic identity* (pp. 1–14). Clevedon, Avon, UK: Multilingual Matters.

Hecht, M. L., & Ribeau, S. (1988). Afro-American identity labels and communication effectiveness. In W. B. Gudykunst (Ed.), *Language and ethnic identity* (pp. 1–14). Clevedon, Avon, UK: Multilingual Matters.

Jourard, S. (1978). Education as dialogue. *Journal of Humanistic Psychology, 18*(1), 47–52.

Kalia, S. (1991). Addressing race in the feminist classroom. In J. Gaskell & A. T. McLaren (Eds.), *Women and education* (2nd ed.; pp. 275–282). Calgary: Detselig.

McLeod, K. (1984). Multiculturalism: Life style, way of life, life chances. *Multiculturalism, 7*(2), 19–21.

Paul, D. N. (1993). *We were not the savages: A Micmac perspective on the collision of European and Aboriginal civilization*. Halifax, Nova Scotia: Nimbus.

Sachs, S. (1998). Negotiation skills: A platform for success. *Risk Management, 45*(4), 70–76.

Stewart, H. J. (1996, Spring). Collaboration: Towards improved education practice: Lessons learned from Brock University's Centre of Collaborative Research. *Education Canada, 36*(1), 20–25.

CHAPTER 4

Cooperative versus Collaborative Research: Assessing the Difference

Andrea Toepell

INTRODUCTION

Much of the literature on collaborative research focuses on partnerships created for a specific research project. Typically, such partnerships involve academics working closely with agents external to the university, or researchers involved in participatory action research. For example, Harper and Carver (1999) describe a collaborative project involving university and community-based partners teaming with youth to develop an HIV prevention program. Corse, Hirschinger, and Caldwell (1996) undertook a project involving university-based researchers and clinical staff in a community mental health center as collaborators for researching service outcomes.

When reading about partnerships and research projects, I often question the use of the term "collaborative," when I feel, based on the description of the research, that the term "cooperative" would be more appropriate. When research participants are encouraged to assist researchers in making decisions about a project that impacts them, I agree that such participation is an element of collaborative research. However, when a contributor's role is mainly to assist in carrying out a project without participating in the decision making, I view the relationship as cooperative. Unfortunately, in research discourse, the terms "cooperative" and "collaborative" are frequently interchanged and used uncritically as synonyms; this usage may explain why the distinction between the two types of research has seldom been discussed.

This chapter provides a framework for exploring differences between collaborative and cooperative research from a perspective that is spurred by my own experiences. I define these terms and present models that schematically illustrate the distinction. Upon describing my research experiences, I discuss how they fit the models of cooperation versus collaboration, and, finally, I compare the quality of my experiences by examining the assumptions, expectations, and outcomes associated with them.

BACKGROUND

My experiences as a researcher stem back many years. Before completing my graduate degree, I conducted research as an independent consultant. This role brought with it many advantages that I later appreciated when I began working with others. My collaborative experience is more recent, having developed since I became a faculty member at Brock University. Although I have functioned collectively with a variety of partners on common projects, this chapter focuses on two research projects that have involved working with other university individuals. My experiences with these two projects were very different, as were the eventual outcomes. The first one was a difficult and negative experience (an infectious diseases case study) that was cooperative in methodology, while the second was more positive (a rowing case study) and more collaborative.

Generally, several factors motivated me to work with others. Collaboration offered an opportunity to expand my research focus, a chance to broaden the circle of researchers I know and connect with, a likelihood that I would accumulate more publications, and the promise of working more closely with people I enjoy in my faculty. Some of these reasons are necessities for survival in academia; others are more personal.

As any faculty member will attest, research and publication productivity is what drives a professor's success (and perhaps survival) at a university. Tenure, promotion, and merit are determined primarily using these measures of accomplishment, while teaching performance along with administrative and/or committee contributions and community services are also weighed. A new faculty member must quickly establish an active research portfolio, and collaborative research efforts can assist junior faculty members in establishing a research focus (Nichols, 1998). Considering the competition for external research grant funding, it is not surprising that most faculty, and in particular new faculty, carry out research and publish as a member of a team. In fact, increasingly more granting agencies require that research projects be designed as collaborative initiatives and/or include an interdisciplinary perspective (which by definition implies collaborative efforts with others).

DEFINING THE TERMINOLOGY

According to the *Oxford English Dictionary* (1986), to collaborate is to "work in conjunction with another or others to co-operate, especially in a literary or artistic production, or the like" (p. 613), and to cooperate is to "work together, act in conjunction with another person or thing, to an end or purpose, or in work" (p. 963). Here the only distinction between the terms is that one refers to working collectively "to an end or purpose." I argue that the definitions provided above are essentially identical, as the rationale for "working together" always has a purpose; therefore, nothing unique differentiates the terms as defined.

When people work together cooperatively, they involve themselves with tasks to help each other out. When people work together collaboratively, they participate to meet a common goal. In defining collaborative investigation, McTaggart (1991) argues that collaboration means "sharing in the way research is conceptualized, practiced, and brought to bear on the life-world. It means ownership . . . production of knowledge . . . improvement of practice" (p. 171). Cooperative involvement in research, however, may include various roles short of the complete sharing McTaggart describes. Participants may, for example, advise about a research protocol or "simply go along, politely co-operating with action researchers" (Peters, 1997, p. 67). Such an arrangement is one of cooperation and not collaboration because not all contributors have control over the research or make decisions concerning it.

Collaborative inquiry is often understood as an activity that involves input from research participants; in collaborative investigation, the research and action are woven together in practice (Torbert, 1981). In both, the term "collaborative" implies contributions from participants, but it can be incorrectly used when participants are only playing a cooperative role. However, the literature on action research is filled with terms such as "collaborative action research," "collaborative inquiry," and "collaborative learning" (Brooks & Watkins, 1994), when what is described as collaborative is actually more cooperative.

Building on McTaggart's (1991) idea of constructing knowledge, it is apparent that researchers working together with the intent of creating new knowledge are collaborating (Peters, 1997). However, people working together without the intent to construct new meaning, who are simply assisting one another in a task, are cooperating. Bosworth and Hamilton (1994) give an example wherein the teacher has a lesson plan, tells students what they need to learn, and allows them to work together in whatever fashion necessary in order to have the learning mastered. In this case, the students work cooperatively, as they have had no influence over the teacher's agenda or material to be learned, and individual learning is the focus.

Nichols (1998) provides a definition of collaborative research that focuses on degrees of responsibility. He alleges that collaborative research functions best with a principal investigator who accepts the duty of completing the bulk of exploration and the research process, while other team members contribute in their areas of expertise. I would consider such a model as cooperative, unless all participants have input into both the design and the interpretation of the research.

The natures of participation, accountability, and ownership are significant factors when distinguishing between cooperative and collaborative research. A participant may take on a task-related role in the research project, such as a statistical consultant, be accountable to the project concerning the accuracy of her/his work, own none of the data, and remain removed from the interpretation of the data. This person is working cooperatively with the research team. However, should this person be a team member who has also shared in all aspects of designing and implementing the research, participated in making decisions concerning the project, and invested in data collection and interpretation, then this person is working collaboratively with the team. When working cooperatively on a research project, the responsibility of a team member is restricted to the task(s) assumed or the guidance sought, and there is no ownership of the project's process or outcome. For some people, working cooperatively on a project means acting in the role of counselor and not as collaborator. For these members, research and action are not constructs that direct their involvement in the project, as this level of commitment to research inquiry is neither expected nor sought from them.

As illustrated in Figure 1, the cooperative research model involves two types of individuals: the primary researchers, who assume ownership and responsibility over the research experience, and the cooperating assistants, who take on and are responsible only for their specific tasks. Completed tasks are directed back to the primary researchers, who make all the decisions concerning the project. In such projects, the outcomes and benefits may or may not be shared. For example, co-authorship on publications may be negotiated, or the primary researchers may publish alone.

As demonstrated in Figure 2, the collaborative research model offers the potential for more continuous flow of communication and decision making because the primary researchers are involved in almost every part of the project. From the beginning, the primary researchers, all working together, make collective decisions concerning the scope and direction of the project and define their contribution abilities as they assume equal responsibility, accountability, and commitment to the project. Instructions for tasks come from the group, and results are directed back to them. Communication between members undertaking tasks is more likely as they have an equal investment in the project. Co-authorship on publications is assumed as part of the joint responsibilities and rewards of collaboration.

The distinction between cooperative and collaborative research has been examined here from the perspective of the research team. I define collaborative research as a process in which team members share all aspects of the research project, including ideas, design, implementation, data collection, analysis, and writing, and who collectively own the data and share

Figure 1
Cooperative Research Model

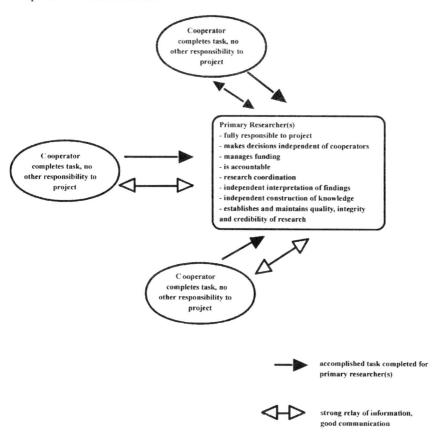

the responsibility and accountability to funding agencies, the studied population, and the field of research. I define cooperative research as the process by which some members share an interest in the research but are
responsible for single tasks, work together in an effort to accomplish the
tasks, but have no influence over the project's design, direction, or interpretation of findings.

MY RESEARCH EXPERIENCES WORKING WITH OTHERS

The research focus I had prior to my university appointment was one I
developed and honed independently in the field of HIV/AIDS and prisons.
Upon coming to Brock University, I was unable to find colleagues who
were working on projects similar to my own areas of interest. Wanting to
expand my research focus was a natural progression, but I lacked the con-

Figure 2
Collaborative Research

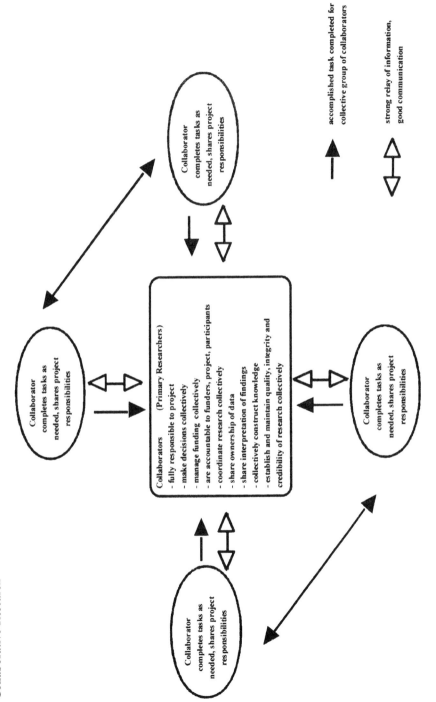

fidence to branch out independently into fields entirely unrelated to my "mainstay" subject area. It was a logical choice to explore other subject areas with the intent to collaborate with colleagues.

The first case study described involves a project that began prior to my appointment at the university and reflects a "cooperative" research project.

An Infectious Diseases Case Study

While still employed as a consultant in the field of HIV/AIDS and prisons, I was approached by a hospital physician cross-appointed to an Ontario university. He had received government funding to conduct a study examining the attitudes and perceptions of correctional staff concerning infectious diseases (including HIV). Aware of my work, he asked if I was interested in collaborating with him and another researcher, who was a masters student and employee of the Correctional Service of Canada, on the project. I did not know him but happened to know her, and was eager to become involved as a consultant and collaborator on the research project. As an independent researcher, I would be paid for my contribution, while the masters student would have use of the data for her thesis.

We three team members met once to discuss the project in detail, define the research questions, and divide the tasks based on our skills and expertise. Our goals were to evaluate institutional perceptions (the research focus), and write manuscripts describing the findings and policy recommendations to the government, correctional institutions, and journals.

What Transpired

My experiences with the Primary Investigator (PI) on this project were good initially but then declined from bad to worse. As the study progressed, I took on most of his responsibilities in order to complete the project. Along the way, he assured me and the third partner of his commitment to the project, but continually referred to his demanding work schedule. Despite his promises to complete the tasks needed, he failed even to begin them, and the burden fell on the other researcher and me.

During the project, I developed and prepared the lengthy interview questionnaire, collected some of the data (most of which was collected by the other coresearcher), constructed the coding manual, coded all the questionnaires (169), and designed and set up the database for data entry. The other woman studied the policy development in the field, coordinated all the interviews in five penitentiaries, conducted most of the interviews, and wrote a manuscript, her own thesis, describing the study with recommendations for policy development. The PI later hired an individual to enter the data and carry out descriptive statistic analyses. As far as I am aware, the PI did nothing else to participate in this collaborative research effort, but he did present some preliminary data at a ministerial correctional meeting.

More than two years passed. A report was due to the founders, which was repeatedly promised by the PI. I was particularly concerned about how the delay would affect the reputation I had developed over the years in the field before the start of this project. Eventually the PI modified the thesis manuscript that the coresearcher had prepared for her masters program (which he requested on disk from her) as his report to the government. I felt disgraced that he "borrowed" the other team member's work and presented it as his own, was inexcusably late with this submission, and included my name on the report.

After several years and to the best of my knowledge, no article has yet been written describing the study, nor has any substantive data analysis beyond the earlier simple descriptive type been completed. I offered to take the leadership in these initiatives (data analysis, writing of articles) and was assured that I would receive from him all the data in order to fulfill these tasks, but the data have never arrived and remain in his possession. It is unfortunate that they are not better analyzed and that journal articles are not published, as the findings from the study are pioneering and of great interest to policy developers in the field. Also, participants in the study were promised a report of the findings, as the issue studied directly affects them in their workplace, and this promise has still not been fulfilled.

If ever there was a "research experience from hell," this one is close. As a researcher embarking on a collaborative project with people I did not know well, I should have been wary of being used or abused, of having to do all the work without receiving any of the credit, and of being held at arm's length from the data. In this case, I even had to fight to be paid for my work.

How Collaborative Was This Experience?

Although I was invited to "collaborate" on this project, it became more of a cooperative than a collaborative arrangement. The PI clearly did not share the same vision, commitment to the tasks, or ethical concern about the project as did the other coresearcher and I. His role, as it later evolved rather than as we agreed at the outset of the project, was one of director with sole ownership of the project. In other words, he had two "cooperators," or assistants, who carried out the research while he made all the decisions concerning data analysis and dissemination. Perhaps it was his perception that since he was awarded with funding for the project it was his research project and the data belonged to him.

Usually when data are collected, the standard research protocol is to make copies of the raw data, coded data, and all data sets. In this study, copies of the raw data (completed questionnaires) were made and sent to me for coding. After the questionnaires were coded, I sent them back to the PI, who was to enter the data into the database and do the analysis. In hindsight, I see that I should have made a copy of the questionnaires *after* I coded them to (1) prevent having to recode all the copied raw questionnaires should they not have arrived safely, and (2) ensure I had a copy of the coded data for myself. It was foolish of me to continue trusting the primary researcher, as I would have had a copy of the data that I could analyze on my own, and possibly have published a journal article co-authored with the other research member. Such a tactic, however, raises ethical concerns. The project functioned cooperatively despite my initial expectation that it would be collaborative, and although I might have protected myself by keeping copies of the data, they rightfully belonged to the primary researcher. My taking ownership of the data would have been in violation of the cooperative model presented in Figure 1.

I approached this project as a "collaborator," and was encouraged to assume this role, when the PI apparently saw my role as a "cooperator." Preliminary discussions regarding the sharing of design ideas, tasks, and data analysis implied collaboration, but these plans did not unfold as such. Although role clarity was determined at the beginning of the project, as stressed by Nichols (1998) to be an important process among collaborative researchers, unexpected shifts in role responsibility occurred. Also, considering that I was hired as a consultant, I should not have presumed to be treated as a collaborator but rather have understood that I was working as an assistant to the PI and cooperating on the project.

My coresearcher and I were equally concerned about the lack of communication and commitment from the primary investigator, and she and I worked collaboratively in whatever capacity necessary in order to complete the project. We were able to rely on one another, work independently, and work without direction from him, and since I had experience in conducting research I took the lead whenever necessary. Further, the PI's communications with me and the coresearcher were singular in nature (to be expected in cooperative projects) as opposed to collective, whereas communicating with both of us together would have been expected in a collaborative effort. The other woman and I cooperated with him by fulfilling the tasks and carrying out the research, but we were neither perceived nor respected as "collaborators" by him. His owning and not sharing the data, as well as failing to fulfill previously assumed responsibilities, are also not characteristic of collaborative intentions. Figure 3 illustrates the dysfunction found in this research project when applying the cooperative research model to this experience.

As identified by Tom and Sork (1994) and Torbert (1981), there is a difference in the type of knowledge gained when research results are interpreted collaboratively among all practitioners and researchers on a project, as opposed to interpretations made by a single researcher. Each team member contributes to the process of understanding the results, and thereby influences the knowledge gained. In the case of the infectious disease project, the interpretation of the results became the sole responsibility of the PI, the team member most detached from the research process. It is

Figure 3
Dysfunctional Cooperative Research Model, Infectious Diseases Case Example

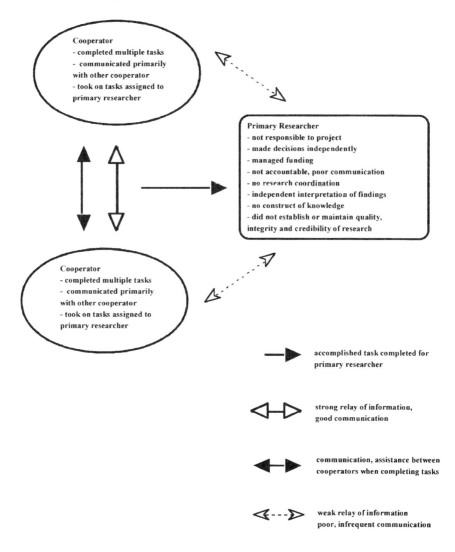

therefore likely that the interpretation will lack the reflective insight that could enrich the findings were I or the other coresearcher involved in the interpretation process. However, interpersonal dynamics can also interfere with the research process, and the results might then be flawed (Jarvis, 1999), a plausible outcome for this study were I and the other coresearcher involved in the data interpretation.

Although this study generated a high amount of cooperation between the two coresearchers, collaboration on productivity (e.g., journal writing) was nonexistent. In examining collaboration on academic research productivity, Landry, Traore, and Godin (1996) note that geographical closeness to partners influences the outcome of published articles (i.e., the further away in distance, the less likely it is that collaborators will publish). Although this finding may have influenced the lack of collaborative productivity in the infectious diseases project, I believe that the PI's hidden intention not to work as an equal partner played a larger role, as did differences in work ethic. Collaborative researchers recommend that methodologies, motives, and expectations be discussed and clarified prior to the onset of a collaborative project (see, e.g., Nichols, 1998; Tom & Sork, 1994), but the implied assumption is that individuals are honest with the agendas at the time and that they aim to honor their agreed-upon plans when the research project is underway. Unquestionably, the research experience would have been much more pleasant had the PI fulfilled his assumed and agreed-upon tasks, or at the very least acknowledged his inability to take on necessary tasks, and the project would have finished with all commitments met in a more timely and professional fashion.

A Rowing Case Study

Female colleagues with whom I am friendly at Brock University were jokingly discussing the supposed benefits we could reap were we to collaborate on a research project. One said, "Oh, I'd have the research profile and publishing track record I need to get into a doctoral program." Another said, "I'd finally spend time working with people I actually enjoy." And I added, "Yeah, and I'd have some friends!" As we discussed research ideas we discovered a mutual interest in the topics of women, aging, health, and the sport of rowing. When we described what particular skills each of us could bring to the project, we collectively planned a research project that met all of our interests. According to Landry, Traore, and Godin (1996), such circumstances enable the research experience to be a productive one. This project began quite differently from the infectious disease project, in that the coresearchers already knew each other and worked in close proximity. Our goals were to study the perceived health benefits of rowing among older women, further develop the research scope to include additional areas of interest (e.g., aging and/or obstacles to rowing), and publish journal articles describing the results from all projects completed.

What Transpired

The rowing project started with much enthusiasm, and during the initial data gathering, even more energy was brought to the project. A rowing regatta was quickly approaching, which offered us our first opportunity to collect data. We met frequently and with relative ease since we worked in the same institution, even in the same faculty. The research focus was defined and the project's implementation and data collection strategies were collaboratively determined.

The four coresearchers collectively designed the four-page survey instrument. I took the leadership in organizing and creating it while others brought the literature review, theoretical framework, and health models to it. All members were involved for the data collection at the rowing event. One coresearcher created the database spreadsheet, had a student input the data while she herself did the statistical analyses, and shared the results with the remaining research members. All expenses up to this point were incurred privately by the research team. Several opportunities to submit for conference presentations arose, and all four team members contributed to this forum. Different components to the research have already been presented at varying conferences. The research group also worked together on a grant and was successful in receiving funds to continue with the project.

With every new opportunity to collect data, the original questionnaire was collaboratively revised to reflect a new or different aspect of research to explore. Meetings were set regularly and organized with an agenda in order to ensure a productive use of time and keeping the project on track. This research project is still ongoing, although journal articles describing the findings have not yet been written.

Although the above describes a positive collaborative research experience, it is not without problems or difficulties. As can be expected when collaborating with several people, differences in working styles and attitudes toward meeting times can raise tensions. Meeting mutually agreed-upon deadlines remains a problem for some members, although all of us have had to postpone a promised commitment due to teaching or other responsibilities. Despite the meetings being organized with set times and dates, it often happened that one or two members were unable to attend the meeting or arrived very late for it without previous notice. When preparing for conference presentations, the prior communication between the copresenters was at times poor, and the presentation experience was not as satisfactory as expected. Such behaviors may be a result of members feeling relaxed about commitments because they were friendly with team members prior to embarking on a research study together.

When I began a year's leave from the university, we all agreed to prepare journal articles for submission, but none of us achieved this goal. During that year the group did not meet, nor were additional data collected when possible opportunities arose. After my year's absence we regrouped as a research team and planned for an upcoming and significant opportunity to collect new data. A new questionnaire was designed for this purpose. One member, suitably connected with the rowing event at hand, negotiated the pragmatics of our collecting data and having the questionnaires copied for the site. As the regatta date approached, she became increasingly overwhelmed with other work duties and family obligations. I offered support to her in order not to miss the opportunity to collect data, but she insisted that she could manage all of her research responsibilities. At the last moment, she was not able to collect data at the regatta. Although she felt bad about the turn of events and suggested an alternate opportunity for data collection, the preparation involved for the regatta was wasted and the chance to collect data during a unique rowing competition was lost. The support system needed to prevent such a missed opportunity was obviously not in place.

How Collaborative Was this Experience?

Clearly, the rowing project is much more representative of collaborative than of cooperative research. This is a team of four primary investigators who share the same vision and commitment to the project and who collectively make decisions concerning the research. Coresearchers are seen as neither assistants nor cooperators, but rather as equal partners. Landry and colleagues (1996) showed that incentives for researchers to work together increase with geographic proximity; this was the case for the rowing research team, for both personal and intrinsic incentives (as described earlier).

Collective efforts were made to receive funding; hence, all team members have access to the funds awarded. Communication between co-investigators is much better than for the previous case study, although there remain areas for improvement, and members speak freely with one another concerning task outcomes, results, continued research ideas, and other concerns.

Data are shared among and owned by all team members. Collective interpretation of the data provides a richer explanation of the findings because each member contributes her unique understanding and experience of the research to the analysis (Tom & Sork, 1994; Torbert, 1981).

Work ethics are fairly consistent among the four members; however, there are clear personal differences in how team players handle stress, multiple duties, and time management. Although geographical closeness has facilitated convenient and frequent meeting times, it has not had an impact on publishing productivity (as noted by Landry et al., 1996), and a journal article is only now being drafted. It appears that this outcome has until now not been a high enough priority for any of the team members to undertake it and fit it into their schedule.

EXAMINING THE COOPERATIVE/COLLABORATIVE PROCESSES

When functioning as an independent researcher, one can only count on oneself to accomplish all tasks, unless assistance from others (who are not collaborators but rather assistants or cooperators) is arranged. Overall, the researcher makes all decisions about the work and can anticipate certain outcomes that are within the control of the researcher. The act of working independently creates complete autonomy and control over the work. However, when working collectively with other researchers there are shifts in the assumptions, expectations, and outcomes as they relate to the research process.

Assumptions

Unless it is otherwise stated and made explicit, partners entering a collaborative working relationship assume that all team members are equally committed to the project. It is hoped that members will be respectful, understanding, motivated, and prepared to work at least at the same level or with the same amount of effort. In the initial negotiations for both projects described in this chapter, each team member's strengths were discussed and each person's roles were defined with their skills in mind.

I made several assumptions when I became involved in the infectious disease project. I assumed that the leading researcher was experienced, professional, and honest. I assumed that he understood what was entailed in conducting research and that he had previously dealt with large volumes of data. Because he is a medical doctor and was awarded research funds, I assumed that he was attentive to meeting deadlines for reports and preserving his credibility. I later learned that it was wrong for me to make all of the above assumptions.

For the rowing project, I also made several assumptions, not all of which, luckily, were incorrect. I assumed that the four coresearchers would share the workload and responsibilities equally (which we did), and have a vested interest in meeting our goals and objectives. I also assumed that we shared the intent to keep the momentum of the project going to welcome continual research developments, and that all aspects of the project were known and accessible to all the researchers (funds, data, writing opportunities, etc.).

Expectations

Perhaps the largest expectation when collaborating with other researchers is that almost every aspect of the project is shared among the team members, unless other arrangements are negotiated early on. That is, writing for funding, conference presentations, and publications is shared, as are collecting, coding, analyzing, and owning data. If the activities themselves are not completed jointly, then at the very least their progress or outcome is shared among members.

For the infectious disease study, I expected the PI to honor deadline dates and commitments as well as possible and to treat his coresearchers with respect. I expected the primary researcher to be forthright with me concerning his abilities, skills, and intentions, and did not expect to learn later that he was unable to complete promised tasks because he lacked the skills to do so and had no intention of sharing the data or collaborating on a journal publication. For the rowing research example, I expected that working with female colleagues whom I had known for a short while and whose company I enjoyed would be a positive experience and that we would support one another. I also expected that despite our relationship as friends, we would treat our collective work seriously and professionally, and meet deadlines and commitments. For the most part, all of this has happened.

Although I expected that I would be able to speak candidly to the rowing research team members about differences (e.g., not informing others about coming late to meetings, or waiting to the last moment to prepare for conference submissions and presentations), I was unable to do this. I feared souring my relationship with team members with whom I had an issue, and I either ignored the issue or accepted the disappointment. In my previous collaborative research experience (the infectious diseases project), I was also not able to speak frankly with the PI about his behavior and standards, and I thought my hesitancy was a function of my not knowing him well enough. With the rowing research group, my continuing friendship, interestingly, actually hindered my saying what I needed to say as well. I surmise that the problem lies with me, as I chose not to assertively address the disappointments I encountered with coresearchers for both projects.

Outcome

The final outcome of the infectious diseases case example remains a mystery, as I am unaware of any progress made with the project. I have not been able to bring closure to the project, as the PI has yet to share the data with me in order for me to further analyze it and prepare journal manuscripts. To my mind, the project remains incomplete, but I accept that my involvement with it is over. I am not content with how the research progressed nor with how it concluded, as journal articles (a shared and promised goal) have not been published. I do not foresee working with the PI any longer, as I suspect he has either given up on preparing such articles or has already done so without my knowledge.

The outcome of the rowing case example so far is also not entirely satisfactory. Although much has been accomplished as a team and the process has been positive, the way in which we operate is at times harried. Preparing article submissions has not been accomplished by any of us despite this being the most critical collective outcome, although a brief report was published in a rowing magazine. We have, however, remained friendly and our relationships have strengthened due to our collaborative involvement. I continue to work with the rowing research partners, and although I no longer take the leadership in organizing new research opportunities, I am supportive when we collaboratively discuss and plan for them. Instead, one of the coresearchers has taken the leadership to prepare manuscripts for journal publications, as past attempts to do so individually have failed.

THE REALITIES OF WORKING COLLABORATIVELY IN RESEARCH

The truth about collaborative or cooperative research is that the satisfaction of such efforts is largely dependent on who is involved in the project. As with any collective effort, personalities, working styles, approaches, values, and attitudes all influence the ease with which people function together and the satisfaction experienced by all interested parties.

Working cooperatively or collaboratively on a research project can give each team member a sense of belonging, being valued, and even liked (in most cases). These feelings are beneficial to the collective process and to the team members, as they nurture the senses of commitment and motivation that are necessary to forge ahead as the project unfolds. For many people, working collectively is far more satisfying and more rewarding than working independently.

Working collaboratively also offers team members a chance to contribute toward a common goal, a process that is affirming for most people. Being productive, accomplishing tasks, sharing resources, meeting objectives, and reaching goals collectively, are healthy and empowering. All researchers need to feel a sense that there is external approval for their efforts, that there is significance for their findings and contributions, and that their work brings about change or advances a cause, effort, or knowledge. Collaboration makes such events more likely than does working independently or cooperatively because large-scale outcomes necessitate the pooling of resources, expertise, multiple skills, and great efforts. The commitment involved in collaboration also contributes to the likelihood of project completion.

Establishing research partnerships has become the "wave" of today as granting agencies are expecting that such links are made prior to awarding funds. Universities offer wonderful opportunities for researchers to collaborate, especially if the university is located in a community where external agencies are also interested and able to cooperate on particular research efforts. Nichols (1998) defends the roles that professionals from different disciplines can play in collaborative research efforts, giving strength and enrichment to a project.

Some negative realities also exist in working cooperatively or collaboratively. Perhaps the most annoying aspect of working collectively is that not everyone will fulfill the responsibilities they intend to. Even the most committed and motivated individual will have times in her/his life (involving career and family) that make it difficult to follow through with agreed-upon tasks. This reality becomes problematic when an incomplete task prevents other team members from moving forward with their responsibilities or agendas. When activities are built upon one another as a means to completion (as most collaborative projects are), one or two incomplete responsibilities can create havoc and halt a project temporarily or even end it prematurely. In such a case, none of the anticipated outcomes are met, and fellow collaborators are left unsatisfied or even disillusioned by the process.

Challenges and benefits to conducting collaborative research have been identified in the literature. Warner, Hinrichs, Schneyer, and Joyce (1997) maintain that some challenges include ensuring that the collaborative efforts are useful to all parties, that time to be invested by members is negotiated and not assumed, and that the focus of the research does not sway while the project is in progress. In some research, politics and political costs to some partners may be higher or more of an issue than for other partners. Some benefits to collaborating on research are obvious (in particular, the sharing of costs, resources, expertise, time, and accessing otherwise hard-to-reach populations), but Rovegno and Bandhauer (1998) describe the significance of experiencing shared empowerment for individual transformation as researchers, and for writing for publication when working collaboratively.

Yamane (1996) describes two distinct difficulties that can occur when conducting collaborative research: transaction costs and free riding. He explains that there are direct costs to completing research (e.g., time and energy spent on surveying the literature, constructing the research question, gathering the data, etc.) as well as transaction costs (results from interacting with group members, scheduling meetings, negotiating differences, etc.). In the infectious disease project, the direct and transaction costs were very high for me, while for the rowing project they were mostly shared equally among members. Yamane cautions against the "free-riding" problem, wherein coresearchers do not participate equally in the process but assume equal credit. This certainly was the case with the infectious disease project.

When working on a team, one typically shares control over the project or delegates it to one or two key members. This shift in power can be difficult for some people, especially for those who are accustomed to functioning independently. "Going with the flow" is an obvious way to avoid power struggles, but if a project is heading in a direction some participants find inappropriate, or if an aspect of the research is handled in a way that is not satisfactory to all, then difficulties will arise. Handling differences, working them through, and finding suitable resolutions are themselves skills that must be brought to the team effort by at least one member. Warner and colleagues (1997) emphasize the importance of developing trust among collaborative research partners prior to the onset of the research, while Tom and Sork (1994) acknowledge the difficulties that "mistrust" can create when working collaboratively.

Often a researcher considering participating on a cooperative or collaborative research project must weigh the anticipated quality of output against the amount of effort required from her/him. An independent researcher must see to all necessary tasks and does not have the luxury of dividing labor among several members, but is also solely responsible for the caliber of the work and outcome. This is not so when one works collectively with others. As has been my experience, working on a cooperative project can threaten a researcher's credibility, especially when another team member(s) behaves in an unethical or not mutually acceptable manner. Often researchers must accept that the quality of a project may be less than what they are able to achieve when working independently, and that not everyone shares their rigorous work standard.

MAKING THE COLLABORATIVE EXPERIENCE POSITIVE AND PRODUCTIVE

It would be presumptuous of me to declare any profound insight concerning collaborative research, considering my little experience in the area. I can, however, present personal "lessons learned" that suggest ideas about working collaboratively and cooperatively.

Being clear about what strengths or expertise each person brings to the collective effort is valuable. With the rowing project, I have taken control over setting meetings and agendas, and I am content with this role, as my contributions in this area have ensured that the research has moved ahead and stayed on track, and that we have collaboratively accomplished a lot. I am aware that I have strong organizational skills (and do not have difficulties taking charge) and use them in ways to advance the research and not (hopefully) alienate my fellow team members. I found that when I took some control over aspects of the shared research agenda, I was being constructive within the project and enjoyed my involvement in it. However, for the infectious diseases research, I took charge when it was clearly necessary, but I did not feel good about doing so, as the roles and responsibilities shifted continuously without an acknowledgment or discussion of these adjustments with the PI.

Corse, Hirschinger, and Caldwell (1996) identify several aspects to successful partnerships when conducting collaborative research. These include expressing appreciation for the complementary contributions of partners, frequent and effective communication, high levels of commitment and consensus concerning goals of partners, and clearly negotiated credit of the collaboration. All of the above features were missing from my infectious diseases research experience, but the majority were and are present during the rowing project.

A major personal weakness I have is that I do not enjoy writing research reports for publication. I can write and I *must* write, but I hate to do it and I know that I am not alone. Working collaboratively can help someone like me through this impasse, but not when all members on the research team share this problem or are too busy to make writing a priority. Typically, others on a research team can encourage or assist in the writing process, but one must consciously select members with such abilities to ensure that publishing becomes a final outcome (as is critical in the field of academia). It is not helpful when all team members share the same weaknesses, but it is helpful to be honest about them in order that support or prevention strategies are put into place.

Other aspects of working collaboratively that contribute to a positive experience include working with a group of individuals who treat one another with respect and as equals. Personalities need to be harmonious with one another, and if they are not, then they should at the very least be agreeable. Knowing people before organizing a research project together is ideal but not always possible. In the case of the infectious diseases project, I did not know the PI, but I could have searched his publication history and noted that he had very few publications and was the last coauthor on most of them. This piece of information would have alerted me to the fact that he did not have much research experience, and I could have assumed a larger organizational role right from the start rather than taking on more of his responsibilities as the project progressed and his weaknesses were revealed over time.

Working in the same institution or city has a large impact on the flow of working collaboratively. For the rowing project, meeting times and dates and locations were easily organized, enabling us to continuously feel connected with the progress of the project. The infectious diseases project relied heavily on e-mail communication and the occasional telephone conversation, primarily due to the travel distance required for the three coresearchers to meet.

Finally, being able to maturely and reasonably address difficulties or differences is always a welcome strategy when working with others, and one that helps propel the work forward while keeping the group's effort united. Personally, I have not been able to approach team members about the poor organizational skills that have caused the project to miss opportunities, nor have I been able to confront individuals who have shirked responsibilities and forced others to carry a heavier load. Dealing with disappointments and finding resolutions is a skill that needs to be applied in a way that will not strain relationships with team members but will promote a positive research experience for all involved.

REFERENCES

Bosworth, K., & Hamilton, S. J. (Eds.). (1994). *Collaborative learning: Underlying processes and effective techniques*. San Francisco: Jossey-Bass.

Brooks, A., & Watkins, K. E. (Eds.). (1994). *The emerging power of action inquiry technologies*. San Francisco: Jossey-Bass.

The compact edition of the Oxford English dictionary (12th ed.). (1986). Oxford: Oxford University Press.

Corse, S. J., Hirschinger, N. B., & Caldwell, S. (1996). Conducting treatment outcome research in a community mental health center: A university–agency collaboration. *Psychiatric Rehabilitation Journal, 20*(1), 59–63.

Harper, G. W., & Carver, L. J. (1999). "Out of the mainstream" youth as partners in collaborative research: Exploring the benefits and challenges. *Health and Education Behavior, 26(2)*, 250–265.

Jarvis, P. (1999). *The practitioner-researcher: Developing theory from practice*. San Francisco: Jossey-Bass.

Landry, R., Traore, N., & Godin, B. (1996). An econometric analysis of the effect of collaboration on academic research productivity. *Higher Education, 32(3)*, 283–301.

McTaggart, R. (1991). Principles for participatory action research. *Adult Education Quarterly, 41(3)*, 168–187.

Nichols, J. D. (1998). Multiple perspectives of collaborative research. *International Journal of Educational Reform, 7*, 150–157.

Peters, J. M. (1997). Reflections on action research. In B. A. Quigley & G. W. Kuhne (Eds.), *Creating practical knowledge through action research: Posing problems, solving problems, and improving daily practice* (pp. 63–72). San Francisco: Jossey-Bass.

Rovegno, I., & Bandhauer, D. (1998). A study of the collaborative research process: Shared privilege and shared empowerment. *Journal of Teaching in Physical Education, 17(3)*, 357–375.

Tom, A., & Sork, T. J. (1994). Issues in collaborative research. In D. R. Garrison (Ed.), *Research perspectives in adult education* (pp. 39–56). Malabar, FL: Krieger.

Torbert, W. R. (1981). Why educational research has been so uneducational: The case for a new model of social science based on collaborative inquiry. In P. Reason & J. Rowan (Eds.), *Human inquiry: A sourcebook of new paradigm research* (pp. 141–151). Chichester, UK: Wiley.

Warner, M. E., Hinrichs, C., Schneyer, J., & Joyce, L. (1997). *Collaborative research between community development practitioners and university based researchers: Challenges and benefits*. Unpublished paper available from ERIC Document Reproduction Service, No. ED 419 124).

Yamane, D. (1996). Collaboration and its discontents: Steps toward overcoming barriers to successful group projects. *Teaching Sociology, 24 (4)*, 378–383.

PART II

The Assumed

CHAPTER 5

Collaboration as the Foundation for Negotiating New Models of Education

Susan M. Drake

This study explored what happened in four Ontario school boards from 1994 to 1998, a turbulent period in education. The Common Curriculum (Ontario Ministry of Education and Training, 1995) was being implemented from kindergarten to ninth grade. This radically different curriculum model took an integrated, outcomes-based approach demanding many new teaching skills. As well, grade nine was being destreamed (detracked). Collaboration was officially recommended as the preferred organizational process for implementing the new curriculum.

The purpose of this chapter is to explain what happened during this period and how it happened. What role did collaboration play in the unfolding events? How did educators respond to being put in positions where they were expected to collaborate? What were the results? What factors contributed to successful collaborative approaches?

THE CONTEXT

In many ways, this period was typical of the difficult times that educators find themselves facing daily. We are in the midst of unprecedented change in our school systems. Traditional curriculum models are being challenged in light of such factors as technological advances and the knowledge explosion. The old models of leadership no longer work (Fullan, 1998). Teachers receive little in-servicing to prepare them to meet new, unprecedented expectations, and have only a few concrete models for the changes. Across the globe, educational systems are being dominated by a market economy (Dei & Karumanchery, 1999; Dempster, 1998; Nelson, 1998). Never has it been so clear that politics and education are inextricably in-terrelated.

In another sense, however, the time frame of this study was unique. Although teachers were expected to do things in different ways, there was no one dictating to them exactly what this meant in practice. Students were to achieve the outcomes mandated in the Common Curriculum, which was intended to be interdisciplinary. How this would happen was not pre-scribed. It was up to teachers, schools, boards, and larger collaborative bodies to define what education would look like when it was translated into the classroom. By 1998, a new government had declared the Common Curriculum dead and enacted a much more directive policy. Thus, this period of time offered a brief window of opportunity to observe how ed-ucators made sense of the world when given both massive changes and the responsibility to carry them out.

THE METHOD

In our study, our research team collaborated with four boards of edu-cation. Each board was distinctive in its size and nature. We had worked with all these boards on various projects over periods as long as 12 years. As a result, we believe this allowed for easy access to the schools, admin-istrators, consultants, and teachers to carry out this study. As well, we worked collaboratively with each board for the duration of this study. We met with key personnel each year to determine how the research design could incorporate what would be useful information both for them and for us.

The study focused on how educational personnel dealt with changes re-lated to outcomes-based learning, alternative assessment procedures, inte-grated curriculum, and the collaboration process related to these changes. As we proceeded, it became impossible to limit our observations to this process. Teacher experiences indicated that we must also explore the con-texts in which the study was occurring. We extended our observations to explore the role of the teacher, leadership, personal and professional de-velopment, and stress management in the educational culture where the changes were being implemented.

The inquiry process was guided by the theory, technique, and practice of interpretive inquirers such as Bogdan and Biklin (1992), Gleshne and Peshkin (1992), and Lincoln and Guba (1985). The study took a multisite, case-study approach. Interviews were the primary research tool. Also in-cluded were data from invited activities at different sites, including at-tendance at events such as an advisory board meeting, staff meetings, board-wide teacher meetings, central office curriculum department meet-ings, and one meeting of the community and the board. A second prong of the research was an indepth ethnographic study conducted at one high school. One of the coauthors worked part-time at one high school for three years in the role of a change agent. She was also a member of the board-level evaluation committee for two years. Here, she also acted as a participant observer and these data were included in the study.

In each board, people from at least one elementary school and one high school, as well as various people working at the system level (e.g., superintendents and consultants), were interviewed. One interview a year was scheduled (most participants were involved over three years). Over 180 interviews were conducted with people with a wide range of age, experience, and teaching styles. Indepth, unstructured interview techniques were guided by the work of researchers such as Spradley (1979), Mischler (1986), and Seidman (1990).

As a part of the collaborative process, we fed back our data interpretation to the boards involved. We shared our interpretations with educators involved and they were free to make necessary changes. We sent out a regular newsletter and a yearly report to all the schools and each central office involved. This interpretation was offered back to the schools and boards in the form of a newsletter and a yearly report.

WHAT HAPPENED

The results of our study (Miller, Drake, Harris, & Molinaro, 1998) indicated that changes came in pockets. There was no site where a school had totally shifted from a traditional model to one that operated in a fundamentally different way. There was, however, a large variance in what was occurring at different sites. We found that labeling practices as being "old story" or "new story" helped us to assess what was happening in different sites. We developed a continuum of practices to identify different schools' efforts. This directional shift from old story to new story has also been reported in other jurisdictions undergoing restructuring (see, e.g., Lipsitz, Mizell, Jackson, & Austin, 1997; O'Hair, 1998).

The continuum ranged from:

- Old Story–Traditional: schools that followed the conventional model;

- Transitional Story: schools that were in transition from the old story to the new story; and

- New Story–Transformational: schools implementing a fundamentally new model of education.

We identified "old story" schools as having the following characteristics:

- isolated culture
- disciplines offered rigid curriculum boundaries
- lectures and conventional teaching practices
- traditional evaluation
- factory model
- administration as managerial leaders
- change perceived as an event (often to be resisted)

Schools moving toward the "new story" demonstrated varying degrees of the following characteristics:

- collaborative culture
- integrated, standards-based approaches to curriculum
- community involvement
- alternative assessment practices
- shared leadership
- teacher leadership
- teachers as learners
- ongoing in-house professional development
- change perceived as continual
- positive attitudes of educators

Although collaboration represented only one of the criteria in the new story, it appeared to be central to the success of schools that were able to negotiate change. Collaboration was highly valued in the Ontario context. As previously mentioned, collaboration was a working principle of the Common Curriculum (Ontario Ministry of Education and Training, 1995) itself. Here it was defined as an approach where "school-board and school staff, students and the community work together to develop programs that effectively meet local needs" (p. 2). The document also referred to partnerships that recognize that education is a responsibility shared among the Ministry of Education, teachers, students, parents, school trustees, and business, labor, and other organizations. The Report of the Royal Commission on Learning (1995) recommended collaborative processes. Other education publications, such as *Beyond the Glitterspeak: Creating Genuine Collaboration in the Schools*, published by the Ontario Teachers' Federation (Morgan & Morgan, 1992), promoted collaboration as a salvation for schools involved in positive change.

The literature supports collaboration as a building block necessary to successful change, often using the terms "reform" and "reculturing" interchangeably to denote times-of-change efforts. Sirotnik (1999) differentiates between reform and renewal. Reform refers to changes in structures or curriculum policies that are mandated from above; reform does not work. Renewal, on the other hand, is ongoing and has a collective moral purpose; this continual critical inquiry has the possibility of improving education. It is a collaborative venture. "Renewal is about the process of organizational change, about nurturing the spiritual, affective and intellectual connections in the lives of educators working together to understand their practice" (pp. 607–608). In terms of this chapter, reform and restructuring as a way of effecting major change occur in the "old story"; renewal is a fitting term for the "new story."

The work of Fullan (1998) and Hargreaves (1994) focuses on the process of change and tells a similar story. After studying various school systems undergoing the process of change, they concluded that reform or restructuring was doomed without reculturing. Traditional schools operated in a traditional culture that did not value collaborative efforts, and teachers worked in an isolated culture, as typified in the old-story portrait given above. Schools that wanted to effect substantive change needed to reculture, that is, mandates from above could only be effectively implemented in a culture that was truly collaborative. Efforts at collaboration that were mandated (contrived collaboration) were also doomed. As Sirotnik (1999) maintained, reculturing that involved true collaboration needed to be driven by commonly held principles and come from the heart.

Thus, teachers' experiences with collaboration as a road to change fitted with the literature on effective renewal and reculturing. Collaboration in this study can be seen as foundational to effective change.

FACTORS INFLUENCING COLLABORATION

Over the three years of the study, it was impossible not to notice the power of collaboration. We noted that the greater the degree of implementation of new models, the stronger the network for collaboration seemed to be. This same relationship has been noted by others (Rosenholtz, 1989; Veslilind & Jones, 1998). Collaborative processes are known to be very difficult, even at the best of times (Hatch, 1998; Leiberman, 1995). Different parties come to the table with different needs, agendas, and understandings about the nature of collaborative efforts. Why, then, did collaboration stand out as the foundation for developing new models of education? The following factors emerged as relevant to building a foundation for collaborative efforts.

Positive Perceptions of Collaborative Experiences

An excerpt from the third-year report summarized the extent of collaboration (Miller, Drake, Harris, & Molinaro, 1998).

From year one, the aspect of reform that teachers enjoyed the most was collaboration with colleagues. Indeed the collaboration energized them. This satisfaction with collaboration was echoed throughout the three years of the study. The other outcomes of the study emerged over time. Collaboration differed in definition. For some, it meant talking to colleagues at the water cooler (a new activity), while for others it was full blown collaboration occurring over a long period of time. This type of collaboration usually meant a team of teachers developing and implementing an interdisciplinary curriculum. Collaboration at the elementary school level tended to revolve around divisions. At the high school level, two or three teachers usually reported collaborating around integrated curriculum projects.

Collaboration was woven through the negotiations at all levels and included the central office personnel, teachers, administrators, students, parents, local businesses and organizations, and the general public. As in the literature (Ross & Hogaboam-Gray, 1998), there seemed to be levels of collaboration moving from information exchange, through joint planning and participation, to concurrent implementation and joint implementation. Those we interviewed reported the greatest satisfaction with this aspect of the changes occurring. Even those who strongly opposed the mandated changes reported the newfound reward of collaboration as one of the few positives on the landscape where they found themselves.

Some comments that describe teachers' experiences were:

I've learned the value of working with a colleague. That's inspirational and supportive.

It's an important way to share ideas and make sure you have a grasp of what you are doing and why.

Working with another teacher helps to motivate me.

In the words of John Donne, "No man is an island," and teaching is very much a collaborative enterprise, a communal activity.

I guess the biggest thing I've learned is how to collaborate with other people.

I've learned you can't do it alone.

You know it's funny, I find the more I work with other teachers, the more I want to work with them. It's becoming natural in this school.

It's just too difficult to do alone. You need someone to bounce ideas off of.

Obstacles to Collaboration

In spite of positive attitudes toward collaboration, teachers did report some difficulties with the process. For example, one obstacle mentioned was the difficulty in finding suitable people with whom to collaborate. By far the most common barrier mentioned was the lack of time available for collaborative activities. Time had to be scheduled for such things as planning, practicing, curriculum development, sharing successful practices, and selling the innovation (Adelman & Panton Walking Eagle, 1997). Scheduling time was done in a variety of ways by innovative administrative personnel. Typically, some collaborating teachers were scheduled for similar work breaks; others were allotted time for curriculum development.

Time was also needed to develop relationships and maintain them. Principals were aware of this need. As one said:

The nature of this organization is very much based on relationships and that actually becomes an extra burden. It is a very important and special quality of this school, but it does have its challenges. The challenge is to find the time to build and maintain these relationships.

Many teachers agreed with this stance and did the best they could to foster a collaborative culture. A typical comment was:

I really see it as a process of being proactive and building relationships with my colleague on an ongoing basis. So if I see a teacher that I don't know that well at the photocopier, I will go up to that person and introduce myself and begin a conversation. I think that is the kind of stuff we have to do.

Philosophical Agreement

Perhaps the most central factor in moving toward a new story in education was a similar philosophy held by many stakeholders. It often seemed that everything was changing everywhere, and that there was not much to connect the changes. However, an underlying philosophy was embedded in most aspects of the required reform. The acceptance of this philosophy facilitated the initial acceptance of government mandates, and ultimately, collaborative efforts toward implementation of these mandates.

Essentially, the philosophy involved revisiting the basic questions of education: What is the purpose of education? What is worth knowing? How do people learn best and therefore how do we best teach them? Who is in control of education? The answers to these four questions were radically different from the conventional answers that have served educators and the public for the last century. They moved from the old story to the new story.

The purpose of education in the new story was no longer to support the status quo but to ensure "success for all." This required a vastly different definition of success that honored principles of equity, rather than ones based strictly on merit. What was considered worth knowing shifted from a wide content base to generic skills that moved toward self-direction and lifelong learning (Parker, Ninomiya, & Cogan, 1999). Constructivist learning principles (Fosnot, 1996) replaced traditional thoughts on how people learn. Such principles demanded a classroom that looked very different. In this classroom, students constructed meaning through social interaction, feedback was ongoing and hands-on, and reflective activities were the norm.

The last question revolved around who was in control of education. In the new story, education was no longer in the hands of the few giving direction from a centralized site. Rather, education was a *collaborative* effort among stakeholders at a particular site; these stakeholders included administrators, teachers, students, parents, and the community.

This new philosophy was clearly fueled by a strong set of beliefs. It would lead to principled changes in how schools operated and how students were taught. This was in the spirit of renewal rather than one-shot reform (Sirotnik, 1999).

Creating New Networks

One of the ways in which teachers learned about the new-story philosophy, new techniques, and approaches was through new networks that sprouted up across Ontario. These collaborative networks, unlike traditional professional development efforts, developed trusting relationships and built commitment by having teachers and administrators actively pursuing answers to their own questions (Leiberman & Grolnick, 1997). Each board became involved in a network or consortium that combined with other boards and local universities. These networks were funded by the Ministry of Education and Training. They sponsored events like in-service sessions with experts and curriculum-building ventures. A wider network funded by the Ministry was called the "Culture of Change." This network connected educators electronically through several listservs on a wide variety of topics. It also trained facilitators to work with staffs on any change venture that they wished. This was an ambitious project revolving around changing the culture of schools into collaborative ones. Those who took up this offer did venture into more collaborative territory (Castle & Drake, 1997).

Whole Community Negotiation

An important component of the change process was that all voices were considered and valued. This principle honored collaborative decision making, and although it was a complex and messy process, it ensured that people were on-side. The Ministry set this precedent with their consultation process for the Common Curriculum. However, different boards applied it in different ways.

The one rural school board participating in the study invited community members to meetings to decide what was important for students to learn in school. These meetings allowed for dialogue among parents, students, educators, secretaries, bus drivers, and other community members. Involving everyone reduced resistance to innovations and developed a clearer understanding of why changes were happening. This rural community took charge of the direction of the changes, rather than just blindly following mandates.

Another example was provided at a new school, where the principal created an advisory board before the school even opened. This board involved representatives of all possible stakeholders. They became the decision-making body who decided on a whole school philosophy. Before the school opened, open community meetings were held. At these meetings, it was members of the advisory council who defended decisions that had been made for innovation. Again, this school felt in control of what was happening. Most of their innovations corresponded to Ministry guidelines, but the school went beyond necessary requirements.

Board Attitudes Toward Collaboration

Different school boards responded very differently to the mandates of the Ministry. There was a continuum of board acceptance of the new policies, but four factors, in particular, influenced its success.

1. Although all the boards at least went through the motions of implementation, the "culture" of a board seemed to determine the extent to which it actually tackled its execution. There appeared to be a direct connection between the attitudes of the central office toward collaborative ventures and what was happening in the schools we studied.

2. One participating board, a separate (Catholic) school board, had a strong unified policy that was determined collaboratively and permeated the entire system. This policy worked with outcomes, and all planning and problem solving was outcome-based. The board created different committees to deal with board issues that were made up of personnel from all facets of education. A collaborative culture was in the making. As a separate school board, it had conducted intense discussions about its philosophy, and a holistic approach had been adopted. This initiative aligned neatly with the Ministry mandates. This board seemed to have succeeded with the most widespread adoption of these mandates.

3. The three other boards had varying degrees of success. Two of them had strong programs in place at the central office level. However, severe cuts in Ministry funding meant the depletion of central office staff and resulted in internal chaos. This affected the level of implementation. In both boards, despite the dedication of remaining board-level staff, the pockets of implementation reflected the administration policy of each school. Without a collaborative unifying strategy, implementation was not as consistent as in the separate school board.

4. In the fourth school board, educators saw themselves as mavericks who "did their own thing" and would not be told what to do. At this central office, curriculum officers worked diligently to understand and disseminate new materials that captured the Ministry's philosophy. There were also several days

devoted to county-wide in-service sessions to promote the new policies. Those in the central office held a perception of being in the forefront of curriculum change. However, little concerted or unified effort toward change appeared to be actually occurring in the schools. There was some change, but it depended entirely on the will of the administration or the people at that site. At those sites where change did occur, a collaborative culture had emerged rather than a maverick one.

Collaboration Through Restructuring

In some schools, structural change facilitated the reculturing of the school. This was particularly true in high schools. Traditionally, high schools worked within a department structure that guaranteed allegiance to a discipline and not to a collaborative culture (Siskin & Little, 1995). The most dramatic example of effective structural change was in a new high school that was built with the new story of education in mind. Here the traditional department offices were gone; in their place were offices that housed individuals from many different departments. This strategy, along with others, fostered the building of a collaborative culture in the school.

The pockets where the new story was adopted most completely had leaders who believed fully in its philosophy. These administrators were transformational leaders. Informed by the literature, they shared decision-making power and allowed time for teacher talk to explore philosophical issues (Telford, 1996). They supported their teachers in efforts to implement change as the quotes below illustrate:

I would have to say the administrators I'm working with now are very encouraging.
    Well, I think we are fortunate here. She [the principal] is just an excellent leader. She motivates us. She has high expectations for us.

Recognizing that collaboration alone could lock systems into the status quo (Little, 1990), this administrator developed norms for continuous improvement to accompany collaborative processes.

I have deliberately done all I can to establish a collaborative culture in this school. And it's worked. I have enthusiastic teachers who work together on all aspects of the school. We have set high standards for ourselves and our students.

Not all principals tried to change the culture of the school or to bring in the mandated changes. In one school, for example, the two administrators decided it was "better not to rock the boat" and so did not push for change. This was in spite of the fact that they both philosophically believed in the changes being asked of their teachers. A few others who had not bought into the "new story" paid lip service to the new curriculum but did nothing to bring about change. But the times required some change from even the most die-hard of resisters. Most teachers found themselves re-quired to do something in a new way, even if it was only to use outcomes as indicators for evaluation and reporting. In these schools, the need for collaboration to accomplish such tasks was noted by the teachers as the only real evidence they had that the educational world was changing in a positive way.

In one example, a collaborative culture was created within the larger school culture. The principal believed in the mandated changes and wanted the staff to adopt them. However, this new principal had inherited a school culture that was resistant to change. The staff was determined to avoid all efforts at change and directed their animosity toward the principal. Curi-ously, some change did occur at this school; a group of teachers who were experimenting with new strategies introduced an outcome-based, integrated approach to their colleagues. The principal, remaining in the background, quietly supported this venture. However, the changes were not as wide-spread as they possibly could have been.

Modeling the Process

The leaders who embraced the changes, a group including school and central office administrators and teachers, modeled the process. Modeling is key to collaborative leadership (Telford, 1996). One principal explicitly explained why he and his vice-principal facilitated democratic meetings where teachers were part of the decision-making team. He felt that if the process were not modeled from the top, the teachers would not accept the changes being required. The truth of this was demonstrated in another school, where the principal preplanned his "democratic" decision-making teams. Once the teachers found out that they really had no choice, resent-ment grew, and the process was not as successful as it might have been. The principal realized, too late, that he had not modeled the way in which he wished his teachers would behave. This awakening allowed him to change his approaches to the staff in a way that led to more authentic teacher leadership. This principal commented:

I would like to think that what I've left is a legacy of teachers that are more em-powered. . . . I think that teachers in this school feel that they have a bit more control of this school in terms of what happens in the school and the decisions that they make.

Indeed, these teachers eventually reported that the collaborative process was rewarding (Harris & Drake, 1997). Similarly, Avalos (1998) reported that "contrived collaboration" also led to a collaborative culture with teachers in secondary schools in Chile.

In another school, the teachers led the change process. They worked at convincing their peers of the need for change by challenging their current practices, both in the staff room and at staff meetings. They consistently applied innovative ways of teaching in their own classrooms. These teacher leaders were well respected by their colleagues, and the proof was in the success they were enjoying in the classroom. Students were learning more. Given these models, other teachers came to understand what the innovations could look like in practice and were therefore more willing to try.

Shifting Teacher Beliefs

Gradually, over three years, more and more educators came to accept the new story. A cardinal rule is that people do not change unless they share a compelling reason to change (Schwann & Spady, 1998). Yet our research noted that the most common shift mentioned by teachers was one from transmitter of knowledge to facilitator. How did this happen?

This acceptance came in many ways. Many already believed, as a result of their own experiences, that the "old story" was not working for enough students. These educators tended to go into a classroom and ask, "What can I do to ensure that every student in this class can learn?" These educators now had the freedom to experiment with innovations. Many of them collaboratively shared their excitement with others. As a result, some teachers witnessed the success and energy generated in their colleagues' innovative classrooms and ventured to experiment themselves. Others were forced by administration to try a new methodology and found that it worked. Some became involved in collaborative efforts and were swept along in the enthusiasm. Still others were challenged by students to make the curriculum more interesting, as other teachers were doing.

Slowly but surely, we found that teachers acquired subjective meaning for the changes, sometimes almost subliminally, as if they did not realize they had made the change. After three years, a significant number of the teachers in our study shifted their understanding of teaching in major ways, although often they did not articulate this. Rather, the shift was demonstrated through changes that they had made in their practices. For example, many teachers had started to use rubrics and found they worked well with students. Rubrics were taken for granted as a good way to "do" education. One elementary school teacher stated:

I have started to use more performance criteria and rubrics. I went over it [the rubric] with the students before they did the main work so that they knew what to expect, and then I used it to grade that way. . . . Then I sent that home with my comments to the parents, and used that in conferencing when they were in last week for their parents/student conferences. I was really surprised. I thought I would have to explain it more to the parents, but they really got the hang of it pretty quickly, and I think the students felt more ownership over it because they could actually see where they were.

Teacher Leadership

One of the most significant findings of our study was the shift in teacher roles. Over the three years, teachers began to perceive themselves as leaders. Teacher-leaders can be identified as those who reach out to others with encouragement, technical knowledge, and enthusiasm to learn new things (Nias, Southworth, & Yeomans, 1989). Sometimes teachers saw themselves as being a leader in the classroom. Most often, the perception came from being part of a collaborative effort where leadership in some capacity was required. In these cases, there was no single assigned leader, and leadership would shift according to need (Clift, Veal, Holland, Johnson, & McCarthy, 1995). One teacher put it this way:

I see myself as equal, I guess, to other colleagues and sitting down and doing some problem-solving around whatever happens to be [of concern] . . . I guess a leader is somebody who is willing to take things on and try their best, and work in collaboration with their colleagues.

These collaborative opportunities were often facilitated by strategic restructuring efforts on the part of the administration. Teachers acquired more responsibility as new decision-making bodies evolved. One school had action research committees dealing with general school issues; every staff member was expected to belong to one. Other schools created school-wide committees for different ventures, such as assessment and curriculum issues. These were often headed by teachers rather than department heads. Another school banished the label "department head" and experimented with other ways of assigning responsibility.

Teachers became responsible for professional development in the school. Those who had successfully implemented a new strategy or who had been sent for in-service outside the school often assumed responsibility for teaching others on their staff. This shared responsibility for professional development led to more collaborative cultures where everyone was working toward the same goal. One teacher summarized it this way: "Working collaboratively, there is more sharing and ownership. People feel like they're all part of it rather than someone just doing it and saying, 'Yeah, now do this.' "

Teacher leaders do not need to have the goal of becoming administrators, but they do need to wish to have an influence on policies beyond the classroom (Ryan, 1999). Research over the last 20 years has indicated that teacher-leaders make a positive difference on school change and student achievement (Hallinger, 1999).

Educators as Learners

One of the most influential concepts surrounding effective change is the "learning organization" (Senge, 1990). Given the relentless pace of change, organizations that survive are ones where the personnel can adapt to change by learning new ways to do things. A learning organization has a collaborative culture. People in learning organizations learn together, and collaborative cultures turn individual learning into shared learning (Hargreaves, Earl, & Ryan, 1996).

At the start of our study, huge changes were demanded of teachers. After initial resistance, many educators began the task of learning what the changes meant and how they could apply them in their contexts. Much of the learning occurred because educators perceived themselves as "all in this mess together." No one was really sure what outcomes based education meant in practice. No one was the expert on integrated programs. It was the quest for understanding of how to do these things that acted as a catalyst for learning. Collaborative sharing facilitated learning from each other. Individuals experimented in their classroom and shared what worked with others at the school level. Committees built new curriculum; committee members implemented it. Some boards offered seed money for projects in different schools. Observations showed that not much money actually had to be offered. Rather, teachers appreciated that they were given something for their services. This money was usually spent on time off to plan new curriculum.

Boards created opportunities for teachers to demonstrate their innovative products. For some, this was done through one of the new collaborative networks that were created at this time. For others, the board sponsored a day where teachers presented their work and others viewed it. Some presentations were also displayed at provincial conferences. This helped educators to gain new meaning and see new possibilities. A great deal of energy was generated at these events, and teachers were renewed and eager to return to the classroom.

At the end of three years of this study, educators at all levels described themselves as learners. They were both tired and energized by the steep learning curve they found themselves navigating. One common goal that focused this learning was to make school a better learning experience for the students. This focus allowed teachers to feel in control within their own domain, rather than just being angry at the government for mandating such great changes. It also facilitated the acceptance of the new-story philosophy, since the considered conclusion reached by many teachers was that many of the mandates could actually improve students' school experience.

Learning was at all levels. Several of the teachers commented that they learned from their students:

I always learn from the kids. I mean, I learn from them what I'm doing wrong. If they are just not getting it, I think, "Gee, I didn't handle that too well."

I probably learn most from my students and their reactions to the various activities.

There seemed to be a difference in the quality of learning in different schools. In schools where teachers were simply told to implement the new mandates, they were certainly learning as they followed new blueprints for teaching. The learning, however, tended to be piecemeal, and educators took one change, such as assessment, at a time and implemented it. However, other schools embraced the new model and developed new curriculum structures based on the Ministry mandates. Here also, the teachers tended to learn one aspect of the change at a time, but there was also a conscious understanding that all the curriculum pieces would link together over time. In these contexts, the learning was accompanied by a great deal of excitement.

During times of change, learning is a prerequisite for changing practice. These were the words of one school principal: "Change is the norm. You aren't going to come to a plateau where you can rest. You will just face more change." This attitude toward change became standard in some of the more successful schools in the study. Although teachers reported being tired with the pace of change, this attitude seemed to focus them on perceiving new demands as a challenge rather than simply as a stress. Negotiating change itself was a skill to be learned and utilized. Collaborative leaders understand change and how to manage it (Telford, 1996).

CONCLUSION

Many substantive changes occurred in most schools between 1994 to 1998. While some schools changed more than others—the amount of change seemed dependent on many interwoven factors—what stood out for us was the power of collaboration to ease the path of those struggling to make changes in often unknown territory. It seems simple to say that without collaborative efforts and attitudes, the magnitude of change that we witnessed would never have occurred. Successful implementation involved learning together in a collaborative culture. The collaborative culture facilitated the hearing of everyone's voice and allowed stakeholders' perceived control by permitting everyone to come to their own understandings.

What is also key to this period of change is that educators were seeking understanding of a "new story" in education. There were no mandates from above dictating every move; educators were encouraged to explore in their own way. Creative efforts abounded, and students seemed to thrive.

It was an exciting time to be an educator. As the pendulum swings and we move into more and more directives from above, it is crucial that we do not forget the conditions that promote real change. Collaboration was the glue that held the parts together.

NOTE

This research was supported by a grant from the Social Sciences and Humanities Research Council of Canada.

REFERENCES

Adelman, N. E., & Panton Walking Eagle, K. (1997). Teachers, time and school reform. In A. Hargreaves (Ed.), *Rethinking educational change with heart and mind* (pp. 92–110). Alexandria, VA: Association for Supervision and Curriculum Development.

Avalos, B. (1998). School-based development: The experience of teacher professional groups in secondary schools in Chile. *Teaching and Teacher Education, 14*(3), 257–271.

Bogdan, R., & Biklin, S. (1992). *Qualitative research for education* (2nd ed.). Boston: Allyn & Bacon.

Castle, J., & Drake, S. M. (1997, May). *Teacher as change agent: Exploring process and product in one Ontario project.* Paper presented at 17th Annual International Seminar for Teacher Education, Brock University, St. Catharines, Ontario.

Clift, R. T., Veal, M. L., Holland, P., Johnson, M., & McCarthy, J. (1995). *Collaborative leadership and shared decision making.* New York: Teachers College Press.

Dei, G. J. S., & Karumanchery, L. L. (1999). School reforms in Ontario: The "marketization of education" and the resulting silence on equity. *Alberta Journal of Educational Research, 45*(2), 111–131.

Dempster, N. (1998). *Challenging teacher education: Under stress: Professional values in a competitive educational environment.* Paper presented at the annual seminar of the International Society for Teacher Education, Kruger Park, South Africa.

Fosnot, C. (1996). Constructivism: A psychological theory of learning. In C. Fosnot (Ed.), *Constructivism: Theory, perspectives and practice* (pp. 8–33). New York: Teachers College Press.

Fullan, M. (1998). Leadership for the 21st century: Breaking the bonds of dependency. *Educational Leadership, 55*(7), 6–10.

Gleshne, C., & Peshkin, A. (1992). *Becoming qualitative researchers: An introduction.* New York: Longman.

Hallinger, P. (1999). School leadership development. *Orbit, 30*(1), 46–48.

Hargreaves, A. (1994). *Changing teachers, changing times.* London: Falmer Press.

Hargreaves, A., Earl, L., & Ryan, J. (1996). *Schooling for change: Reinventing education for early adolescents.* London: Falmer Press.

Harris, B., & Drake, S. M. (1997). Implementing high school reform through school-wide action research. *Action in Teacher Education, 19*(3), 15–31.

Hatch, T. (1998). The differences in theory that matter in school improvement. *American Educational Research Journal, 35*(1), 3–31.

Leiberman, A. (1995). Restructuring schools: The dynamics of changing practice, structure and culture. In A. Leiberman (Ed.), *The work of restructuring schools: Building from the ground up* (pp. 1–17). New York: Teachers College Press.

Leiberman, A., & Grolnick, M. (1997). Networks, reform, and professional development of teachers. In A. Hargreaves (Ed.), *Rethinking educational change with heart and mind* (pp. 192–215). Alexandria, VA: Association of Supervision and Curriculum Development.

Lincoln, Y., & Guba, E. (1985). *Naturalistic inquiry.* Beverly Hills, CA: Sage.

Lipsitz, J., Mizell A., Jackson, A., & Austin, L. (1997) Speaking with one voice: A manifesto for middle-grades reform. *Phi Delta Kappan, 78*, 533–550.

Little, J. (1990). The persistence of privacy; Autonomy and initiative in teachers' professional relationships. *Teachers College Record, 91*, 509–536.

Miller J. P., Drake, S. M., Harris, B., & Molinaro, V. (1998, May). *How real schools change.* Paper presented at Canadian Society for Studies in Education, Ottawa, Ontario.

Miller J. P., & Seller W. (1990). *Curriculum perspectives and practice.* New York: Longman.

Mischler, E. G. (1986). *Research interviewing: Context and narrative.* Cambridge, MA: Harvard University Press.

Morgan, G., & Morgan, J. (1992). *Beyond the glitterspeak: Creating genuine collaboration in the schools.* Toronto, ON: Ontario Teachers' Federation.

Nelson, W. W. (1998). The naked truth about school reform in Minnesota. *Phi Delta Kappan, 79*(9), 679–684.

Nias, J., Southworth, G., & Yeomans, R. (1989). *Staff relationships in primary schools.* London: Cassell.

O'Hair, M. J. (1998). *Restructuring conventional schools for democratic education: Implications for teachers and teacher education.* Paper presented at the annual seminar of the International Society for Teacher Education, Kruger Park, South Africa.

Ontario Ministry of Education and Training. (1995). *The Common Curriculum.* Toronto: Government of Ontario.

Parker, W. C., Ninomiya, A., & Cogan, J. (1999). Educating world citizens toward multinational curriculum development. *American Educational Research Journal, 36*(2), 117–145.

Patton, M. (1990). *Qualitative evaluation and research methods* (2nd ed.). Beverly Hills, CA: Sage.

Report of the Royal Commission on Learning. (1995). *The educators: For the love of learning* (Vol. 3). Toronto: Ontario Ministry of Education and Training.

Rosenholtz, S. (1989). *Teachers' workplace: The social reorganization of schools.* New York: Longman.

Ross, J., & Hogaboam-Gray, A. (1998). Integrating mathematics, science, and technology: Effects on students. *International Journal of Science Education, 20*(9) 1119–1135.

Ryan, S. (1999). Teacher leaders. *Orbit, 30*(1), 12–15.

Schwann C., & Spady, W. (1998). Why change doesn't happen and how to make sure that it does. *Educational Leadership, 55*(7), 45–47.

Seidman, I. (1990). *Interviewing as qualitative research.* New York: Teachers College Press.

Senge, P. (1990). *The fifth discipline.* New York: Doubleday.

Sirotnik. K. A. (1999). Making sense of educational renewal. *Phi Delta Kappan, 80*, 606–610.

Siskin L., & Little, J. (1995). Introduction. In L. Siskin & J. Little (Eds.), *The subjects in question* (pp. 1–22). New York: Teachers College Press.

Spradley, J. P. (1979). *The ethnographic interview.* New York: Holt, Rinehart & Winston.

Telford, H. (1996). *Transforming schools through collaborative leadership.* London: Falmer.

Vesilind, E. M., & Jones, M. G. (1998). Gardens or graveyards: Science education reform and school cultures. *Journal of Research in Science Teaching, 35*, 757–776.

CHAPTER 6

Is Collaboration in the Classroom Possible?

Karen Krug

This chapter treats two major questions related to collaboration in the classroom: What are the barriers to collaboration in the classroom, and how can they be overcome? Images of an engaging and interactive learning climate lead many educators to adopt the goal of developing collaborative learning strategies in their students, but the key to doing so is an understanding of the barriers and routes to authentic, socially useful collaboration.

COLLABORATIVE LEARNING APPROACHES

To contribute to this understanding, I reflect on three types of teaching models used in my own academic context, drawing out both the elements that lead to positive, productive learning, and the elements that hinder it. Because the observations are contextually based, a description of the context is essential; however, a general theoretical model that corresponds closely with the approaches taken in the Environmental Policy Institute (EPI) at Brock University will follow.

My immediate teaching context is the EPI, which is explicitly interdisciplinary. All students are comajors in environmental policy and another discipline. The core EPI courses emphasize an interdisciplinary methodology and concepts such as sustainability (which attends to economic, ecological, and equity factors) that combine and transcend various spheres of knowledge from the disciplinary backgrounds of students. Elective courses provide opportunities to practice interdisciplinary approaches to problem solving in relation to specified topic areas (such as agriculture, waste, or pollution).

Two key features of "interdisciplinarity" (Stefanovic, 1996) shape the approach taken to teaching in the EPI. First, it is assumed that the problem faced defines the kinds of expertise required to address it. For example, to deal with pollution of agricultural lands, interdisciplinarians may need team members such as the following: someone with an understanding of chemical interactions; a plant physiologist; a soil scientist; a person who understands how policy changes can be implemented; a person experienced in motivating individuals to embrace change; and a person whose income is generated from farming. Second, it is assumed that each team member is committed to understanding how the factors others recognize as significant interact with the ones with which they themselves are most familiar, and each is committed to collectively identifying appropriate methodologies and solutions. This is different from both multidisciplinarity and transdisciplinarity. In the former, experts from various disciplines may be brought in to provide advice in their narrow fields, leaving the use of their information to others. In the latter, contributors would assume that disciplinary boundaries are too narrow, and hope that everyone could simply look for the best solutions by transcending traditional theoretical limitations. Interdisciplinarity, however, requires full collaboration, and practitioners of interdisciplinary work confirm the validity of this theoretical perspective (Krug, 1999). Participants in interdisciplinary endeavors must be able to understand how others' disciplinary expertise is relevant to common problem solving, and must be committed to collective knowledge and action. Three collaborative learning approaches that are consistent with this understanding of interdisciplinarity and that are routinely used in the EPI's interdisciplinary setting are discussed below.

The first approach consists of a series of environmental policy courses that are structured with clusters of presentations by guest speakers from various backgrounds (usually two or three over the same number of weeks) followed by synthesis sessions. The expectation is that in the synthesis sessions, students will collectively look for ways to combine the insights provided by the various speakers and begin to piece together a more informed view of how to address a particular theoretical or practical problem. An example of a theoretical problem would be: Should nature be assumed to have intrinsic value or be seen primarily in terms of its utility for sustaining human life? An example of a practical problem would be: Is organic agriculture the best way to maximize social, economic, and ecological well-being? The problem itself will determine how the students use the speaker's information to develop meaningful solutions. After a series of synthesis exercises, students usually prepare a final synthesis project that all can support, critically appraising and then building on the ideas they have collectively generated.

A second approach, designed as an alternative to lecturing and having students imbibe information for "regurgitation," is the use of intensive group projects as the primary learning tool. They may be several weeks long, or may run the length of the term. In one course, students were asked to redesign the EPI workshop to be more environmentally sustainable, and to explain how they would obtain the resources to achieve this plan. In another, they were asked to come up with an urban design for a third-world city of their choice, and to explain why it would be appropriate for that context. In these courses, students must move beyond their disciplinary training because the various facets of the issues interact with one another. Oral presentations provide a mechanism for each group to share its research and analysis with other students. Using this process, students are motivated to ask their own meaningful questions and to find avenues to collect relevant information for policy decisions. Again, they must process the information collectively to arrive at solutions all group members support.

The third approach incorporates a process designed to implement the interdisciplinary, collaborative learning assumptions of the EPI program at the honors level, rather than expecting honors students to work in isolation. Students may elect to do a single policy course or two thesis-related courses. In either case, collaborative learning is intended to be inescapable. In the policy course, students work collectively on a research project that is to result in concrete policy suggestions for improving sustainability within the international biosphere reserve in which the Brock campus is located. They are expected to use their disciplinary expertise to research the background information required to make informed policy choices. In order to reach agreement with one another, they must understand the implications of the disciplinary-based research for the ecosystem as a whole; hence, collaboration is essential. While the thesis course is similar to most in that an individual student works alone on a major written document, collaborative learning is at the core of this process as well. Each student must proceed according to a preestablished framework: proposal, methodology, preliminary results, troubleshooting, final results, policy conclusions, and defense. Although this framework sets some limits, because all students follow the same schedule, they are able to meet together with the supervisors to share information as they go along, identify problems they are facing, offer each other solutions to problems raised or overlooked, and share their disciplinary insights. Each student learns about the others' projects and benefits from colleagues' and supervisors' insights on one another's projects.

While the first of these three approaches is a special collaborative learning model developed for an interdisciplinary learning context, the other two approaches are consistent with the "group investigation" approach to collaborative learning. As noted above, interdisciplinarity requires collaborative learning. The methodology of the synthesis-based guest speaker courses offers a distinctive approach consistent with the two main assumptions of interdisciplinarity described above and with a policy orientation. Policy is defined as a plan of action that allows one to move from the current situation to the desired situation. The synthesis course model is therefore highly appropriate for the particular variables of the EPI, but could be adapted to a range of interdisciplinary settings. The remaining two approaches are modifications of the classic group investigation model. In particular, they are consistent with the six stages of implementation of group investigation outlined by Sharan and Sharan (1992). The ideal model includes the following steps: the class determines topics and organizes research groups, groups plan their investigations, groups carry out their investigations, groups plan their presentations, groups make their presentations, and then the teacher and students evaluate their projects. In the thesis course, all these steps are followed, but each student works with the group only in the class setting. In the other courses, this methodology is followed closely, with minor alterations consistent with specific course contexts.

Of the many forms collaborative learning may take, the general characteristics of group investigation are most consistent with the approach taken in the EPI. The theoretical principles that underpin the practice of group investigation are also consistent with the collaborative learning approach undertaken in the EPI. According to Sharan and Sharan (1992), the simultaneous integration of the following four key elements is foundational to authentic group investigation: an orientation toward investigation (characterized by a quest by students to seek answers to their questions), ongoing interpersonal interaction (distinguished from isolated reflection), constant group and individual interpretation of information (distinguished from memorization and reproduction), and intrinsic motivation by all individuals (distinguished from primarily external motivators, such as grades or other rewards or an entertaining teacher). These are the methodological underpinnings of the group investigation approach.

Several additional theoretical rationales are characteristic of both the group investigation approach and the EPI activities described above. In particular, the speaker-and-synthesis courses are consistent with a basic concern of group investigation; that is, knowing that students have "pieced together, that is, *synthesized*, the information so as to make sense out of it" (Sharan & Sharan, 1992, p. 12, emphasis added). This approach is predicated on the belief that the act of interpretation (as contrasted with memorization) makes recall of significant ideas almost effortless. Another key assumption shared in both approaches is that controversy can be used creatively, for instance, that "debate among students about ideas contributes to their ability to interpret the information and make meaning of it" (Sharan & Sharan, 1992, p. 14) and contributes to the development of students' intellectual and social skills. The EPI approach shares with advocates of the group investigation model the assumption that students are intrinsically motivated. Good assignments will unleash students' natural curiosity so that they will voluntarily choose to invest their energy into learning more about areas that they recognize as important and relevant. The emphasis placed on relevance is also consistent with Dewey's philosophy of education, which assumes that what happens in a classroom should be closely connected to activities in the real world and particularly to the structures and values of society. This democratic education approach highlights the importance of preparing students to be good citizens in society, that is, citizens capable of thinking critically for themselves, and able to exchange ideas and opinions with others (Dewey, as discussed in Sharan & Sharan, 1992, pp. 3–4). Finally, it is a noncompetitive model of education that is supported, in which improvement of all students is encouraged, rather than the success of a small group of the "best and brightest" at the expense of the average student. These philosophical assumptions differ significantly from the philosophy implicit in the mainstream forms of education in schools and universities.

BARRIERS TO COLLABORATION

Participatory learning is the broadest term I use to characterize the kind of teaching approaches employed in the EPI. Such an approach to teaching and learning requires that both students and professors be actively engaged, interacting with one another and with the learning materials in the classroom. Students can engage in learning in ways that require active participation, without necessarily collaborating with one another. Collaborative learning is a specialized form of participatory learning. Genuine collaboration must involve a meeting of persons who see themselves as equal partners in a common endeavor committed to establishing and sharing in a process together that will result in some mutually derived creation. However, just as one cannot guarantee full participation in every activity intended to be participatory in nature, neither can one guarantee full collaboration in every collaborative-based pedagogical opportunity.

The success of collaborative learning opportunities must be judged on the basis of their process, purpose, and products. It is self-evident how process is related to collaboration, for classroom methodologies must create a space for common endeavors among equal participants. In particular, the group investigation model fosters interaction among students, helping them integrate pieces of information into coherent structures. The purpose of an assignment can also suggest something about its underlying pedagogical principles. For instance, if the sole purpose of an exercise is to show how well a student has mastered a skill or an essential bit of knowledge, then it is unlikely to be collaborative in nature. By contrast, a collaborative assignment would encompass a purpose such as finding a solution to a social issue or building on the strengths of disciplinary backgrounds. When students understand and believe in the purpose of an investigation, one observes a qualitative difference in the way they interact that can be distinguished from their behavior during an activity being done for the sake of the activity alone.

Products can indicate the depth of collaboration by revealing a lack of integration of pieces of information or showing lacunae that might have been filled had collaboration occurred. For example, in an exercise to design a sustainable workshop for the program, students in all work groups ignored a basic component of sustainability: namely, the complex of social relations and means to order them. For example, they did not refer at all to systems for keeping the workshop equipment clean and organized, or for tracking reservations so that the space would not be double-booked. Yet these dimensions of sustainability would have emerged easily had they seriously thought about their day-to-day use of the facility. Instead, they tried to do the exercise for grades, and focused on technical information such as lightbulb wattage to the exclusion of human factors. The lacunae in the final reports revealed their failure to follow the group investigation method fully. Products can therefore indicate whether an exercise has led to collaboration.

While the approach taken in the EPI is designed to foster collaborative learning, whether or to what extent collaborative learning actually occurs is another question. The experience of the students is not always as anticipated by instructors. Two significant factors affecting collaborative learning in the classroom are power differences between students and teachers and among students themselves, and assumptions made in and about the academy. Preconceptions and entrenched perspectives about the role of university professors and students, about what counts as knowledge, and about the value of applied versus pure knowledge, affect collaboration. Both sets of factors are intertwined and involve complex interactions.

One power imbalance that is present in any classroom is that which exists between professor and students. Simply by virtue of the prescribed roles, a difference is established. Add to this the professor's responsibility for evaluating student learning and the gulf widens. Whether this gulf can be bridged to allow genuine collaboration to occur is a significant question. In EPI's fourth-year honors course, even though conversation among students is expected and explicitly encouraged, when a question is raised it seems to be an automatic reflex for students to look to faculty to respond rather than to their peers. Sharan and Sharan (1992) recommend systematic development of discussion skills through practice in communicating a thought concisely, listening carefully, summarizing and reflecting the contributions of previous speakers, and including everyone in the conversation. While practicing discussion skills may help break down these barriers, in part this tendency to defer to professors is due to ingrained academic assumptions that require deconstruction. Off-hand comments made by second- and third-year university students reflect learners' expectations that instructors will earn their salary by playing the role of experts. "Doesn't this professor know anything? She is always trying to make us find all the answers. Why do we pay all this money to do all the work ourselves? What does she get paid for, anyway?" The expectations implicit in such statements support a traditional pedagogical approach. However, if learning is to be truly collaborative, it is not possible for a single person to presume to know all the answers beforehand. When faced with problems for which no definitive answers exist, students can become frustrated, thinking that they are there to be told answers rather than to learn how to collectively find—or, more accurately, to create—answers for themselves. These realities pose dilemmas for students who are used to the pervasive "banking model" of education (Freire, 1970/1983) and to professors, who are trained through the system to become "experts."

The question of expert knowledge is complex. As people who have spent their professional lives focusing on a particular area of study, instructors will have accumulated knowledge that a novice may not possess. However, this knowledge cannot be transferred directly from the teacher to the learners in a straightforward way. To be meaningful, the knowledge must fit into students' personal and social contexts. Students have not had the time to accumulate and process the information currently possessed by the teacher. Since students' learning experience is necessarily abbreviated, teachers may be able to convey the historical development of key concepts only. This transfer of information is not really learning, but rather a prelude to it. True learning occurs when students have assimilated the information and are able to use it to generate new ideas and applications. The advantage the novice has over the expert is the ability to furnish insights from outside the academy that can shed new light on familiar problems and spark radically new ideas. At the same time, an expert can contribute to the group's understanding because novices do not always recognize or grasp nuances, subtleties, and complexities. Assuming that the goal of education is to advance meaningful understanding, the expert and the novice are ultimately interdependent. However, the expectation in the university is that the expert has little, if anything, to learn from students and that students are there to acquire the insights and information held by the expert. In such a system, if one takes seriously a belief in collaborative learning, one is casting doubt on one's own academic credibility. Furthermore, there is the paradox of how to evaluate work as an individual while maintaining belief in collective understanding; of how to be a learner-teacher and be omniscient enough to evaluate others' work.

Peer evaluation has been used in the EPI to correct for this, but because grades and peer approval are very important to students, grading is distorted. The "better" students tend to be more self-critical than the "poorer" ones, who may not have the critical skills to recognize their own limitations. While teachers may not always be objective, ultimately they are more likely to make useful distinctions than students, who have other incentives. Another problem is that few students are motivated to move beyond the transfer-of-information stage. Students have been socialized to be receptacles and earn rewards for being intact and nonleaky (albeit unoriginal) vessels. To break out of this mold is difficult for teachers and for learners, and therefore the established power imbalances restrict collaboration from occurring naturally and frequently.

Students have less power than instructors by virtue of their role as learners. However, collectively and even individually, they can have and use other forms of power. Differences of race, gender, age, or sexual orientation can shift the balance of power. A young female teacher can be perceived by students to have significantly less power than an older male teacher. Should the young teacher be dealing with unconventional subject matter or material that challenges the dominant view, the fulcrum may shift even further away from the teacher. Working with two older male colleagues trained in ecology and biology, I am aware that students regard me differently. They do not assume that I have something to contribute to their education. Because my background is in ethics rather than in "hard sciences" or traditional areas of environmental study, I am not always viewed as credible by those for whom these "soft knowledge" areas are perceived to be secondary or unimportant. Introducing a collaborative learning model based on discovering or developing answers to questions with no single, correct answer provides few opportunities to build credibility of the kind that impresses students trained to receive knowledge through direct transfer. The combination of age, gender, and a nontraditional approach leads students to perceive power differences between me and my colleagues, and to increase students' power in relation to me.

When teachers like myself open the classroom to collaborative learning, they give away some of the power they would otherwise hold over students by virtue of their role. Shifting the balance in favor of students means that if students wish to use this power to disrupt the learning process, they are able to do so. Students collectively are able to sabotage a carefully structured collaborative learning process. For example, one class activity, the redesign of the EPI workshop, was turned into a meaningless exercise because few students took it seriously or bothered to invest much in it. The research project was intended to be meaningful and directly relevant to students, and to provide opportunities for creative integration of fundamental principles of sustainability. Unfortunately, students convinced one another that it was a waste of time. This poor attitude resulted in such uniformly weak final reports that the project was never attempted again. By contrast, in similar group projects such as the third-world city planning course, students have been highly motivated and the final products inspiring. Group projects done in seminar classes over an entire term of a third-year course on human-services planning showed a mixed result: some groups produced creative and very useful products while others submitted uninspiring work. In all these group exercises, the attitude of students made the primary difference to the value of their accomplishment. These observations suggest that, in the end, collaboration can only be voluntary.

Because educational methods that require active participation place demands on students not required by more passive pedagogies, motivation is of the utmost importance. If students are not motivated, collaboration will not occur, no matter how much the learning model may invite collaboration. In a lecture-based course, unless the lecturer's presentations were extremely bad, students who do not do well tend to look to themselves as the source of the limitations. A collaborative learning exercise that is not entirely successful, on the other hand, is likely to elicit scathing critiques of the instructor and the learning environment. Ironically, this is because in a course requiring collaborative learning, students are more inclined to fault the learning method than to criticize their participation in it.

Resistance is a tool enabling students, collectively or individually, to thwart collaborative learning. My own experience has shown that students may resist collaborative learning in any of the following situations: when there is a large discrepancy between the teacher's expectations and their understanding of the role of teacher and students, when they are not convinced an exercise is of value, or when an exercise pushes them in a direction they perceive as too "radical." The kind of education done in the EPI is consistent with the problems-based learning that Paulo Freire (1983) advocates in that it is premised on engagement, involves learning designed to be recognizably relevant and to accomplish a desirable end, and allows the problem itself to determine the kind of expertise required for successful resolution. By definition, it is radical in both the etymological and the more colloquial meaning of the word. I distinguish between the two versions here because, while etymologically, "radical" refers to the root, in common usage it is taken to mean that which is "way out" or extreme. The pedagogical approach taken in EPI supports a three-part methodology: to identify how things are now and why they are thus, to imagine how things might otherwise be, and finally to identify the plan of action that could enable a move in the preferred direction. The approach is radical in the etymological sense because to be successful one must identify the root problem and develop strategies to correct it. It is radical in the colloquial sense because a shift from the status quo is anticipated. The motivation leading to this approach is illustrated by Freire's philosophy of education. Freire wrote his work on pedagogy of the oppressed in a politicized context characterized by extreme injustice and oppression, in which receptiveness to consciousness-raising and motivation for social change were high. In contrast, observation by colleagues and me suggests that the typical university student in Canada tends to minimize or deny inequalities of class, race, gender, or sexuality, reject theories of social injustice, and resist consciousness-raising, political action, and radical social change. It is not surprising to encounter resistance to the pedagogical approach itself, since it is designed to foster radical analysis and action—a goal seldom aspired to by typical Canadian students. However, when students use their power to resist collaborative pedagogies, learning opportunities in the classroom are diminished.

While the power difference between students and professors is the most obvious factor limiting collaborative activity, there are also power dynamics among students that have this undesirable impact. As in society at large, power imbalances among students result from differences in sexuality, age, race, gender, and economic status. Among classmates, factors such as physical attractiveness, size, and voice can make a difference. However, variables such as perceived intelligence (indicated mostly by verbal participation), students' academic records, and the kind of relationship students have with the instructor have an even more direct impact in most classrooms. Each of these factors influences power relations and can affect the success of collaborative endeavors. Students who speak frequently in class or in seminars may be perceived by their peers to be stronger students, even if their comments are not very enlightening. Students often know one another's standing in courses, and make judgments about one another's academic abilities and intelligence. They also watch each other relate to professors, and make assumptions about who is favored or not favored. In a system in which grades are of paramount importance, students' observations about one another's academic ability shape the power dynamics in a classroom-fostering competition rather than collaboration, and suspicion rather than support. Predictable dynamics occur in group projects when students with differing academic abilities are expected to work together. Students with a high stake in the outcome may take over a group process, overcompensating for the weaker contributions of those who are less concerned about the outcomes. Groups with few motivated participants may simply submit inferior products; those composed of highly invested students often produce outstanding products. These dynamics, which stem from what Robert Slavin calls "diffusion of responsibility" (1992, p. 154), create tensions either within groups or between groups and restrict the possibility of maintaining an atmosphere of collaboration in a classroom.

OVERCOMING THE BARRIERS

Power dynamics among students, like those between students and instructors, may restrict collaboration in the classroom. Traditional assumptions about the proper role of students and teachers can also limit the possibilities for collaboration. For collaborative learning to thrive, one must acknowledge and correct for power imbalances, and change both the assumptions of students about what constitutes learning and the traditional assumptions about scholarship upon which the academic system is based. Can collaboration happen in a classroom with a division of responsibilities that by its very nature creates power differences? Can collaborative learning initiatives be orchestrated to move beyond, or to capitalize upon, existing power differences? Ultimately, these questions matter to teachers.

As a teacher, one can provide a space for collaborative learning in a classroom, but cannot guarantee it actually occurs. Beyond simply providing pedagogical methods that allow for collaboration, one can also seek to limit or change the factors that are known to disrupt collaboration. One of the barriers to collaboration dealt with in this chapter is the plethora of problematic power imbalances. A second barrier to collaboration discussed is the dominant assumptions about teaching and learning, and the structures that produce these narrow understandings. While negative power discrepancies cannot be eliminated altogether, most can be minimized. Many of the unhelpful assumptions and structures in teaching institutions can also be altered to produce a climate more conducive to collaboration.

Various strategies may be implemented to minimize the impact of power differences among students. There is a growing body of literature on gender and race dynamics in the classroom, and strong recognition that who speaks and how often they speak correlates with access to privilege and power (Moyer & Tuttle, 1983). Acknowledging the way that power dynamics at the societal level influence what happens in the classroom, and then seeking to implement strategies that compensate for natural biases is important if collaboration is to be possible (DeDanaan, 1990; Montecinos & Tidwell, 1996). Sharan and Sharan (1992) point out that cooperative learning methods actually create conditions that help rectify power imbalances because they allow all group members to participate and provide opportunities for minority students to acquire status and acceptance. In particular, they note that "the group investigation approach succeeded in correcting an imbalance in the participation of children from two ethnic groups" (pp. 143–146). The same positive influence would be expected to empower other minority or marginalized groups.

Comparable beneficial impacts of group investigation may be made to ameliorate the power differentials that arise from perceived or real academic differences (Hamm & Adams, 1992). Teachers cannot necessarily change the fact that some students excel in particular activities or that students' perception of these differences among their peers prevents collaboration. However, there are several ways to minimize the impact that academic differences make. One is to acknowledge the value of a full range of skills (research, writing, analytical, oral presentation and communication skills, group process and interaction activities, practical experience) that could be used collectively to produce useful knowledge, and to build on the strengths and minimize the weaknesses of all students. For example, a student who has poor writing skills would probably receive a grade lower than expected in an individual assignment because of this factor alone, but might be able to contribute beyond this level in a group assignment where someone else did the writing. If collective learning strategies are used to build on existing individual strengths, it is also imperative to identify, as early as possible, areas in which students could use remedial help and then to recommend specific ways those students might develop such skills. For example, assessing students' writing skills can be done at the beginning of a term through a short writing exercise, and those in need of help could be referred to a writing skills program or be cotutored by other students. Slavin (1992) cautions that teachers must distinguish between individual learning and group products. Since learning is something that takes place in the mind of an individual, a product that reflects the compilation of all group members' work does not necessarily correspond with the individual learning accomplished by each person in that group. Authentic group learning will only occur if all members of the group learn roughly what every other member knows. An intriguing approach that reflects this learning focus is to teach those who are weakest in a certain area before the rest of the class and then have these students teach their peers the new concepts. In such a scenario all students would advance at the same time.

For collaboration to occur, one must help students understand that learning can be a cooperative effort, rather than a competitive one. One approach is to offer learning assessments with incentives or rewards based on the sum of group members' individual performances or on the lowest individual performance. Another assumes that the group experience offers an inherent incentive to cooperate and help, and that external rewards are not required. The underlying belief in both approaches is that education need not encourage competition.

Education should strive to have students acquire a profound sense of belonging to social groups, without losing their individuality, rather than fostering disconnected individualism through competition for artificially limited resources (e.g., to be the "first" one in class, or the one with the "highest" grade). This view of education seeks to provide as many students as possible with the opportunities to develop their abilities to the fullest and excel in their knowledge and grasp of matters. The message is that excellence need not be realized at someone else's expense. (Sharan & Sharan, 1992, p. 5)

Collaboration rather than competition can be the cornerstone of education.

Collaboration works best when learners see themselves as equals and when the power held by professors over students is minimized. When it comes to collaborative teaching, the distinction between power over others and power with others is useful. While teachers will always have some form of power not held by students, this power can be used to shape the collective experience in a way that empowers everyone—that enhances power with others, that is, collaboration.

One way to create an atmosphere conducive to collaboration is to encourage students to deliberately reflect on the group process, their successes and failures, and the process of group collaboration, as well as on how they feel about the process and the learning they did (Sharan & Sharan, 1992). I usually build this type of reflection into the grading scheme in my courses so that students are challenged to assess their role in the learning process rather than being permitted to facilely attribute failures to something external (often the professor or "problem" students). If the students are there to learn (not just to get a good grade or obtain the credit), they usually see the benefit of this type of reflection. Sharan and Sharan (1992) also point out that for novice group investigators, it is necessary to offer evaluation to the groups on their progress, indicating if there are problems they may need to solve, providing help when necessary, and maintaining students' incentive to achieve their objectives.

Establishing learning goals that can later be evaluated is also a good technique for fostering student interaction and limiting the control of the teacher. If students are responsible for articulating what they want to learn, they can be purposeful about how to achieve their goal, and can critically assess how successful they have been. This process of intentionally setting learning objectives gives students ownership over the learning process, shifting control away from the instructor to the collective (Sharan & Sharan, 1992).

Setting group norms is another strategy that addresses both student–teacher and student–student relationships (Briskin, 1999). When both students and teachers help shape and define these norms they understand one another's roles and responsibilities more clearly and can view one another as allies in an exercise that is mutually beneficial. They can then become collaborators. Setting group norms actually increases a sense of freedom. Although constraints and boundaries are set, this is done not in a dictatorial, heavy-handed way, but in the spirit of cooperation. There is more freedom within the boundaries because it is clear that everyone understands the goals and can recall the norms if it seems the class is straying from these guidelines. Teachers are freed to be creative within the constraints established. Students are freed to experience the classroom in a new way, with a clear sense that they have a genuine role in the way things proceed.

In general, fostering freedom is likely to encourage collaboration. Students feel the constraints in a classroom quite acutely, which those of us who have not been students for some time tend to forget. In a typical classroom, students must participate in the type of activities dictated by the teacher, must meet the teacher's criteria for assignments, and are constantly evaluated by teachers. "Traditional instruction in schools is directed by what the teacher wants the students to know and what the teacher has planned to present. It is not typically directed by what the students may or may not know, understand or wish to learn about a given topic" (Sharan & Sharan, 1992, p. 11).

After not getting the results that I wanted in my own courses, I began to specify with increasing detail my expectations for all dimensions of the course. To thwart students' attempts to find loopholes that would allow them to avoid doing work, I found myself trying to anticipate their moves and adding more layers of regulation. However, the result was that students began to spend more time trying to figure out what I, as the person to grade them, wanted and less time actually thinking about the course material and how the learning could be useful to them. Precisely the opposite tack is taken by other colleagues whose approach I find increasingly appealing. Tactics that maximize freedom for students include allowing students to choose the books they use, the questions they use to focus their research, and the ways they wish to present their material; letting students choose both which type of assignments within a certain range they would like to do, as well as the weight of each assignment; and deciding collectively in class the evaluative criteria for assignments, learning goals, and discussion topics. Such actions increase students' freedom and allow for some open learning to emerge. Requiring students to make choices is critical in group investigation, as collective decision making enables students to connect what and how they study with their interests and ideas (Sharan & Sharan, 1992).

Actions explicitly geared toward promoting freedom in the classroom can reduce power imbalances between students and teachers. In the EPI honors courses, in which we want students and instructors to act as peers, this message must be explicitly and repeatedly conveyed to students. Students have been conditioned for so long to accept the power differences between students and professors that they automatically respond with deference. The forceful message that students and instructors are colearners must be repeated frequently and must be accompanied by a consistent model of respect for student input in which students are as likely as professors to have the first or last word. Teachers must refrain from evaluating each statement made, instead offering more opportunity for students (Sharan & Sharan, 1992). Grades are another route via which the message of inequality between students and teachers is conveyed. To reduce the significance of marks, it is helpful if an assignment has some value in itself. When students are convinced that there is a purpose for an assignment, especially one that extends beyond the classroom, they are much more likely to focus on the learning required to do the assignment well than on the grade they will receive for it. For example, one of the best projects I have seen was done by a group in a third-year course. They conducted research and then prepared radio advertisements, a video, posters, and information sheets for a student referendum on incorporation of bus passes into tuition fees. Similarly, the fourth-year honors project, which is geared toward applied policy suggestions for fostering sustainability on the Brock campus and its surrounding area, takes on a life of its own. Students work collectively with their peers, view faculty as resources, and focus less on marks and teachers' expectations than on creating useful end products. Typically the process becomes collaborative, and there is usually reduced anxiety about the roles played by individuals. Building in reflection on the group process as a requirement of group assignments is another approach that serves to integrate the process with learning objectives, to make students aware that it is their responsibility to interact with one another and problem-solve as a unit, and to redirect energy away from the teacher's role in adjudicating students' input. All such strategies reduce the power teachers hold over students, and make it possible to increase the power of learning through collective experience.

Although lack of motivation on the part of learners can thwart the collaboration process, Sharan and Sharan (1992) report that group investigation models are actually more likely to tap into students' intrinsic motivation than are whole-class learning approaches. Studies confirm that motivation is linked with achievement, and is tied to students' level of pleasure in formal learning settings and to their perception of the relevance of their education (Sharan & Sharan, 1992). Problems with motivation may reflect an implementation failure on the part of teachers. One of the primary reasons collaborative-learning approaches may fail is that students do not have the skills or have not been taught how to work together successfully. If a teacher is to intervene in groups to increase their learning effectiveness she must be able to identify the problems taking place and help students practice their cooperation skills. Johnson and Johnson (1994) identify five elements that are essential for success: (1) positive interdependence (recognition that an individual's success is tied to the success of the group); (2) face-to-face promotive interaction (students help each other to succeed by encouraging, praising, and assisting one another); (3) individual accountability (the group is made aware of which individuals require more assistance so every individual can reach the level the group achieves); (4) social skills (precise social skills such as trust-building and conflict management must be taught as purposefully as academic skills); and (5) group processing (groups can assess the extent to which they have reached their goals and can maintain relationships). These five essential elements of collaboration, Johnson and Johnson insist, must take place not only in a classroom, but system-wide.

INSTITUTIONAL SUPPORT FOR COLLABORATION

While exceptional teachers are able to devise ways to make collaborative learning happen in the classroom, there is much about the system that works against collaboration. Many of the strategies that are successful teaching and/or learning tools are at odds with the assumptions that predominate in educational institutions. For example, preparing assignments that can be used elsewhere reduces students' excessive concern about grades. However, in most educational institutions, most assignments are intended to be useful only as pedagogical exercises. Praxis, or action-reflection, learning models are not normative (Corcoran & Pennock, 1995). A hopeful sign is the growing interest in co-op learning programs in which students are involved in the workplace during the course of their studies, but even this approach does not allow for praxis-based learning in all courses throughout a student's academic career. Students who choose to apply their learning and reflect on its utility can do so, and teachers can propose to facilitate reflection on action or action following reflection, but the structure of the institution does not promote it.

A second example of the gulf between collaborative learning assumptions and the assumptions that prevail in educational institutions is the expectation that teachers will be experts with answers, not posers of as-yet-unanswered questions. At the level of graduate studies, it is recognized that significant advances in understanding result from what were once unanswered questions, yet at the undergraduate level and below, the mandate of teachers is to transmit knowledge rather than to enable students to uncover it. Sharan and Sharan (1992) cite a study showing that an entire classroom of students tends to ask only one-twentieth of the questions a teacher would typically ask them, and go on to observe that "the flow of information, and even of questions, is primarily from the teacher to the students, the obvious purpose of these questions is not to seek a solution to a problem. Teachers ask questions of students not to obtain an answer that is unknown but to determine whether students know the answer the teacher considers to be the correct one" (p. 11). Sharan and Sharan emphasize that teachers are enriched by students' contributions, and encourage interactive learning as an alternative to the expert/nonexpert division. However, in the existing system, because teachers are assumed to be experts, they are expected to rank students with grades. This entrenches a power-over dynamic that emphasizes differences in ability and promotes lack of collegiality, thereby thwarting collaborative learning.

Another example of how institutional expectations impede collaborative learning approaches relates to student involvement in shaping courses. One reason it is not easy to encourage students to help shape the courses they take is that administrators (and therefore, also students) expect course outlines to be available at the beginning of the term and assume it is the obligation of faculty alone to prepare these outlines. The predominant system also discourages student involvement in shaping courses through the evaluative systems it uses. When student evaluations are of primary importance in assessing one's success as a teacher, yielding control is risky; it rests in others' hands whether the course is successful in the end, yet faculty are perceived to be solely responsible. This system of evaluation may be effective in lecture-based courses in which faculty have a greater degree of control, but not for more collaborative learning contexts. Careful examination of the teaching philosophy underlying a course, as indicated by course outlines and assignment descriptions, may offset any imbalance created by students' resistance to collaborative learning, but it is not routinely done. Evaluating faculty performance annually may not leave a wide enough horizon for successfully revamping courses to facilitate collaborative learning, since several iterations may be required before sufficient feedback has been acquired from students to allow for an approach that meets their needs. In this case, some minor adjustments to the operating procedures normally undertaken may enable collaboration to occur.

If collaborative learning were to become normative, however, the assumptions and approaches taken in the academy would have to be rethought, precipitating more radical change. In the current climate, collaborative learning approaches emerge only if faculty members go out of their way to make them happen. Graves (1994) emphasizes the importance of creating a community context for cooperative learning. She observes that students best learn to participate collaboratively if these skills are emphasized from classroom to classroom and beyond, from year to year, and by all teachers. Since there is so much pressure to teach in competitive hierarchical ways, students' learning can be undermined if the values of collaboration are not reinforced consistently. Instructors also need support to develop and modify programs so that they work effectively, and to encourage collaborative relations among themselves and with other staff members. Both students and staff must feel they genuinely belong and have a role to play in a common community enterprise if they are to remain committed and to take full responsibility (Graves, 1994). Collaboration is an approach that flows from a matrix of community support, preferably a support network not only within all levels of the school system, but outside it as well. With effort, commitment, and ingenuity, it is possible to devise strategies that limit power imbalances and circumvent barriers in educational institutions. Only if there is a groundswell of opposition to the status quo, however, will collaborative learning replace the individualized, competitive system of learning that has conditioned almost all of today's teachers.

REFERENCES

Briskin, L. (1999, June 18). *Using ground rules to negotiate power collaboratively.* Workshop at the Society for Teaching and Learning in Higher Education 19th Annual Conference, "Creating Collaborative Learning for the 21st Century," Calgary.

Corcoran, P., & Pennock, M. (1995, October–November). Democratic education for environmental stewardship. *Green Teacher, 44,* 6–10.

DeDanaan, L. (1990). Center to margin: Dynamics in a global classroom. *Women's Studies Quarterly, 1*(2), 141–143.

Freire, P. (1983). *Pedagogy of the oppressed* (M. B. Ramos, Trans.). New York: Continuum. (Original work published 1970.)

Graves, L. N. (1994). *Creating a community context for co-operative learning: Handbook of co-operative learning methods*. Westport, CT: Greenwood Press.

Hamm, M., & Adams, D. (1992). *The collaborative dimensions of learning*. Norwood, NJ: Ablex.

Johnson, D., & Johnson, R. (1994). *Learning together: Handbook of co-operative learning methods*. Westport, CT: Greenwood Press.

Krug, K. (1999, June 18). Teaching in interdisciplinary contexts: Possibilities for and difficulties of collaborative learning strategies. Workshop presented at the Society for Teaching and Learning in Higher Education 19th Annual Conference, "Creating Collaborative Learning for the 21st Century," Calgary.

Montecinos, C., & Tidwell, D. (1996). *Teachers' choices for infusing multicultural content: Teacher thinking in cultural contexts*. Albany, NY: State University of New York Press.

Moyer, B., & Tuttle, A. (1983). *Overcoming masculine oppression in mixed groups: Off their backs . . . and on our own two feet*. Philadelphia: New Society.

Sharan, Y., & Sharan, S. (1992). *Expanding co-operative learning through group investigation*. New York: Teacher's College Press.

Slavin, R. E. (1992). *When and why does co-operative learning increase achievement? Theoretical and empirical perspectives*. Cambridge, UK: Cambridge University.

Stefanovic, I. L. (1996). Interdisciplinarity and wholeness: Lessons from eco-research on the Hamilton Harbour ecosystem. *Environments, 23* (3), 74–94.

CHAPTER 7

Searching for Collaborative Balance: Negotiating Roles in School–University Partnership Research

Linda L. Lang

INTRODUCTION

The differences between the cultures of the university and the school often create challenges that must be considered by teachers and university researchers who intend to embark on collaborative research ventures. These differences may also create wonderful opportunities for both teachers and university educators to experience personal and professional growth, explore new educational ideas, and form valuable and life-enriching collaborative relationships. Teachers and university researchers who enter into partnership projects with open minds and a strong shared commitment to the same educational goals and values may discover that the opportunities provided by this type of research more than compensate for the challenges that must be faced.

One research purpose for the study (Lang, 1998) that comprises the primary data source for my discussion of school–university collaboration was to explore how a university researcher/drama specialist could support classroom teachers who wished to expand their instructional practice to include process drama teaching strategies. An important corollary of this purpose was that the teachers would be empowered to define the nature and extent of the researcher's participation in their exploration. The researcher and both classroom teachers who participated in the collaboration agreed that the pedagogical purpose of our collaborative work would be to explore how educational drama experiences could be used to enhance students' response to and engagement with selections of literature.

In order to achieve successful collaboration, the research partners from both school and university cultures must be willing to negotiate research roles in a spirit of flexibility and compromise. Although the overarching research study involved two classroom teachers, my original conception of one research narrative that involved three interrelating coresearchers, two from the classroom and myself from the university, proved to be unrealistic when the realities of both teachers' lives and their differing expectations of my role in their individual explorations emerged during one of our early collaborative meetings. The conversation that inspired us to change the research design to accommodate these realities and expectations is explored in detail later on in this chapter. One result of our mutual decision to alter the original research design was that three narratives rather than one emerged from our work together: (1) the story of my collaboration with Carol, (2) the story of my collaboration with Mary Ellen, and (3) the story of our three-way collaborative meetings. The third story became a briefer part of the research narrative rather than the key and overarching research story I had initially expected it would be.

To tell all three stories in sufficient depth would expand the scope of my discussion to three chapters rather than one. The story of my work with Carol evolved in a pattern more consistent with the notion of researcher as "pedagogical adviser" (Perez, Blanco, Ogalla, & Rossi, 1998) and class-room teacher as learner or apprentice. Even though I resisted assuming a teaching role, Carol's lack of experience and training in educational drama and her expectation that I would "evaluate" her drama teaching practice with her students made the evolution of a mentor/apprentice relationship almost inevitable. Since I had encouraged both teachers take responsibility for defining my role in their respective classrooms, I made the decision to put this commitment ahead of my own preference for a more egalitarian professional relationship.

Mary-Ellen, on the other hand, was a very experienced drama teacher who was interested in adding process drama to her teaching repertoire. She had worked primarily with a theater arts or performance-oriented approach to drama teaching in the past, an approach consistent with secondary drama curricula. My own teaching experience as an elementary school drama educator had centered on nonperformance or improvisational "process" drama teaching approaches. Since we came from different places in our approaches to drama education, we often expressed differing perspectives about how an instructional issue should be handled. Achieving collaborative balance was a changing dynamic in our working relationship and thus the narrative of my work with Mary-Ellen provides a richer opportunity to explore the nuances of teacher–researcher role negotiation. Our partnership story comprises the main focus of this chapter.

Negotiation and renegotiation of research roles continued from the project's inception until its conclusion. That we were both able to engage in the negotiation process with a positive and constructive attitude is probably due, in part, to conditions that may be essential in school-university partnership projects. These conditions include: (1) a flexible research design that accommodates the demands faced by school-based practitioners, (2) a willingness on the part of both researcher and teacher to experiment with different research roles, and (3) shared researcher/teacher commitment to the ultimate goals or purposes of their collaboratively generated action plans. Our success in maintaining each of these three conditions throughout our collaborative study may well have contributed significantly to our perception that our research and pedagogical goals were successfully achieved. The following brief overview of school–university partnership literature supports the importance of each of these three conditions being present when teachers and university researchers decide to work in joint collaborations.

THEORETICAL FRAMEWORK

Small volunteer relationships between one or two teachers and one university-based researcher are often established to explore questions of instructional practice (Calhoun, 1993; Hollingsworth, 1994; Johnson, Hughes, & Mincks, 1994; Lieberman, 1986; Macaul, Blount, & Phelps, 1994; Raywid, 1993). Some partnerships are structured around specifically defined roles for the various participants in the project. These roles may include university educator as coach (Joyce & Showers, 1983, 1995), as service provider (Macaul, Blount, & Phelps, 1994), as critical friend (Costa & Kallick, 1993), or as resource provider and demonstration teacher (Raywid, 1993).

The partnership structure utilized in this research study was defined by a shared purpose of critical inquiry rather than by role. The construct of critical inquiry as a governing purpose in school-university partnership research has been explicated in various ways by different researchers. Joyce and Showers (1995) describe critical inquiry as a method involving continuous data collection, analysis, and interpretation. Sirotnik (1988) describes it as "a process of self-study—of generating and acting upon knowledge, in context, by and for the people who use it" (p. 169). Feldman (1999) postulates that the very act of entering into sincere, extended, and goal-directed conversation constitutes critical inquiry and that when the results of this conversation are made public, conversation can be seen as a viable research methodology in and of itself.

Supportive conditions must exist, however, before the process of critical inquiry can meet the expectations of both school- and university-based collaborators. Participants—teachers and researchers alike—must recognize that even though teachers and university researchers may bring different goals and purposes to a shared collaborative venture, the collaboration can serve educators from both cultures as long as participants from both communities have a definite understanding of what partnership research can offer them (Goodlad, 1988). When collaborative ventures are aimed at the professionalization of teaching, Schlechty and Whitford (1988) argue that an organic principle may emerge, because the common good and common interests of both teachers and university educators are considered as equally important and mutually supportive. It is essential, therefore, that teachers and university researchers be honest and forthright about their expectations for the research project from its inception until its conclusion.

Specific benefits identified by school-based teachers who have participated in school–university partnerships include the support to take risks and experiment with new instructional practices (Christensen et al., 1996; Johnson et al., 1994; Lieberman, 1992; Macaul et al., 1994), the opportunity for growth-enhancing dialogue about instructional practice with educators who hold different perspectives (Christensen et al., 1996; Feldman, 1999; Johnson et al., 1994; Macaul et al., 1994; Sirotnik, 1988), and an impetus to creativity created by bouncing ideas around with interested colleagues (Johnson et al., 1994; Lieberman, 1986; Macaul et al., 1994).

Both school-based and university-based educators may also achieve transformative understandings about themselves and their profession through shared collaborations. Knowledge about teaching may be both enriched and extended through the conversations conducted by collaborative partners (Feldman, 1999; Hollingsworth, 1994; McNiff, 1992; Stewart, 1997). When teachers and researchers meet frequently to explore common concerns and purposes, an atmosphere of mutual respect develops as participants sincerely listen and respond to each other's ideas and experiences. Through these shared experiences of being heard, self-esteem grows (Lieberman & Miller, 1984), friendships form, and communities that enhance participants' feelings of belonging and having something worthwhile to contribute are formed (Drake & Basaraba, 1997; Hollingsworth, 1994; Stewart, 1997).

School–university partnerships seem to experience the best opportunity for success when all participants are aware of and sensitive to the challenges and demands they will face during the course of the research project. Although we believed we knew what we wanted and how we would get there at the beginning of our research journey, the road we walked together through the seven months of our collaboration contained some unexpected roadblocks. The tools we used to circumvent and overcome unanticipated obstacles may be located within the "toolboxes" of commitment, flexibility, and negotiation. These toolboxes are unpacked in the following description of our journey.

DATA SOURCES

Data sources for the overarching study included the researcher's reflective journal, field notes, full transcripts of all teacher/researcher planning meetings and collaborative meetings, transcripts of interviews with each teacher, and students' written responses to the literature and to the research project. Excerpts of data incorporated into the present discussion are drawn primarily from collaborative meetings and teacher/researcher planning meetings.

NEGOTIATION IN THE EARLY STAGES OF PLANNING

Our research study utilized a research design based upon the Kemmis and McTaggert (1988) action research cycle, which includes phases of reconnaissance, planning, action, and reflection. This cycle was adapted to meet the needs and purposes of all research participants.

We initially formed our collaborative group from our joint participation in a University of Alberta summer school course entitled "International Studies in Process Drama," in July 1997. I was searching for teachers who had a basic knowledge of process drama methodology and an interest in integrating this methodology into their instructional practice. Mary-Ellen was searching for new ways to challenge and engage the students in her middle-years English and drama classes.

We met as a trio four times before moving our work into classroom action. These early meetings allowed us to share our teaching stories with each other (Connelly & Clandinin, 1988), to establish our joint purposes for the action research study, to explore possible researcher roles, and to discuss methods of data collection. This period of reconnaissance (Kemmis & McTaggert, 1988) clarified conditions that would influence how we conducted our work together over the ensuing seven months. It was during the reconnaissance phase that we first discovered the need to be flexible in all aspects of our collaborative work together. This need for flexibility emerged as a most important condition in the success of our school–university collaboration.

FLEXIBILITY IN RESEARCH DESIGN AND PROCESS

The need for a flexible research design was the first condition to emerge as crucial to the success of our project. The initial plan for the research assumed that most or all of our collaborative planning would occur in meetings among all three collaborative partners. Besides the fact that Carol and Mary-Ellen taught at different grade levels and were using different selections of children's literature, each began the project with very different levels of drama knowledge and drama teaching experience. Carol had no drama training or knowledge of drama pedagogy prior to the summer school class, while Mary-Ellen had been teaching drama (from a theater arts perspective) for over two decades. It became clear in the early planning stages that each teacher required very different forms of researcher support and assistance.

We decided collaboratively at our third meeting to change the research design so that specific planning decisions and classroom action plans could be developed in teacher and/or researcher dyads. This decision was borne out of both teachers' frustration with the second meeting. Carol described how her examination of the transcript of the second meeting confirmed her feeling that both she and Mary-Ellen were spending large amounts of time listening to conversations between me and the other teacher. She identified the reasons for this situation as (1) differences in the amount of drama teaching experience she and Mary-Ellen brought to the research project, (2) differences in the grades taught by her and Mary-Ellen, and (3) differences in institutional structures (scheduling, student enrollments, school size) of the two schools in which they taught. An excerpt from the transcript of our conversation demonstrates how Mary-Ellen and I responded to Carol's concerns:

L: My purpose is to create a supportive context for you two to work with these strategies in your classrooms. That's really what the research purpose is: How am I helping you? Is this process helping you? That's what I want to talk about.

M: Well, I agree with Carol. You and I dialogue and Carol and you dialogue and I'm not sure that the two of us are getting much of a chance to work together. Or, in fact, if that's even possible, with the difference in background and classes.

L: And the structure of the school too. I mean, you and I are wrestling with times for periods and location and working with a set, specific period of time in a junior high setting, where the periods are just so long.

M: If there were some way that the two of us were involved in each other's projects, but that's not possible, so . . . maybe we should meet separately. Maybe that's the answer, to meet separately. (collaborative meeting, November 24, 1997)

Although we met as a trio twice more during the course of the research project (to reflect on classroom action plans and share common concerns), all subsequent meetings were conducted in teacher/researcher pairs. This instance of negotiation clarifies the importance of university researchers' readiness to adapt their purposes and plans to the specific needs and circumstances of the teachers with whom they work.

ESTABLISHING ROLES: MARY-ELLEN AND LINDA

Before we began our first action cycles, I considered the participant–observer continuum (Hammersley & Atkinson, 1983) and assumed that I would probably position myself as researcher, close to the participant end of the continuum. What I did not consider, before beginning the research, was that my researcher role might shift back and forth over time within the same classroom context. This was, in fact, what happened when our action research plans became a living practice.

Mary-Ellen taught in a large school and was responsible for teaching several different classroom groups of students. Buzzers that signaled students to move from one classroom to another and from one teacher to another governed her days. Mary-Ellen was confident and experienced teaching drama to early adolescent students. My own school teaching experience had been primarily with students in Grades 3, 4, and 5. It seemed appropriate to both of us, therefore, that I would assume an observer role when we began working with the Grade 9 students in our first action cycle. This was a role that was familiar to me as a teacher educator with extensive experience gathering data for student teachers. Mary-Ellen could continue in a role that was most comfortable and familiar to her, the role of sole teacher in charge of the classroom. Thus, our initial choice of teacher and researcher roles seemed appropriate to both Mary-Ellen's and my own comfort levels.

As the research project progressed, however, I became more confident working with the junior high students and Mary-Ellen became more confident working with me. Because Mary-Ellen was facing increasing professional pressures in the spring months, it seemed appropriate that I take a more active participant role in the third action cycle. Traditionally, the "expert" demonstrates new teaching strategies with students and then gradually turns the classroom back over to the teacher as the teacher's skill in working with new teaching strategies gradually develops. By the time the third action cycle occurred, Mary-Ellen and I were comfortable enough with each other to eschew traditional ideas about what our roles *should* be and establish roles that served our immediate needs most effectively. Our shared process of negotiation and decision making meant that I, as researcher, moved from the role of observer to the role of participant—a sequence of researcher roles that would traditionally be reversed.

Mary-Ellen described her response to my shifting researcher role in our final three-member collaborative meeting in April 1998:

M: And you saved me with the Grade 8's. I mean I was too tired.

L: I know you were.

M: I was finished. There wasn't anything left to be creative. I knew I wanted to do something, but I didn't know what I wanted to do. So when you presented those—what do you call those things?

L: Role cards.

M: Role cards. I just thought, "Isn't this wonderful." I didn't have to be creative, I didn't have to do anything. And it was so much fun, I just wished I didn't have to be a teacher, that I could be a student and do this stuff too. It was wonderful. You freed me right up—it's in my notes—and you took an enormous weight off my shoulders. I wanted to do it. I wanted to do it because I had promised you. I wanted to do it because I knew it was the right thing to do. I wanted to do it because I'd promised my students. I wanted to do it because it was a creative process that was valuable and I knew it was valuable. I was living up to my religious zeal, but my physical and mental and emotional energy was spent, was gone. I said to my husband "I can't do this. I don't want to do this." And Earl said, "Well, call Linda and tell her you're not going to do this." And I would look at the phone and I would think "No, maybe I'll feel better tomorrow. I'll do it, I'll do it." And then when I'd get into the classroom I'd say to the kids, "Now we're going to be doing this drama," and the words would be out of my mouth and I'd be thinking, "Why are you saying this? Why are you doing this to yourself? You silly twit. You just nailed the coffin shut. Now you've got to do it. Now where am I going to come up with the ideas?" Then Linda calls and says, "How about this?" and I'm thinking "Thank you, thank you, thank you." (collaborative meeting, April 27, 1998)

Although one might expect that a drama specialist would be more actively involved when a teacher was first experimenting with new teaching strategies, then gradually move into a more passive, observer role, this pattern was not appropriate to Mary-Ellen's specific needs. When we first began the classroom research, Mary-Ellen had more time to plan and to exercise her own ideas and creativity. She expressed her satisfaction with my initial role as moral support and creative foil:

M: We were talking on the telephone and you made some comment that "I just let her talk and she starts coming out with all kinds of ideas. She said she was tired, but then she comes up with all these ideas." And I'm thinking, "Yeah, and part of that's just because I had so much to look at" . . . you gave me that opportunity to start creating. Even though I was tired in that phone conversation, beat at the end of the day, the adrenaline started to flow because I was creating.

L: Yeah.

M: And so you say, have you been a help? Absolutely, because that allowed me the chance to be creative. That was fantastic. (Planning meeting with Mary-Ellen, January 15, 1998)

From the beginning, the collaborative ethic had been that the research project would serve the teachers rather than the teachers serving the research project. Teachers were frequently reminded not to feel bound by predetermined expectations of how the project would unfold. Perhaps the ethic of serving teachers' needs combined with a freedom from rigid expectations influenced both of us to adjust our roles in response to contextual factors rather than presupposing our roles should evolve in a preconfigured pattern. Although our roles did vary and shift in a variety of ways, our mutual commitment to the pedagogical purpose of our research project remained stable. This shared purpose created a third condition that contributed to the project's success.

Shared Commitment as Inspiration and Influence

When we use drama as an instructional practice, we use our total selves as the primary "tool" of instruction, perhaps more than in any other method of teaching. We move, speak, think, and feel within "drama time" at the same time as we are working with our students in "real time." It follows, then, that a teacher's sense of self is heavily invested when teaching with drama. Ross (1992) suggests that the extra demands that drama teaching practice places on teachers require them to attend to students, support their efforts, and "enable their becoming" while still remaining sensitive to and supportive of the dramatic roles they have constructed within the dramatic reality. Teachers must, therefore, deeply believe that teaching with drama will enable them to achieve instructional goals and learning objectives that they could not otherwise achieve using less demanding teaching approaches.

Mary-Ellen and I shared this deep belief in drama as an important and powerful teaching approach that could enhance students' response to literature. Mary-Ellen reiterated her understanding of how drama could encourage students' heightened response to literature in a conversation we had during the early stages of planning.

L: Thinking back to our summer school drama class, what do you think you might bring from that class to our research project?

M: Well, I think what I've come out of the process drama course with is a desire to use that. Not perhaps as a psychological tool to delve into psychological situations, but as a tool to help students gain that deeper appreciation of literature.

L: Mmm hmm.

M: Just as this student was able to make connections because of the information she gleaned in a couple of courses that I taught her. I think that using a drama approach to literature can deepen a student's understanding and response. And if it deepens their understanding and response to the literature, then the next step should be that it will help to deepen their understanding of interpersonal relationships, because they'll have to delve into this in order to fully explore the piece of literature.

L: That makes sense to me. (conversation, October 8, 1997)

Mary-Ellen's view more than "made sense" to me; it echoed a belief that had guided my practice as both an English language arts educator and educational drama specialist throughout my career as an elementary school teacher, curriculum developer, and university lecturer. We were on the same "wavelength" from the beginning, and shared the same level of excitement when we found supporting evidence for our beliefs in the students' written response to a short story they had explored through drama.

M: Look at this [*reading*]: "When you see a member of a gang walk by, what do you see? Do you see a Royal, or perhaps a Guardian, or do you see a person with a name, like Andy?" [*Continues reading into the next paragraph.*] Oh, some of the questions she poses! And she quotes everybody in here.

L: She really got into it.

M: [*reading more*] "Now the Royals are planning their revenge to even the score. The saga is continuing. Some say, 'Hey, one dead body's better than two, right?' But the thing is, it's not one or two. It keeps building up and up. Think how many lives were affected by this one person's death. There was one Andy didn't even know about. What do you see? A person or a jacket?"

L: Oooh. Isn't that powerful? That's tremendous work. How does it compare to some of her other writing?

M: She's good. She's a strong writer. But this is *good*.

L: Good stuff. That's what we wanted. And what did they think about it?

M: Oh, they loved it. (planning meeting, January 15, 1998)

Our shared excitement about the students' response to our work with drama and short story carried us through many more stressful moments in the weeks that followed this conversation. When we reflected on the entire project at our April wrap-up meeting, we agreed that the creative energy and commitment generated by our shared excitement had contributed significantly to the success of our work together.

M: The work with you was sort of keeping me creative, keeping me young, keeping me looking at other alternatives and new ways of doing things. Because if you had sat me in a room and said, "Okay, now here's a number of pieces of literature, be creative," I'm not sure that I would have.

L: I wonder if anybody can, though? Like, I wonder if you can do that in isolation? Because I know when we get together and talk about things or talk on the phone, I find that—

M: The ideas really start to flow.

L: Yeah, yeah. Somebody says something and it bounces something and that—

M: Yeah—that sharing of ideas. (collaborative meeting, April 27, 1998)

Since Mary-Ellen's teaching schedule was extremely full, most of our planning and reflection did happen on the telephone or in evening meetings. Although we didn't find many opportunities to discuss classroom events immediately, the time between classroom action and shared reflection probably allowed us to achieve a more deeply considered response to our classroom work together. In spite of outside pressures and demands, this shared response was consistently characterized by mutual enthusiasm about the results of our collaborative efforts. We knew what we wanted to do, we believed it was worth juggling demands and schedules, and we were willing to adapt and change the structures of how we conducted our work and the roles we played within that work to create the best possible conditions for success. Our discussion at our final collaborative meeting indicates that we were successful in meeting our own needs as well as the needs of the students:

L: Isn't it funny how much emotional satisfaction it gave me to be able [to participate] in that collegial relationship? And you know, you sort of take what we've built over the course of six months and think about what teaching would be like if that were built in.

M: Oh, God.

C: Very encouraging; wouldn't it be very encouraging?

M: It would be nice to go to school in the morning. . . . But we were lucky—we were lucky. There are thousands out there that aren't lucky. (collaborative meeting, April 27, 1998)

We *were* lucky, but an analysis of the data we generated over seven months of meeting, planning, teaching, observing, and reflecting on our work indicates that factors other than luck were operating during the time we functioned together as a collaborative unit. Changing the research design, adjusting our research roles, and sharing a commitment to the purposes of our work were conditions that helped us achieve success. But what led us to create those conditions for ourselves? The following section discusses themes (attributes and attitudes) that characterized our interactions with each other and with the students.

Achieving Balance in Collaboration: The Interplay of Themes

My search for themes began with three successive attempts to code and categorize the data generated in collaborative meetings, in two-way planning conversations, and in classroom interactions. In my first attempt, I established categories according to interactions that took place in the school context and interactions that occurred in collaborative meetings. This system of categorization was too broad and provided little direction or clarification in detecting research themes. My second categorization system included categories for resources, relationships, and responses to the research process and classroom action. This structure enabled me to revisit the data from another perspective and provided new insights and thematic possibilities but was still limited in its scope. The final structuring of data categories relied on the Kemmis and McTaggert (1988) action research cycle and included categories for (a) planning, (b) action, (c) data collection, and (d) reflection and response. This structure provided the most effective approach to examining and exploring the data, but left me feeling dissatisfied with its explanatory power.

When I realized that I was attempting to impose one thematic structure on three very different stories I was able to clarify the essential problem with my data analysis. Although the themes that emerged were common to all three stories, they played out differently in each context. It was the interplay of themes that revealed the nature of our collaborative relationship and provided a context for understanding why we were able to create the conditions for a successful school–university partnership.

The seven themes that were revealed through my analysis of data included: (1) creativity, (2) authority, (3) accountability, (4) constraint, (5) connections, (6) praxis, and (7) concern. These themes that pervaded the progress of our collaboration from beginning to end resembled the notes in a musical phrase or melody. They were always there but in different combinations, different volumes, and with different tonal qualities at different times in our work together. Our achievement was not in playing the notes, but rather in the way we combined them to achieve harmony and balance in our collaborative "composition."

The theme of creativity emerged as very important to Mary-Ellen's articulation of her own growth throughout the course of the research study. Although she seemed overwhelmed by other professional responsibilities during our first meeting, as soon as we began talking about creating an instructional plan for her first action research cycle she entered into the process with energy and enthusiasm.

Once we got into brainstorming ideas for working with "On the Sidewalk, Bleeding," she blew me away with the speed at which she could generate ideas and tie the strategies we used in Neelands's class to the story. It was really interesting for me because I see that I naturally go into taking the lead in brainstorming, but she had so many ideas and they were so right on that I just sat back and wrote notes instead. (research journal, November 4, 1997)

Mary-Ellen's enthusiasm for creating her instructional plan was evident at our second collaborative meeting in October, where we spent time discussing ideas for "On the Sidewalk, Bleeding" (Hunter, 1983), the first short story Mary-Ellen chose for drama work.

M: Yeah but I'm picking up on that idea. I think you could break the talk show down . . . I'm thinking of something written I want to have come out of this: a newspaper article, either a straight report of the death or an editorial . . . a newspaper reporter that goes and talks to various people.

L: Interviews.

M: Interviews—this is an investigative reporter. He's picked up just the one-liner or two-liner that appeared on the last page of the newspaper. You know, "Another gang slaying." And he's decided that this isn't going to be just another gang slaying. That he's going to make Andy a person. And therefore he's going to interview people. . . . (planning meeting #2, October 27, 1997)

The telephone quickly became our most important collaborative tool as we communicated ideas about the story Mary-Ellen would explore through drama with her Grade 9 students. She had clear ideas about where she wanted to go with "On the Sidewalk, Bleeding" but suggested that she needed the interplay of ideas between us in order to get there.

M: I'm not getting anywhere, I want to get to—

L: We want to make a transition.

M: Transition to investigative reporter. Okay, how are we going to get there?

L: Oh, here's an idea. What about doing a teacher-in-role thing where they have the players, the group, the people who've been involved in this who've been called together by the police—well no, maybe by an investigative reporter. You know, the meeting thing where you have a meeting of people? And he says that this is a very important story and that he wants to get—

M: As much background as he can—

L: As much background as he can about it and asks the different people who are involved to tell him a little bit about what happened from their perspective. And you could do it with that meeting format and you could do it as a teacher-in-role with the teacher-in-role as the reporter. There's an idea.

M: Where are the kids going to be and which kid is going to come forward? That's my concern.

L: Well that might be something that they might agree on before. One of the ways of working that—

M: I'm thinking it's got to come out of the "role on the wall." (planning with Mary-Ellen, November 16, 1997)

Mary-Ellen's delight in the creative energy she experienced during our first action cycle led her to invest a great deal of time in creating her instructional plan and in creating props to be used as focus objects in the students' small group work. Her enthusiasm about the project inspired me to embrace the role of teaching assistant in gathering and creating the props she had suggested for the groups. This new researcher role as assistant was rewarding because I was working with someone who was as committed as I was to the pedagogical purposes of our project. The opportunity to work together creatively thus inspired us to experiment with new roles, just as it deepened our shared sense of commitment to collaborative planning for instruction.

But Mary-Ellen's enthusiasm was tempered by her experience of the other demands that remained ever present in her role as classroom teacher. She explained the tension that had been created within her as a result of taking time away from her other professional responsibilities:

I tried not to let my mind think about the marking that was sitting there that should have been done and didn't get done. I tried not to let that spoil what was happening for me with the creative juices flowing and my getting totally involved. . . . I like that kind of thing. And the kids liked it. (meeting with Mary-Ellen, January 15, 1998)

The conflicting feelings that are evident in this excerpt continued to influence our work together over the next four months. Yet the ideas we generated as a team created a synergistic energy that was strong enough to maintain our commitment to working together closely on instructional planning. When I was trying to make sense of where this creative energy originated, I discovered another important theme that seemed to influence our ability to create brand new ideas from very different starting points. The theme of authority seemed to support and influence our experience of creativity.

Mary-Ellen and I drew on different kinds of authoritative resources to inspire the creative ideas that characterized our collaborations. I drew heavily on the process drama literature and the summer school class as support for my creative contributions. Perhaps because of her extensive experience in teaching English language arts and drama, Mary-Ellen relied upon her own experience as a primary authority from the very beginning stages of the research process. She did ask for my theoretical input occasionally during our planning process but usually it was for the purposes of labeling or explaining a strategy we had not used in the summer session class with Dr. Neelands.

M: . . . the "role on the wall"—you'd better go over it again—I had it sitting here and I've lost it. So could you go over how that's done?

L: The role on the wall? Okay. Well the way Neelands describes it in the book, you put up a piece of paper or you could hand out individual papers with some sort of an image or an outline of a character. Okay? And then the students fill in what they know. He says "role on the wall" because you put up a poster or something with an outline of the character. You know maybe draw around a body or something. But that's just one way of doing it. (planning meeting, November 16, 1997)

The authority for decision making in our instructional planning was but one aspect of the authority theme that emerged in our collaborative work together. Another aspect of this theme related to classroom authority. Mary-Ellen did share classroom authority with me on a few occasions, although my usual role in her classroom was that of observer. In the early stages of the project, we reached an unspoken agreement that it was appropriate for her to retain the authority role with her students for those reasons that have been discussed previously. The first time she shared the teacher role with me, I was both surprised and challenged.

As the class begins, Mary-Ellen tells the students I'm in charge while she leaves the room for a moment. Help! It has been a long time since I've been in charge of Grade 8 students but they all bustle around and get their scenes ready and I only have to speak once to a couple of girls who are both pulling at either end of the same sweater. I'm surprised that the old "teacher voice" comes back so immediately—it must still be lurking pretty close under the surface! (research journal, February 18, 1998)

Mary-Ellen was more willing to share the teacher authority role with me at the end of the research project than she was in the beginning stages. Also, I was more willing to assume that role in her classroom during the last action cycle. The caring relationship we had with each other may have developed successfully because we communicated our professional respect for each other's roles from the beginning of our work together. We talked, at our last meeting, about what might have happened if we had reversed our roles during the first action cycle. My acknowledgment of Mary-Ellen's authority as a teacher—especially as a drama teacher—is evident in our interchange.

M: I don't think I'd have you do anything differently. Except it might have been neat—just from my own perspective—to see you in role. Just to see you in role, just for the fun of watching you do it, and sharing that experience with you.

L: Oh sure, I could have done that. I love it.

M: But in my situation, it didn't seem to lend itself—

L: I would have done it if you'd asked me. But I felt, in your classroom, that you had as many skills as I did in terms of taking on a role. (collaborative meeting #5, April 27, 1998)

Both Mary-Ellen and I explicitly acknowledged that she contributed an authoritative voice in our collaborative work with drama teaching practices. But Mary-Ellen also believed that her role as teaching authority in drama and English language arts was accompanied by a responsibility to take a leadership role in these areas of teaching practice. Thus, her experience of authority was influenced by an equally strong experience of accountability and constraint. These two themes are so tightly intertwined in Mary-Ellen's story that it is impossible to explore one without reference to the other.

Mary-Ellen set very high standards for herself as a teacher but often found that she was exhausted and stressed as a result of striving to meet those standards. The tension between her desire to achieve excellence in her professional practice as an English language arts and drama educator and her feelings of being bound and constricted by added professional responsibilities emerged in our first collaborative meeting in October. At this meeting Mary-Ellen explained that she was involved in a writing project with her students that involved them in interviewing and recording the stories of the senior citizens who lived in a senior citizens' residence across the street from the school. She felt accountable to the students, to the school administration, and to the senior citizens involved in this writing project but she also stated her sense of accountability to her teaching and to our collaborative research project. Mary-Ellen seemed to experience her extensive responsibilities as a form of constraint.

First of all, Linda, I have to decide if I'm going to succumb to the pressure. This is a lot of extra work for me as well, because I end up doing all the proofreading. . . . So somewhere in there I've got to fit our research work as well and I want to get into this when the students have already gone over short stories and the elements of a short story. (collaborative meeting #1, October 7, 1997)

As the school year continued, Mary-Ellen seemed to experience her professional commitments as increasingly more stressful. She had some health problems in the winter months and had also undertaken the supervision of student teachers in the fall term. During the winter and spring terms, Mary-Ellen had agreed to take a group of students to Greece during the March break and was responsible for coordinating and producing the school's variety night in May. These extracurricular responsibilities were important to her but she considered her students' achievement in exams to be equally important. The success of her first action research cycle seemed to create additional stress, even though Mary-Ellen was thrilled with the students' response.

Well, you know what's suffered for me is marking. I had to steal from Peter to pay Paul. And there was guilt attached with that. . . . I want to do more of this kind of work, and I'm thinking, "Well, the marking doesn't—." But then, you see, I have a very high standard with regards to my marking. I like a turnaround of a week, and I haven't been able to do that. And I think personally, morally, that's wrong, because the kids need to have it back as quickly as possible so they can make sense of it all. And I haven't been able to do it. (collaborative meeting #4, February 9, 1998)

By March, Mary-Ellen was seriously considering whether or not she could finish her third action cycle. She communicated her distress to me in a phone message.

As regards the class, I've continued working with The Proof. I've already told them that I'm going to do something in a dramatic vein but I don't know what yet. I haven't had a moment to even really think about it. I'm sorry to let you down but I'm completely overwhelmed with work this year. (phone message, March 9, 1998)

The result of this phone call was that I stepped in and prepared the written instructional plan and teaching materials based on earlier conversations Mary-Ellen and I had had in reference to this particular short story. Mary-Ellen taught from this plan and was relieved to have received tangible support in the form of prepared materials since she felt committed and accountable to her students and to me. She was not prepared, however, to undertake another action research cycle without a definite and structured plan in place.

It seemed that Mary-Ellen's need to carefully structure learning experiences and be able to predict how students would respond to those experiences also constrained her experiments with new drama teaching approaches. She was especially nervous about working with the "teacher-in-role" convention during her first action research cycle. This convention requires the teacher to play a role inside the imagined reality of the drama so that she may guide students' work from within the drama. She commented on her feelings about using this convention for the first time.

I was really tense, and part of it was because I was in fear. I was about to perform. And I took that quite seriously and I . . . did intellectually understand that I had been concerned about this but I don't think I really understood emotionally to that depth. I was concerned because for me this was performance. I was going to perform, and my ability to perform was going to set the tone for them. And if I didn't get that tone right in the first few sentences, I could destroy it or make it very, very difficult for the class to get on track. (meeting, January 15, 1998)

My presence as an observer may have exacerbated Mary-Ellen's tension to a certain degree but it was her own standards for performance that seemed to be the strongest influence. She was very successful using the teacher-in-role convention, perhaps because she took her performance so seriously.

Mary-Ellen took all of her instructional practice very seriously and this dedication may have influenced her attitude toward making connections between process drama and her goals and purposes as an English language arts teacher. She was very concerned that her students be able to use their drama work to better understand the literature they were studying. When

Mary-Ellen witnessed the Grade 9 students using drama to understand literary themes and devices better, she was especially pleased.

They're making connections with the very Standard English with a capital "E" in their drama, which was very creative. And then they start talking about "I'll never forget this," and "He was a real person, not a fictional character." That is what excites me. It gives me great satisfaction. I feel like I'm smiling all over the place. (meeting, January 15, 1998)

When she reflected on her work with the Grade 8 students, she made further connections between drama work and English language arts objectives.

I think when you look back over those evaluations that the Grade 8's did on their project, a lot of the comments were, "I have a deeper appreciation of the characters and what it takes to create a character." They got an insight into creating a play (it's in the language arts curriculum guide), and they had the opportunity to get into that by using the drama. (collaborative meeting #5 April 27, 1998)

Mary-Ellen also made explicit connections between her instructional planning for the students and our summer school class experience.

Now, when they finish the scene—what did we do in the process drama class—did we not debrief each scene as we watched it? What we did is we played them in a sequence. Maybe that's what we should do next. We should have the kids play their scenes in a sequence. (planning meeting, November 25, 1997)

Over the course of our research together, I watched Mary-Ellen achieve that place where theory informs practice and practice transforms theory that Freire (1970) defines as praxis. She made the connections between English language arts purposes, the performance-oriented drama teaching strategies with which she was very familiar, and the process drama teaching approaches we had explored in the summer school class and then lived out these connections in her work with the students. I described one experience of observing her new understandings in action in my research journal.

Mary-Ellen explained that they would be using their research notes to do the drama work and the writing project that would follow it. She explained that the drama work would prepare them for the writing project and she would be giving them some questions to answer in their writing. She also told them that they would have their own choice of writing form and listed a few possible forms: poetry, journals, letters, etc. She said they had read the story, researched the period, and now were going to "live it in hopes you'll have more source material at your fingertips to write." She summarized by telling them they would be using three areas of knowledge to prepare their drama work: their own ideas, knowledge of the story, and the knowledge of history and witchcraft they'd learned during their research. She explained, "Once we've watched the vignettes, we'll have the total story." (research journal, March 11, 1998)

Mary-Ellen commented about how our joint planning and my presence in her classroom had supported her in being able to live out the connections between theory and practice that constitute praxis.

My work with you was what I needed to do. It's helping me to formulate and play around with ideas for my own work, and I think it also has opened me up, kept me looking at other alternatives and new ways of doing things. Because if you sat me in a room and said "Okay, here's a number of pieces of literature; now be creative," I'm not sure that I would. (collaborative meeting #5, April 27, 1998)

It is possible that this "opening up" Mary-Ellen mentions relates to another role I was able to play as the researcher. By being present for instructional planning and classroom action, I was able to contribute an "external view, new 'eyes' to see certain aspects [she] might have overlooked in everyday practice" (Perez et al., 1998, p. 247). But my "eyes" were concerned rather than evaluative, and Mary-Ellen responded to my concern for her well-being and success with an equal level of concern for me and my research purposes.

Mary-Ellen's concern for me and my research needs emerged on different occasions throughout the course of the research study. She wanted to make sure that the data I was collecting in her classroom would be helpful and useful to me.

M: Can you use the information I've given you without you actually being there to hear what I've said?

L: Sure. I'm doing that all the time.

M: I'm just thinking about material you can use for your dissertation. (collaborative meeting #4, February 9, 1998)

Mary-Ellen's concern for her students related to her strong desire to invoke within them a love of learning. She talked about this concern in our initial conversation prior to beginning the research project:

L: What aspects of being a teacher bring you satisfaction?

M: Well, when you do touch that one child. You see the lightbulb go on and they've grasped the concept; or probably even more than that, when they come back after they've left you, after they've been in Grades 10, 11, and 12, or even gone on to university, and they say "Gee, I'm glad I was in your class. I still have your notes. I remember when . . ." That's a great sense of satisfaction because then you know that you have made a difference. (meeting, October 8, 1997)

Mary-Ellen's concern for her students' needs and for my needs as a re-searcher was probably a decisive factor in her decision to remain in the research project when the stress of other obligations became overwhelming to her in the spring. The interplay of her feelings of concern and account-ability did not eliminate the constraints she was experiencing at this time but instead provided a countering ethic that allowed her to continue on with our work. At our final meeting, Mary-Ellen described how the collab-orative relationship, born out of feelings of mutual teacher and researcher concern and accountability, indeed of caring (Noddings, 1984), contributed to the success of the research project:

You were investing in us so it was a symbiotic relationship. We had made a promise to you. That promise to you was an investment in our own work and in our own students. You had an investment in what we did because it was part of work that you were doing. So all the hands washed each other. (collaborative meeting #5, April 27, 1998)

CONCLUSION

I have touched on several metaphors to assist me in exploring the process of role negotiation in teacher–researcher collaborations. Metaphor does, as Stewart (1997) suggests, create a lens through which we can make meaning from our collaborative process. I have considered the conditions of flexi-bility, shared commitment to educational purposes, and willingness to ne-gotiate roles as toolboxes that contained the tools we needed to engage in collaboration. But when those toolboxes were opened, instead of finding hammers and wrenches, I discovered musical notes that played out in dif-ferent combinations at different times to create the musical composition that emerged as our collaborative story. Mary-Ellen contributed a third metaphor when she described our collaboration as "all hands washing each other." This reference to washing each other's hands crystallizes for me the spirit of caring for each other that allowed the themes and the conditions for success that I have discussed to exist in the first place.

Noddings (1984) characterizes caring as the way we must treat our teach-ers if we expect them to be innovative and creative within the classroom:

We know that teachers are, with students, the heart of the educational process. We know, also, that all sorts of changes and innovations have been effectively blocked, ended, or distorted behind the classroom door. But we still persist in asking how we can crash through this blockade—how we can get teachers to adopt the methods and practices we think they should use. Perhaps we should try more seriously to find out what they are doing, and to work cooperatively with them toward per-fecting the methods to which they are devoted and in which they reveal their talent. (p. 197)

Mary-Ellen and I did take the time to listen to each other and work co-operatively toward our individual and our common purposes. We also chose a pedagogical purpose that we both felt was worthy of our mutual devotion. These qualities of our work together created a successful and positive professional experience for both of us.

Research on teacher change (Fullan, 1991, 1999) and the words of my collaborative partner suggest to me that financial support may not be as important a factor as it is often touted to be in supporting innovation and teacher growth. Concern for the needs of classroom teachers and a passionate belief in models of pedagogical excellence may be far more important attributes for the educational researcher. Mary-Ellen and I both believed that drama-teaching strategies could engage and deepen students' response to literature. We worked together and attended to each other's needs and purposes in order to validate this shared belief in the arena of classroom practice. One of the Grade 9 students who participated in our research project described her own experience of drama in English language arts in words that also characterize the collaborative relationship Mary-Ellen and I developed with each other: "Everyone learns in different ways and this project helped people in their ways of learning . . . I also understand more about thinking before jumping to conclusions when reading a story."

We also understand more about "thinking before jumping to conclusions" and we learned it from working for and with each other, confronting the challenges, and drawing upon our own resources, values, and beliefs in order to achieve collaborative balance.

REFERENCES

Calhoun, E. F. (1993). Action research: Three approaches. *Educational Leadership, 51*(2), 62–65.

Christensen, L., Epanchin, B., Harris, D., Rosselli, H., Smith, R. L., & Stoddard, K. (1996). Anatomy of six public school–university partnerships. *Teacher Education and Special Education, 19*(2), 169–179.

Connelly, F. M. & Clandinin, O. J. (1988). *Teachers as curriculum planners: Narratives of experience.* New York, Teachers College Press.

Costa, A. L., & Kallick, B. (1993). Through the lens of a critical friend. *Educational Leadership, 51*(2), 49–51.

Drake, S., & Basaraba, J. (1997). School–university partnership research: In search of the essence. In H. Christiansen, L. Goulet, C. Krentz, & M. Maeers (Eds.), *Recreating relationships* (pp. 209–218). Albany, NY: State University of New York Press.

Feldman, A. (1999). The role of conversation in collaborative action research. *Educational Action Research, 7*(2), 125–144.

Freire, P. (1970). *Pedagogy of the oppressed* (M. B. Ramos, Trans.). New York: Continuum.

Fullan, M. G. (1991). *The new meaning of educational change* (2nd ed.). Toronto: OISE Press.

Fullan, M. G. (1999). *Change forces: The sequel.* Philadelphia: Falmer Press.

Goodlad, J. I. (1988). School–university partnerships for educational renewal. In K. A. Sirotnik & J. I. Goodlad (Eds.), *School–university partnerships in action: Concepts, cases, concerns* (pp. 3–31). New York: Teachers College Press.

Hammersley, M. & Atkinson, P. (1983). *Ethnography: Principles in practice.* London: Tavistock Publications.

Hollingsworth, S. (1994). *Teacher research and urban literacy education: Lessons and conversations in a feminist key.* New York: Teachers College Press.

Hunter, E. (1983). On the sidewalk, bleeding. In R. J. Ireland (Ed.), *Responding to reading: Level C* (pp. 49–54). Don Mills, ON: Addison-Wesley.

Johnson, C. S., Hughes, M., & Mincks, R. (1994). School–university collaboration: Everyone's a winner. *Reading Horizons, 34*(5), 430–442.

Joyce, B. R., & Showers, B. (1983). *Power in staff development through research on training.* Alexandria, VA: Association for Supervision and Curriculum Development.

Joyce, B. R., & Showers, B. (1995). *Student achievement through staff development: Fundamentals of school renewal* (2nd ed.). New York: Longman.

Kemmis, S., & McTaggert, R. (1988). *The action research planner* (3rd. ed.). Victoria, Australia: Deakin University Press.

Lang, L. (1998). *Teaching with drama: A collaborative study in innovation.* Unpublished doctoral dissertation, University of Alberta, Edmonton.

Lieberman, A. (1986). Collaborative work. *Educational Leadership, 43*(5), 4–8.

Lieberman, A. (1992). Pushing up from below: Changing schools and universities. *Teachers College Record, 93,* 717–724.

Lieberman, A., & Miller, L. (1984). School improvement: Themes and variations. *Teachers College Record, 86*(1), 4–19.

Macaul, S. L., Blount, T., & Phelps, K. H. (1994). School–university partnerships in reading/language arts: Working toward collaborative inquiry. *Reading Horizons, 34*(5), 421–429.

McNiff, J. (1992). *Creating a good social order through action research.* Branksome, UK: Hyde.

Noddings, N. (1984). *Caring: A feminine approach to ethics and moral education.* Berkeley: University of California Press.

Perez, A. I., Blanco, N., Ogalla, M., & Rossi, F. (1998). The flexible role of the researcher within the changing context of practice: Forms of collaboration. *Educational Action Research, 6*(2), 241–254.

Raywid, M. A. (1993). Finding time for collaboration. *Educational Leadership, 51*(1), 30–34.

Ross, C. (1992). *Dwelling in possibility: Using group drama as response to literature.* Unpublished doctoral dissertation, University of Alberta, Edmonton.

Schlechty, P. C., & Whitford, B. L. (1988). Shared problems and shared vision: Organic collaboration. In K. A. Sirotnik & J. I. Goodlad (Eds.), *School–university partnerships in action: Concepts, cases, concerns* (pp. 191–204). New York: Teachers College Press.

Sirotnik, K. A. (1988). The meaning and conduct of inquiry in school–university partnerships. In K. A. Sirotnik & J. I. Goodlad (Eds.), *School–university partnerships in action: Concepts, cases, concerns* (pp. 169–190). New York: Teachers College Press.

Stewart, H. (1997). Metaphors of interrelatedness: Principles of collaboration. In H. Christiansen, L. Goulet, C. Krentz, & M. Maeers (Eds.), *Recreating relationships* (pp. 27–53). Albany, NY: State University of New York Press.

CHAPTER 8

A Committee with Commitment

Jessie Lees and Vianne Timmons

INTRODUCTION

In the education sector, a concern is emerging regarding the retention of new teachers. Many school districts have concerns about the number of new teachers who leave the profession. Clayton (1999) estimates that one third of teachers in North Carolina quit by their fifth year. The Canadian statistics are not available, but 30 percent is the number most commonly presented. It is costly, personally, professionally, and fiscally, to lose potentially excellent teachers in their initial years, and therefore many school districts across the continent are implementing programs that provide support for beginning teachers in the hope that the retention of teachers improves.

In this chapter, we explore the evolution and dynamics of one committee, the Beginning Teacher Induction Committee of the province of Prince Edward Island. This committee was developed in 1996 with a mandate to implement a province-wide teacher induction program to support new teachers. The relationships that developed through the collaborative work and the interactions of committee members are interesting and unusual. One comments, "It's one of the few committees that I have been involved in that you really look forward to going to. It is more like a family coming together."

In the business world, many corporate and agency executives spend more than half of their working hours in meetings (Hawkins, 1997). The same trend is evident in the education system, as educators are finding that, in the university and school system, more and more time is spent in meetings and committees. Some are very effective and others seem to go nowhere. What are the elements in committee work that both produce effective results and build relationships? We consider the question in our study of the Beginning Teacher Induction Committee.

THE EVOLUTION OF THE BEGINNING TEACHER INDUCTION COMMITTEE

During the early 1990s, the Prince Edward Island Teachers' Federation and other teacher federations for the Atlantic provinces were interested in creating a Beginning Teacher Induction Program. In 1994, they commissioned a research report entitled "Invitation to the Conversation" (Samson & Lees, 1994). By June 1995, the Prince Edward Island Teachers' Federation had a volunteer teacher trained in the induction process to aid in the establishment of a program to support beginning teachers in Prince Edward Island.

Representatives from provincial school boards, the University of Prince Edward Island, the Department of Education, and the Prince Edward Island Teachers' Federation took part in a three-day workshop to introduce teacher induction to provincial stakeholders. The need to help beginning teachers in their first year of teaching was foremost in the minds of the participants. The workshop was initiated by the Prince Edward Island Teachers' Federation and the Department of Education and supported by all participants. As a result, there was not one leader, but a group of leaders challenged to reach the goal of establishing an induction program for beginning teachers in the province. The training was motivating and informative. Within the next month, a second meeting was held by participants, funding was procured for the program, and a September workshop for beginning teachers was planned. The participants who were at this initial workshop formed the provincial committee that developed and implemented the Beginning Teacher Induction Program. The members of the committee worked together for three years. During the fourth year, significant committee turnover occurred due to early retirements and position transfers.

Since September 1997, the committee has organized and implemented a province-wide Beginning Teacher Induction Program. Workshops are held each term for beginning teachers and their mentors. These workshops are planned and conducted primarily by the committee members. A handbook was also developed by a few of the committee members and distributed to all beginning teachers. Initially one, then later, two workshop locations were used. It proved to be more cost-effective and generally more practical to hold the sessions within a reasonable traveling distance of the teachers, even though the number of workshops was increased.

The first day-long workshop for beginning teachers was held in January 1996. After a general introduction, short sessions, or "carousels of activity," were offered on a number of topics: classroom management, positive communication, mentoring, teacher wellness, teamwork, and the role of the professional organization. Teachers described the day as informative and found the carousel topics useful.

The first half-day workshop for mentors was offered in October 1996. The induction program was explained, and mentors were given information about experiences and practices of mentoring. The greatest response by participants was given to a beginning teacher from the committee, who described her experiences and difficulties and spoke about the day-to-day importance of her mentor's support. Mentors spoke about her "passionate sharing of her experience." Beyond this, one mentor felt that she "gave a better idea of what to discuss with my new teacher."

The mentors were joined by beginning teachers in the afternoon. A presentation on peaceful classrooms was followed by small-group discussion of lessons learned by beginning teachers and mentors in the induction program. Finally, the teacher-mentor groups were asked to make suggestions about improving the program, continuing support for second-year teachers, and ways in which each could contribute to the program. These were the models utilized for subsequent workshops.

Since the initial workshop, two professional development sessions have been held for committee members. The first was a two-day workshop on the mentoring process in the fall of 1997, while the second was a one-day session on facilitation and creating an action plan for the committee, held in 1999.

COMMITTEE MEMBERSHIP

One of the key elements for a successful committee is the configuration of the group. It is important to establish a membership consisting of people interested in and committed to the objectives of the committee (Jones, Wilker, & Stoner, 1995). Klein (1995) states that when individuals share important common goals they tend to grow as a team even though they have separate interests.

A team could be described as people with complementary skills committed to a common purpose and approach, who work together effectively, and hold themselves mutually accountable (Mendzela, 1997). These teams don't just materialize; selection of the members is a critical element of the team's success. Hawkins (1997) discusses who should be selected to serve on committees. He states, "the simple answer is those people who can best accomplish the objective. Obvious choices for attendees would include people who own the problem, those who will be most affected by the outcome, subject matter experts, problem-solvers and idea people" (p. 33).

As previously mentioned, the Beginning Teacher Induction Committee was developed with members who represented the key constituencies of the education community in the province. The goal of the committee was to establish a mentorship program for new teachers; therefore, it was critical to establish partners who could contribute to this endeavor. The committee had representation from the Department of Education, the Teachers' Federation, the University of Prince Edward Island, the school districts, and the Retired Teachers Association. Each of these organizations represented concerned and committed stakeholders. Each organization had its own responsibility for teachers' smooth entry into the profession and therefore "owned the problem" in a very real way. School administrators, teachers, and beginning teachers were included among the individual representatives. As a result, committee members never lost sight of school realities and constraints.

The inclusion of beginning teachers was crucial, because they brought the immediacy of their own experiences to committee meetings and mentors' workshops. Committee members were reminded of the necessity of their work when they heard day-by-day stories of early professional life. As did all committee members, beginning teachers participated in the twice-yearly mentors' workshops. The value of their presentations was commented on in workshop evaluations. Mentors wrote, for example, that these "brought it all back," and that hearing the concerns of a beginning teacher was helpful because "it gave me a better idea of what to discuss with my new teacher."

Beginning teacher representatives were also important because they provided reinforcement. Together with the positive workshop and questionnaire responses of beginning teachers and mentors, they underscored the value of the committee's interventions. This was extraordinarily motivating. One committee member tells the story of an early workshop after which a participant said, "Please, please keep this going. Don't forget about us. We need you." A dedicated educator, she referred to this as the impetus for all that she did.

In summary, as well as making a general contribution to the committee, the inclusion of beginning teachers had three significant effects: (1) Their ongoing experiences underscored the need for the committee's work; (2) they made a unique contribution to mentors' workshops; and (3) they provided positive feedback that was highly motivating to committee members. These positive outcomes indicate the value of having representation of people affected by the group's activity.

CLEAR GOALS AND DIRECTION

Along with calculated membership criteria, another critical aspect that contributes to the success of a committee is the establishment of clear goals.

Hyatt (1997) describes effective work group performance as possessing a clear, elevating goal, results-driven structure, competent team members, unified commitment, collaborative climate, standards of excellence, external support and recognition, and principled leadership.

The goal-setting is as important as the team selection. Mendzela (1997) states that a team possesses a common vision and purpose that members help develop and in which they take pride. It contains members who feel responsible for the team's work, not just for their individual contributions.

The Beginning Teacher Induction Committee established clear goals and direction at its inception, which definitely contributed to its success. In addition to clear goals, the group worked on developing an ongoing communication network. For informal discussion of issues and plans, the committee members phoned each other regularly throughout the year.

Manthey (1994) identified three elements critical to the building of effective teams: (1) setting, defining, or articulating a goal or vision; (2) empowering team members to handle their work so they achieve that goal; and (3) establishing effective communication channels and healthy relationships. All these elements are evident in the Beginning Teacher Induction Committee. A contribution was made by the initial workshop for committee members, in which the practicalities and research literature were set against a background of personal narrative. This sharing of entrant professional life experiences fostered relationship-building among members as well as an intellectual and emotional commitment to the goal of supporting beginning teachers. Its significance is well summarized by one of the participants:

The three-day workshop provided us with a persuasive rationale for needing an induction program for beginning teachers, got us to do some soul searching about important mentors and their characteristics in our own lives, and introduced us to the literature on establishing successful mentoring relationships. It forged friendships that would sustain us in our subsequent struggles to flesh out the details of the induction program in later meetings.

A FOCUS ON TEAM BUILDING

As its work continued, the team developed a tight bond that stood out as unique in the participants' experiences. This bond evolved as the team developed. A late-joining member was "struck by the fact that committee members genuinely liked and respected each other's opinions, ideas, suggestions, and each other." One committee member wrote, "the chemistry of the committee members has been an important factor in terms of [the committee's] success."

The story of the Beginning Teacher Induction Committee supports Mendzela's (1997) description of the development of a team:

Teamwork is like a salad: Individually, each ingredient maybe tasty and fresh, but they will certainly not add up to a gourmet experience. Put together in the right way, the ingredients enhance one another to produce startling results. Each ingredient retains its character and strengths, but contributes to a more exciting and effective overall result. (p. 67)

Some of the committee's effectiveness as a team had to do with relationships and mutual respect established at the initial workshop. Some had to do with commitment to the committee's purposes. A newly appointed member made the following comments:

Committee members have a deep attachment to their work in this area. Many people spoke of the initial professional development they received, of their personal professional growth, of the joy of being involved with this project. There is something intangible about it all . . . but it works!

Fowler (1995) attributes committee success to a team process that also pays attention to the affective needs. The Beginning Teacher Induction Committee would set up meetings in a variety of venues, including cottages and peoples' homes, and include a social at the end of some of the meetings. Workshops for committee members were designed to include a social component and the second workshop was held over a weekend at a Retreat Center.

LEARNING AND PERSONAL GROWTH

In Haskins, Liedtka, and Rosenblun's (1998) description of an ethic of collaboration, they mention willingness to invest in learning, and value placed on learning. Members of the Beginning Teacher Induction Committee were conscious of their need for greater expertise and professional development. They arranged to spend a weekend in a retreat setting with leaders from the National Association of Secondary School Principals mentoring program to learn more about skills of mentoring. Later, in a day-long workshop, they heard about workshop facilitation and identified future goals. These training sessions were critical to the success of the project because members used their developing skills to improve the planning, implementation, and content of workshops for beginning teachers and mentors. As well, the sessions contributed to team building as members learned more about one another's abilities and beliefs.

The knowledge of one another's strengths was valuable in planning workshops. It also led to mentoring within the committee. Many members refer to their personal growth and to the way in which they mentored one another. One wrote, for example,

I have grown in confidence and acquired experiences that will benefit me in the future. The encouragement I have received from committee members has motivated me to strive to better myself and set goals that are higher than when I joined the group.

Also important for strengthening connections among members was the interplay between planning, organizational, and educational roles. This is a working as well as a planning committee. As a member comments, "the group decides on the manner of support, implements workshops, and meets with individual beginning teachers and mentors on a first-hand basis." Members run the mentors' and beginning teachers' workshops, acting as presenters, facilitators, teachers, role players, and workshop leaders. In the process, they gain respect for one another's professional skills.

THE FACILITATION

Boss (1995) identifies the team leader as the single most important person in determining the success or failure of a team-building meeting. In the Beginning Teacher Induction Committee there were a number of skilled and talented facilitators. Burns (1995) noted that regardless of a team's composition and purpose, most successful teams share the common denominator of high quality facilitation. Jones, Wilker, and Stoner (1995) identified a variety of roles that facilitators take on in meetings. For example:

Facilitators play different roles, from expert, to thought leader, to innovator, to teacher. More minor roles the facilitator will play include cheerleader, timekeeper and barometer. Whether the facilitator is a manager, a group member or an outsider, he or she must help participants generate ideas, keep the flow of ideas moving, and change tactics when discussion lags. (p. 30)

They go on and describe an excellent facilitator as one who makes magic. It often seems that getting the most out of a meeting requires magic. However, facilitators (the people assigned to make the meetings easier and more effective) do not possess supernatural powers. Instead, they have taken the time to learn, practice, and refine their task.

The Beginning Teacher Induction Committee had one member, Arthur, whom all participants described as critical to the success of the committee. He worked diligently on respecting each team member's individuality and the development of the team process. One member writes, "He was able to diffuse the small undercurrents of this diverse group. At the same time, I felt supported by [him] for my particular concerns, confusions, and my attempts to verbalize these." In an interview, Arthur spoke about his contribution to the committee in a way that reflects, and goes beyond, the facilitator's roles described by Jones, and colleagues (1995):

I tried hard on communication, to keep members informed. I also think I contributed to facilitation of the committee work and sometimes I would chair. I always tried to not have my way or my voice dominate but to bring out the voice of all present. I think I made the members feel that they were important. When we planned workshops I tried to make sure that everyone had something to do that day. It didn't matter what it was just so we were all doing something . . . I had good knowledge of induction.

Although he had no formal position on the committee, Arthur's significance was alluded to by almost every member. This, in itself, attributes to the importance of the various tasks he voluntarily undertook and to the value of his people-centered as well as task-centered facilitation.

THE DEVELOPMENT PHASES

The literature presents a number of models that present team process. Mendzela (1997) describes a model that is helpful in an analysis of the Beginning Teacher Induction Committee's development.

Initially, the team focuses on the first stage, which is called Forming. At this time, the new team members demonstrate mixed attitudes: excited, optimistic, reserved, skeptical, and anxious. The team members are often polite, impersonal, and guarded. Members of the Beginning Teacher Induction Committee moved through this phase during the initial workshop. The intensive three-day session and the facilitator's narrative approach enabled members to become comfortable with each other and the project.

As the team embarks on its activities, the second stage develops, which is called Storming. During this time, the team needs to argue about actions and methods. They are testing boundaries and each other. This is when the team develops its decision-making model. The facilitator of a recent workshop for committee members pointed out that the group seemed to have bypassed the Storming phase described by Mendzela (1997). In his opinion, it might be necessary to revisit this phase because, with changes in membership, the committee's way of working was coming under challenge. The Beginning Teacher Induction Committee developed a consensus model of interaction. This took a considerable amount of time. Burns (1997) notes that consultative decision making takes more time than unilateral decision making.

The third stage is referred to as Norming. It is during this period that the group gets organized, develops skills, establishes procedures, and confronts issues. This was evident in the second year of the Beginning Teacher Induction Committee, when the *Handbook for Beginning Teachers* was developed and procedures for the workshops established.

The final stage is called Performing. This is when the team members become synergistic, effective, and cohesive. This is when the action occurs and the committee sees the success of its labor. The third year of the committee saw a special synergy happen. People felt empowered by the success of the program, and the group formed a close supportive relationship. But there was significant personnel change during the last year, and the relationships began to reform.

The Beginning Teacher Induction Committee evolved with a loose, non-hierarchical structure and a consensus-building model of interaction. There was no official chairperson or secretary, although notes were taken and agendas drafted by the same two people on each occasion. Workshops could take hours to plan, as committee members exchanged and refined each other's ideas and suggestions. As Burns (1995) notes, the committee's consultative decision making took a great deal of time. However, the quality of the final decision was often a matter of comment, and there was a general feeling that the process was long but invaluable. The consensual nature of the committee gave it some of its uniqueness.

Members took pride in the fact that beginning teachers, principals, and superintendents met as equals. For one beginning teacher—who made a significant contribution to the committee's work—this was remarkable, "I'm so young and inexperienced and yet these people want to hear my ideas!" This member speaks of her own growth "as a teacher and a person." At the same time, a superintendent writes,

It was also notable that everyone was there (on the committee) on an equal footing. This may be a small point, but it is extremely important because the opinions of the Beginning Teachers on the committee were crucial in the committee formulating plans for the content of workshops.

Perhaps the committee's egalitarianism had something to do with its consensual decision making. Otherwise, it would have been easy for senior administrators to dominate any debate.

CHALLENGE AND CHANGE

Boss (1995) discusses turnover among key staff members:

Changes in team membership, whether caused by turnover or modification in the organisation structure, usually cause off-site agreements to become invalid for the new team members and therefore, require that the team building process begin again. Further, when key members are replaced by those who have no idea of the history of the change effort or the theory underlying those changes, the potential for regression is substantial. This is particularly true if the team gets a new leader, because research has shown that the leader is the single most important person responsible for successful team-building sessions. (p. 175)

The dynamics of the Beginning Teacher Induction Committee are changing as committee members come and go: the leader has retired; other long-standing members have left for a variety of reasons; and soon only one of the original participants is likely to remain. The committee is embarking on a new collaboration with a continuing mandate to build upon and expand its existing work. However, the process is difficult. Tensions are emerging that illuminate previously unexamined concerns underlying the committee's apparently seamless and problem-free working relationship. Significant issues have to do with individual silences, the perceived exclusiveness of a group that has bonded particularly well, pressures toward conformity, leadership succession in an informal setting, complacency, and resistance to change.

It is interesting to notice that many of these issues were articulated during the research process when individual members were asked to write about their experience of the committee. There was an increasing sense of unease in the group and, no doubt, there was talk among individuals, but there was no open committee discussion of some individually significant and strongly felt concerns. Yet long-standing members prided themselves on the group's receptiveness to everyone's opinion. When asked how agreement was reached in the committee, one of the original members wrote, "It is hard to define because we seem always to agree. We made decisions that everybody was happy with. I don't remember once coming away feeling like I wish we did something else." When decisions and workshop outlines took a very long time to make or prepare, it was widely said and believed that the patient collaborative process led to much better outcomes.

"The group's cohesiveness rested, in part, on members' belief that this was a special kind of committee, one composed of a group of very caring individuals." "As well, it was perceived to be egalitarian, so that there was a feeling of belonging and not of any control." These generally accepted and very positive images were supported by the apparent openness of meetings and the generally consensual nature of the decision making. They enabled, and may have been necessary for, the committee's creative, interactive process. In time, however, did they become limiting because they were unquestioned and perhaps implicitly unquestionable? Was there no mechanism for dissent at a level where these basic tenets were established? One relatively new member suggested this, when she wrote that she felt "tentative" about expressing her opinion because "They are a very tight-knit group, so therefore when someone brings up an idea that might be contrary to the way it has been done in the past, I get the feeling that is not really what people want."

The initial workshop played an important part in developing members' sense of closeness but it also isolated newcomers.

When we started we had two days [that] to me gave it the foundation for where we were going. It gave us—it is like a rock—it is a very strong concrete base. And these new people coming on board haven't had it. We haven't had two days to sit down and get to know one another.

From a new member's perspective, "whatever in-servicing they have had as a group was very powerful." She suggests that it represents a challenge. "I think it is hard for them for some reason to open the circle and embrace new people."

Other tensions result from that feeling of closeness and consensus. Wech, Mossholder, and Steele (1998) described pressures toward conformity within a cohesive group. In the Beginning Teacher Induction Committee there were no obvious external pressures, but there may have been an individually felt reluctance to disturb the image of consensus and relationship. One long-term member writes, "I do think that there has been an agreement not to be too controversial in terms of making decisions by consensus and compromise. I am afraid sometimes that I am starting to see group-think." This member feels that the committee must "become more comfortable with vigorous controversy from time to time and confrontation in a constructive way." Some members did not say very much, because they wanted to be explicitly invited to participate in the discussion. A long-term member writes: "I am very quiet and I need to be asked . . . sometimes I would like to be asked more." Somehow, this need was not adequately recognized and it is possible that other relatively quiet members shared her feeling.

The informality and lack of formal hierarchy meant that newcomers did not always know what was going on and may have made them more reluctant to express their concerns. Uncertainty about how things worked increased any sense of exclusion. One new member writes, "I am having trouble . . . trying to figure out exactly what my place is." In this member's view, the committee has done a "wonderful job" but is now marking time rather than moving forward.

The tradition of informal leadership may also have created problems because there were no obvious shoes to fill when the "leader" retired. Moreover, the former "leader" left the committee, whereas Worchel, Hebl, and Michelle's (1998) study found that an optimum condition for leadership transition occurs when an ex-leader stays on and a new leader comes from within the group. Lanza and Keefe (1994), like Boss (1995), comment on a leader's influence in shaping group norms, which do not survive well in times of change. For the committee, other changes coincided with an interim period where there was no obvious leadership—and no obvious lack of leadership because there was no formalized position.

FUTURE PLANS

Although there are concerns and criticisms, there is a very positive feeling about the committee. Its special character is widely affirmed. The newcomer who referred to the "tight-knit group" also described a very sensitive group, welcoming from a personal point of view." The committee's work continues. Workshop evaluations are almost uniformly positive. In their responses to questionnaires about the program, beginning teachers, mentors, and principals are enthusiastic and commend the committee's role. From the outset, this very positive feedback has been a crucial motivating force for the committee, and it continues to inspire new members.

There are financial challenges with the rising number of beginning teachers and the tight educational budgets. There are imaginative challenges as committee members consider how to move forward, building on and extending existing efforts with a new team that has yet to establish its own dynamic. Are there ways to move beyond the existing pattern of workshops and a beginning teachers' handbook without incurring major expense? What does "whole school mentoring" look like, and how can it be fostered? How can opportunities for classroom observation be expanded?

In the committee itself, there is movement toward a more formal structure, and there is a greater emphasis on efficiency. Long-standing members feel a sense of loss as the committee is reshaped. However, the commitment of members, whether newly appointed or long established, is unquestioned. So, the future beckons.

ACKNOWLEDGMENTS

Special thanks to the Prince Edward Island Teacher Induction Committee and the beginning teachers for sharing their experiences with the authors of this chapter.

REFERENCES

Boss, W. (1995). Comment: The challenge of building effective work groups. *Journal of Management Inquiry, 4*(2), 172–177.

Burns, G. (1995). The secrets of team facilitation. *Training and Development, 49*(6), 46–53.

Clayton, M. (1999). First-year teachers spell m-e-n-t-o-r. *Christian Science Monitor, 91*(100), 20.

Fowler, A. (1995). How to build effective teams. *People Management, 1*(4), 40–42.

Haskins, M., Liedtka, J., & Rosenblun, J. (1998). Towards an ethic of collaboration. *Organizational Dynamics, 26*(4), 34–41.

Hawkins, C. (1997). First aid for meetings. *Public Relations Quarterly, 42*(3), 33–37.

Hyatt, D. E. (1997). An examination of the relationship between work group characteristics and performance: Once more into the breech. *Personnel Psychology, 50*(3), 553–586.

Jones, B., Wilker, M., & Stoner, J. (1995). A meeting primer. *Management Review,* *84* (1), 30–33.

Klein, S. (1995). Teams under stress. *Institute of Industrial Engineers Solutions,* 27(5), 34–39.

Lanza, M. L., & Keefe, J. A. (1994). Group process and success in meeting the Joint Commission on Accreditation of Health Care Organizations review. *Journal of Mental Health Administration,* 21(2), 210–217.

Manthey, M. (1994). Team building on the fast track. *Creative Nursing, 1*(1), 5–6.

Mendzela, E. (1997). Effective teams. *CPA Journal, 67*(9), 62–64.

Samson, F., & Lees, J. B. (1994). *Invitation to the conversation: An approach to teacher induction programs.* Research paper presented to the Teachers' Federation of the Canadian Atlantic Provinces.

Wech, B., Mossholder, K., & Steele, R. (1998). Does work group cohesiveness affect individual performance and organizational commitment? *Small Group Research, 29*(4), 472–495.

Worchel, S. J., Hebl, S. M., & Michelle, R. (1998). Changing the guard: How origin of new leader and disposition of ex-leader affect group performance and perceptions. *Small Group Research, 29*(4), 436.

Part III

The Unexamined

CHAPTER 9

Collaborative Mentoring: Insights from a University Research Center

Alice Schutz and Sharon Abbey

INTRODUCTION

This chapter describes a unique process we call "collaborative mentoring," which combines elements from both collaboration and mentoring. The idea for this model began in 1991, when a diverse group of 11 female professors of education decided to form a collegial network based on common research interests. Some of the newer faculty members felt isolated and uncertain about the direction of their careers in the university setting, and believed it might be productive and rewarding to support one another's research and professional growth. At that time, since no similar interactive research model was operating in any of the other faculties at Brock University, the group also decided that it would be worthwhile to study and document its own activities and to investigate elements of its collaborative process as they evolved. Thus began the Centre on Collaborative Research (CCR). For almost a decade now, the CCR has undertaken numerous collaborative projects between schools and universities, across disciplines within one university, and among several universities in Canada, the United States, Thailand, and Germany.

As the advantages of our collaborative work became more apparent, we began to wonder why more group projects were not undertaken in the university, and consider how we might encourage others to try similar interactive research models. Historically, the university has not rewarded coauthored work to the same degree as independent research, and merit ratings, tenure, and promotion still depend mainly on individual accomplishments. These traditions often foster a lonely climate of competition and isolation in which individual faculty members focus on their own personal goals, publication records, and grant awards (Cranton, 1996). CCR members, therefore, wished to counteract the traditional competitive model of university organization with one of openness, collegial support, and shared expertise. At first, however, collaboration was not taken seriously by many of our colleagues, perhaps because the mutual goals and flat structures of collaborative projects were at odds with the hierarchical research practices usually expected for career advancement. Alice Schutz noted, however, that although collaboration might not have found its place at the university, mentorship practices certainly had (Field & Field, 1994; Hawkey, 1997; Mullen, Cox, Boettcher, & Adoue, 1997). Was it possible, she wondered, to take certain elements from mentoring models, familiar in the university culture, and apply them in a collaborative framework? Could connections be made between mentoring and collaborating that would make our CCR work stronger and also more compatible with customary practices in the university? This chapter addresses these questions. The first section begins with an overview of current models of both collaboration and mentorship. The intent is to expand understanding of mentoring, in particular, and show how its essential features are compatible with collaborative structures. The second section considers the similarities and differences between these two approaches and how elements of mentoring might enrich and extend the acceptance of collaborative practices at the university. Finally, the chapter concludes by describing a new model of "collaborative mentoring" and the possibilities CCR members envision for broadening the options of interpersonal research structures within a university setting.

REVISIONING COLLABORATION

Many authors have described what they consider essential features of collaboration. Johnston (1997) maintains that "collaboration is an untidy business, full of uncharted territories, ambiguities, and institutional complexities" (p. 1). Since there is little empirical knowledge on which to draw, we tend to rely on intuition and hunches to form our understandings (Clift & Say, 1988). According to Friend and Cook (2000), the term "collaboration" has become a buzzword, and although many of its benefits, problems, and issues have been described in the literature, few clear definitions have been offered; those that have been are still tentative and difficult. Friend and Cook define collaboration as "a style for direct interaction between at least two coequal parties voluntarily engaged in shared decision making as they work toward a common goal" (p. 6). They also identify the following five key elements of collaboration: it is voluntary; participants are equally valued; goals are mutual; responsibility and decision making are negotiated; and resources and accountability for outcomes are shared. Other researchers agree that equality, egalitarianism, reciprocity, inclusion, and mutually beneficial goals are essential characteristics of this process (Frymier, Flynn, & Flynn, 1992; Hunsaker & Johnson, 1992; Mitchell & Boak, 1997). To this list of collaborative descriptors, Clandinin (1993) also adds mutual trust, shared confidentiality, and openness to listening to one another's voices. As well, she emphasizes that collaborative partnerships are flexible and constantly changing, as participants attempt to develop, sustain, and renegotiate their agendas. Finally, Lieberman (1992) believes that those involved in collaborative projects are "opening themselves to learning from one another, building more long-lasting and trusting relationships, and challenging, refining, or even changing their own frameworks" (p. 9).

In some fields, such as social action and education, collaboration has been viewed as a means of promoting change or of coping with the difficulties of change. There is a growing recognition that collaboration is a desirable and essential process for professionals in diverse settings, for researchers, and for students (Castle & Giblin, 1992; Ross, Rolheiser, & Hogaboam-Gray, 1999). In fact, Fullan (1993) states that "the ability to collaborate on both a small and large scale is becoming one of the core requisites of postmodern society" (p. 14).

Helen Stewart (1997), another founding CCR member, documented the early endeavors of the CCR. She observed that the group's main inclinations coincided with the six critical features of collaboration suggested by Gray (1989): interdependence, constructive response to differences, resistance to stereotyping partners, joint ownership of decisions, collective responsibility for future directions, and interactive procedures, which emerge and are continually restructured. She also identified six principles that best describe the CCR collaborative process: it is an ongoing creative process; change is essential to the process; diversity and tension are realistic and essential to the process; informal, spontaneous conversation is a meaningful and constructive part of the work; the process opens participants to vulnerability and therefore demands trust and commitment; and finally, the vertical hierarchy of power is replaced with horizontal patterns involving symbiotic respect and support. CCR members agree that these positive attributes were all part of our experiences together.

The benefits of collaboration have been described in many fields. It has been linked to enhanced job productivity (Richards & Schutz, 1997a), better job satisfaction (Colling, Grabo, Rowe, & Staneva, 1989; Stewart et al., 1995), reflective decision making (Butler, 1989), and problem solving (Niles, McLaughlin, Magliaro, & Wildman, 1989). Collaborative organizational models have been applied to such settings as preservice and inservice teacher education, research between universities and schools, and exchange programs (Clift & Say, 1988). The array of qualities associated with collaboration is persuasive enough to encourage CCR members to consider it a highly desirable alternative to the traditional university patterns and protocols.

EXPANDING AN UNDERSTANDING OF MENTORSHIP

This section of the chapter briefly describes the structure of mentorship, a model that has always been part of the university structure, in order to compare it with collaboration and to consider ways of combining selected elements from each.

Traditionally, the concept of mentoring suggests a wise and knowledgeable older person assuming a special commitment to instruct or counsel a less experienced person in a situation where both parties are willing to enter into a trusting relationship. This relationship is usually hierarchical, with the mentor in a position of greater power or prestige. Recently, however, the hierarchical structure of mentoring has been called into question, and several authors have argued that this narrow view of mentoring is neither realistic nor useful (Edlind & Haensly, 1985; Gaeddert, Kahn, Frevert, & Ralph, 1981; Gehrke, 1991).

When mentoring relationships are not entered into voluntarily by both parties, difficulties often arise. For example, mentors imposed on others by third parties may be unsuited to their role or to the personality of the protegé. The pairs may be left without any clear goals or procedural plans to follow. As well, timelines are often too short, and implementation expectations unrealistic, controlling, and poorly conceived (Noller & Frey, 1983; Torrance, 1984; Wildman, Magliaro, Niles, & Niles, 1992). Moreover, problematic interpersonal relationships can occur if mentors are limited to one person at a time or age differences are too great. For example, when mentors become too overpowering or domineering, "mentees" may become dependent and have difficulty leaving the relationship. With so many disadvantages, one might wonder why traditional mentoring has remained a valued practice.

Although there has been a great deal of literature developed on educational mentorship in the past 20 years, another serious criticism is that few studies examine in detail how mentoring processes operate or what is actually learned from them (Mullen, Cox, Boettcher, & Adoue, 1997). In addition, the majority of studies are descriptive, "with little analysis or theoretical underpinning" (Hawkey, 1997, p. 325). A few studies, such as Torrance's (1984) work on creativity, provide models of effective mentoring, but most fail to demonstrate that mentoring is a broadly effective tactic.

In an attempt to expand the understanding of mentorship and emphasize that its relational component need not be hierarchical, Mullen and colleagues (1997) explain that the mentoring process consists of multiple intertwining circles involving a complex mix of variables such as trust, reciprocity, compatibility, and elements of genuine care. In many cases, they argue, mentoring can be "a lifelong process that brings mentors and the mentored close together at times, and further away at other times" (p. xxi). In a longitudinal study, Vaillant (1977) also points out that it is sustained relationships with people that help others to develop their unique potential and their ability to overcome obstacles. To this expanded image of mentoring, Kealy (1997) adds that true mentors presumably undertake such responsibilities in order to allow others to see experience through their eyes and their subjectivity, with little thought of their own personal gain. Kealy also asserts that the immediacy of a mentor's guidance and intervention is crucial, as is her/his willingness to inquire into self-practices, to honestly confront, interrogate, and articulate underlying beliefs, and to challenge the status quo. Similarly, Hawkey (1997) argues that mentees must also become conscious of the perspectives, values, and assumptions that they themselves bring to the process, since these orientations all influence the nature of the mentoring relationship that develops. She concludes that the "doing" should not be given greater value than the "thinking." Finally, Moore (1982) adds the notion of "sharing" to this relational focus by describing effective mentors as those sharing power, competence, and self.

Hence, it is suggested by much current thought that mentorship can be reciprocal, reflexive, and self-critical. If both participants learn from one another, the mentoring model may, in fact, come close to our conception of collaboration (Abbey, 1999). In support of this viewpoint, Gehrke (1991) argues that some mentoring projects have resulted in disappointment because of a fallacy in the underlying assumptions about mentoring itself. She suggests that rather than applying an all-inclusive notion based on hierarchical power and outcomes, mentoring should be looked at as an exchange of gifts. By shifting the focus toward a synergetic, inclusive, and reciprocal relationship, and away from a top-down hierarchical model emphasizing power, prestige, and personal gain, Gehrke also moves mentoring toward the spirit of collaboration. This notion of reciprocity is also suggested by Benard (1992). In his study of mentoring programs for urban youth, he concludes that the effectiveness of these mentoring relationships is a result of reciprocity and mutual transformation as well as commitment to providing personalized attention and care.

To deconstruct traditional mentoring practices even further, Gaston (1998) argues that mentoring need not be conceived as an exclusive interchange between an older and a younger person or even be limited to two people. Rather, it can occur between any number of persons who share similar orientations, expertise, or strategies for particular purposes in specific contexts. Flaxman and Ascher (1992) point out that, when "program administrators talk about a 'one to one mentoring,' they are not discussing an essential numerical formula; rather they are describing their intention to provide the personalized attention and care we usually associate with a good interpersonal relationship" (p. 15).

One type of mentoring that attempts to break down power hierarchies is peer mentoring. In this model, the gap between expert and novice is less extensive, the length of interaction is usually of short duration, and the relationship is more reciprocal and egalitarian than in traditional models. Successful peer mentoring has been documented in work with higher education faculty members (Zimpher & Reiger, 1988), with novice teachers (Wildman et al., 1992), with minority women (Johnson, 1998), and with native students and teachers (Smith-Mohamed, 1998). Several studies also report findings on peer mentoring among university colleagues. However, in this milieu, Sands, Parson, and Duane (1991) point out that, "those who are mentored by colleagues put themselves in an unequal and vulnerable position in relation to persons who some time in the future, may be making decisions about their tenure and promotion" (p. 174). Other researchers put forth more positive claims. For example, Harnish and Wild (1994) found that peer mentoring among faculty members resulted in an improved institutional climate, renewed interest in instruction, effective long-term faculty development, and positive support for novices. In addition, Colling and colleagues (1998) discuss a peer-mentored research group that uses collaborative negotiation as the basis for initiating, developing, and communicating research. They claim that this peer-mentored model of collaborative research "promotes collegial participation, maximizes the use of each member's expertise, and enhances skill development within the group" (p. 304). Colling and colleagues come closest to the collaborative climate that developed in the CCR and, as such, support the premise of this chapter that effective mentoring practices utilize many elements associated with collaboration.

DISMANTLING BOUNDARIES BETWEEN MENTORSHIP AND COLLABORATION

In the previous section of this chapter, we suggested that by moving beyond traditional narrow perspectives of mentoring, we may find many qualities consistent with good collaborative models. Building on this premise, we will now attempt to establish a credible rationale to support the CCR's "collaborative mentoring" structure. To do so, we first identify the unique features of each of these organizational frameworks, and then consider related elements that potentially overlap to form a new structure.

We therefore review the question of how mentoring differs from collaborating. At the outset, we believe that mentoring is usually centered around some aspect of task-training or induction, and is therefore focused on the process of attaining specific outcomes. The flow of expertise usually moves one way; one member is considered to have more status, experience, and authority than the other. In contrast, collaborating is more transactional and oriented to broader goals, with mutually negotiated tasks emerging from the participants' own discussions. Expertise is multidimensional and reciprocal, with each member benefiting equally from the shared experience. Moreover, as the collaboration develops, members' roles emerge and change to suit the needs of the group as a whole. Collaboration is typically more informal, more dynamic, and more synergistic than mentoring relationships.

In spite of these traditional differences in purpose and form, the abundance of studies in both fields has gradually dismantled the rigid boundaries between the two models of practice. In fact, as previously indicated, the literature suggests that good mentoring practices also exemplify many of the positive elements of effective collaboration, as in induction projects that involve peer mentors of similar age and experience who work reciprocally toward their mutual goals with trust and respect. The following section of this chapter argues that all mentorship training principles that are acceptable within the expanded framework previously discussed are also compatible with the collaboration principles that emerged from the CCR experience (Stewart, 1997). These principles were formulated as a result of the CCR's explicit reflective study of the interpersonal organization of collaboration itself. The researchers' training involved self-direction and self-study as well as input and guidance from the shared expertise of others. In including elements of expertise and guidance from mentoring, it is our intention to heighten the credibility of collaboration and call into question the narrow range of acceptable research models traditionally rewarded at the university.

ELEMENTS OF THE "COLLABORATIVE MENTORING" MODEL USED IN THE CCR

Although not all CCR members initially expected mentoring relationships to develop within the study of their own collaborative processes, their experience is consistent with many of the aspects of mentorship identified by Edlind and Haensly (1985). Such benefits include career and interest advancement, increased knowledge and skills, development of talent and creativity, enhancement of self-esteem and confidence, development of a personal ethic or set of standards, and establishment of long-term friendships. However, in contrast to formal mentoring practices, these benefits were found to be mutual and reciprocal. In order to describe the unique nature of the interactions more explicitly, three characteristics have been identified that best describe the essence of the CCR's "collaborative mentoring" model: reciprocity, evolving participation and mutual negotiation, and synergy. In this section of the chapter, each of these elements will be discussed with respect to practical, intellectual, and affective domains as they apply to CCR experiences.

RECIPROCITY

Reciprocal sharing of respect, support, and expertise best describes the process of collaborative mentoring as it emerged in the CCR, even though much of this influence is unintentional and spontaneous. Typically, each member is invited to contribute her particular area of expertise, talent, and insight, to learn from others in the group, and also to appreciate common connections, purposes, and visions. For example, one CCR member, Helen Stewart, recalled that it was the shared respect for their profession that eventually removed organizational obstacles and hierarchies for the participants in her curriculum development project, thus allowing collaboration to occur among members of a high school English department, a university English department, and a faculty of Education. Stewart wrote, "While the needs were diverse, they represented the driving force which brought the individuals together" (personal communication, July 8, 1992). It was the commonalties they found across their disciplines that helped the group to move beyond compartmentalization and to transform their own systemic understandings. This group demonstrated that when the strengths and talents of all participants are equally valued and respected, their similarities outweigh their differences, and their commitment is enhanced as a result of their focus on a common goal.

CCR members also agree that mutual support and confirmation are other important aspects of reciprocity. One senior faculty member in the CCR, for instance, describes the support she offers to others as giving the gift she had once wished for as a young faculty member. According to Merle Richards, "This is not a burden; I like working with others, and I don't feel the need to be a director or expert. I am someone with experience who could understand the difficulties of a new faculty member. On the other hand, I find it refreshing to work with people who are still idealistic about university life" (personal communication, June 28, 2000). Sharon Abbey, one of the authors of this chapter, remembers how as a newly appointed untenured faculty member she appreciated the candid advice and positive encouragement of colleagues in the CCR. She was grateful to know that faculty members, who appeared so competent and successful, trusted her enough to share similar doubts and misgivings about themselves and valued her enough to offer positive encouragement and feedback related to her initial efforts as a course instructor and researcher. She believes this "insider" information and cheer-leading were crucial to her survival.

The third aspect of reciprocity that CCR members identified relates to the mutual benefits of shared professional expertise, insight, and knowledge. Observation plays a key role in this kind of mentoring, ranging anywhere from imitation to assimilation. Initially, CCR members brought with them diverse and exclusionary research orientations that were restricted to either qualitative or quantitative paradigms. Intensive and passionate debates ensued in the early days that threatened to divide the group. However, as we worked together on projects and reflected more openly about our theoretical assumptions and beliefs, we learned to appreciate aspects of both research models. Sharon Abbey recalls another novice in the group who clearly exemplifies this experience in one of our recorded conversations:

When I taught my first research methodology course, I worried that my strong background in quantitative analysis would overshadow the qualitative part of her course. However, when another member offered to audit my course in order to learn more about statistical analysis, I was also able to rely on her extensive qualitative background in order to provide greater depth to this aspect of my course. As a result, we both were able to benefit from this arrangement and so were the students. (Reconstructed from meeting notes, March 2, 1994)

On another occasion, Woloshyn recalls another group member with qualitative expertise approaching her to collaborate on a research project that would benefit from an expert in statistical technology as well. The collaborative study that resulted was much richer because of the combined methodologies (Elliott & Woloshyn, 1997). Such experiences showed that to be open to different research orientations, it is necessary not only to respect one another as professionals, but also to welcome and seek new learning opportunities (Castle, Drake, & Boak, 1995; Drake & Woloshyn, 1994).

Over time, the merging of methodological orientations and shared research expertise helped to create strong links between the two research paradigms. Group diversity was recognized as a source of strength, while individual expertise was valued as a resource for the benefit of the entire group. Drawing a variety of standpoints into the conversation also allowed assumptions to be questioned and analyzed, resulting in deeper sensitivity and heightened respect for each other's research (Schutz et al., 1992). Problem-posing, considered to be the most crucial and challenging aspect of the research process (Dillon, 1982), was greatly enhanced by group interactions as well. Ideas were exchanged freely, new problems were generated from the discussions, and research questions emerged naturally as the group grappled with a particular issue. The creation of an inclusive context also provided a safe forum for novices to critique and challenge the perspectives of experts and voice their own tentative ideas.

As the CCR group built stronger bonds of trust and respect, and the potential of readily available experts became more apparent, it made sense to confront our own limitations, to push cognitive boundaries, and to deliberately seek input from others. This began to happen once we felt certain that others would recognize our shortcomings but not use them to betray or take advantage of us (Castle, Drake, & Boak, 1995; Schutz et al., 1992). However, the aim was to remain centered on our goals of research and writing, and not on mutual nurturance. We agreed with Hamilton and Hamilton (1992) that "Warm interpersonal relations are more likely to result from a focus on building competence than from a focus on building relationship. The latter goal is simply too vague and open ended" (p. 549).

Coping with the pressure to write and publish papers was one of the benefits many CCR members gained from the strong alliances built within the group. Alice Schutz, one of the authors of this chapter, recalls that she felt free to ask members in the group who were experienced writers to share their methods and resources, as well as to read and comment on her written drafts. For her, this was a valuable induction into the often confusing and daunting writing process. This sense of security emerged when power and status were downplayed in favor of equality and diversity.

Authentic and heart-felt mentoring, when linked with collaboration, appears to provide both security and affirmation. As Bettelheim (1975) states,

It is not maximum security measures but our importance to others that keeps us going on living in our most desperate moments . . . or rather, knowing how important one is to others who have come to play a significant role in our life is maximum security (p. 162)

Yamamoto (1988) also believes that the sense of worthiness does not depend on prior accomplishment or status, but rather on a positive concept of "the emergent self . . . who one can be, who one is going to be" (p. 184). Such a comment is significant for both mentoring and collaboration, both of which are intended to foster growth of self through relationships with others.

CCR experiences support the findings by Edlind and Haensly (1985) that much treasured knowledge is derived from "watching professionals in one's discipline doing their jobs, seeing them respond under pressure, utilizing their skills and reaping the small rewards from the job" (p. 56). They emphasize that the understanding of the character, the control, and the psychology required to be a successful professional cannot be extracted from textbooks or lectures alone. Alice Schutz experienced the pooling of resources in the CCR, the kind of questioning, tone of voice, ways of conducting a meeting or collecting data, and appreciation of nuances of tone, which have at various times widened and enlarged her personal repertoire of professional practice. Often, the mentoring CCR members are not even aware of the tacit insights they share or of their effect on others.

Evolving Participation and Mutual Negotiations

As previously stated, mentoring arrangements often fail when imposed or predetermined partnerships prove to be incompatible or poorly conceived. Collaboration, in contrast, emphasizes the project or objective, and by inviting volunteers rather than selecting participants, avoids many of these pitfalls. In a study of collaborative organizations, Harnish and Wild (1994) also found that an emphasis on solving problems and completing tasks took precedence over selection of participants on the basis of age or status criteria. They concluded that in collaborative mentoring, "unlike conventional mentoring relationships, there were not always significant age, experience, rank or hierarchical levels between the faculty in mentor projects. Participants achieved a level of mutual expertise, equality and empathy frequently absent from traditional mentoring relationships" (p. 192). This focus on goals rather than procedures also is exemplified by CCR partnerships, which were personally selected, voluntary, and based primarily on the challenge and attractiveness of common visions, interests, and intentions.

Over time, new projects emerged and different combinations of interested members joined forces. Choice played a large part in the process as well. The Readers' Theatre experience discussed in Chapter 13 offers further insight into this dynamic. A few members decided to undertake an alternate format for presenting research that included a short drama production. For most members, the idea of a stage performance was too risky and embarrassing at first. But once we began to write the script and create the props, several others gained a clearer understanding of what we were doing, became intrigued and decided to join us. By influencing each other to take their commitment seriously and to rehearse their lines in a dedicated manner, this troupe of amateur actors succeeded in delivering a successful performance for an audience of enthusiastic colleagues. Creative energy and purpose kept our work ever changing and developing.

Some research undertaken by the CCR involves the same group of people for extended periods of time, while other work is short-lived and quickly accomplished (Torrance, 1984). Still other projects are abandoned or terminated when time commitments are too heavy or when obstacles become insurmountable. For example, CCR members offered to study a model that trained facilitators in schools, but it quickly became apparent that the schools seemed reluctant to have outside observers join them. There was no way to gain entry into this project, which was disappointing at the time. Autonomy of individuals is respected, and CCR members are free to move in and out of projects to some degree. When some members are overloaded with commitments, they are not expected to participate in new projects, and others make an effort to pick up the slack. A certain sense of ethics and fairness at play operates as well, whereby members avoid joining or leaving a project at a point when others would be let down or disadvantaged. Involvement in and withdrawal from projects is freely discussed, with conflicting viewpoints voiced in order to avoid feelings of guilt, resentment, or disappointment. We have learned over time that this type of openness, flexibility, and responsiveness is essential to maintain harmony and productivity in our collaborative mentoring enterprises.

One of the most exciting aspects of collaborative mentoring is the opportunity to work with a manifold range of models, processes, and interpretive frameworks (Mitchell & Boak, 1997). Some members find that they work more productively in pairs when writing joint papers or preparing for conference presentations. They explain that combining research and learning styles is beneficial, and they like the fact that their working patterns are consistent and predictable. Others gravitate to larger, more flexible, and innovative projects, such as the Readers' Theater production described later in this book. In one project, a member might find herself taking on a leadership role, while in another, she might participate in data collection or editing, and on a different occasion, she might take on a minor role as a critic or audience member. Whatever the particular preference, all members agree that such a rich variety of arrangements and possibilities encourages the continual examination and reexamination of one's own points of view, a task that would be more difficult to undertake alone. We find that some degree of personal transformation is inevitable!

Synergy

Synergy, or the combined action and energy of two or more people, best describes another important understanding that emerged from our collaborative mentorship. As a whole, the effect of group efforts far exceeds the sum of our individual contributions, fostering a deeper and wider significance to the work accomplished together. Group members are often propelled to heights that would never have been possible on their own. Over time, research or development projects become more complex, and the interactions become more meaningful (Colling et al., 1998). Achievements of group members are also regarded as beneficial to the group, and we applaud each other even when we dispute or critique one another's work. As one CCR member, who found herself assuming a central role in the theater production, admitted afterward, "I never thought I would be doing that!" We are pleased when we are able to draw out each other's potential and watch each other move forward with confidence.

It is this same type of synergy that allowed Susan Drake, new to the faculty, to convince more skeptical senior members to consider her idea about starting a center to study collaborative research. Although not everyone shared Drake's long-term vision or enthusiasm at first, they were challenged to reexamine their limited assumptions about collaborative processes. There was never any pressure placed on anyone to join the CCR, and those who did so were somehow motivated to share Drake's passion or curious about what might be discovered. As the CCR studied its own collaborative processes, we found a level of inclusiveness, dynamism, and holistic connectedness not usually found in mentoring arrangements (Little, 1989). Membership expanded as a consequence, in part, of this passion, energy, and "call to adventure" continually put forth by group members. This probably accounts for the strong presence of CCR members at local, national, and international conferences, as well as the number of individuals who have either joined the CCR or been influenced by its work. In fact, CCR members were intentionally sought out for their expertise in collaboration at conferences in Kiel, Germany, and Dublin, Ireland, because of the reputation that had preceded them (Castle & Schutz, 1999; Richards & Schutz, 1997b; Sydor & Schutz, 1997).

Over the past decade, the group influence has extended beyond the professional realm and into aspects of our personal lives as well. As Coleman (1987) suggests, professional relationships often provide "a certain degree of intimacy" (p. 38). At one time or another, every member has experienced times of crisis, sorrow, or disappointment, including terminal illness and death. We have opened up to each other, cared about each other, sought solace and comfort, and benefited greatly from advice, sensitive listening, and positive encouragement at times when it would otherwise have been impossible to attend to professional concerns. Hopeful possibilities inevitably took shape.

CONCLUSION

This chapter examines key elements inherent in expanded definitions of mentoring and argues that they are also essential components of the effective collaborative processes experienced in the CCR. Our research suggests that traditional systemic policies, usually favoring individual research and writing, may limit the rich possibilities that can result from projects involving reciprocal modeling, the self-selection of mutually negotiated tasks, and synergistic enhancement. By combining elements from both mentoring and collaborative models, this chapter advocates an expanded framework called "collaborative mentoring," as it is positively experienced at practical, intellectual, and emotional levels. When participants apply the training component from mentoring to the goal-focused essence of collaboration, the result becomes a invigorating reflective study of personal, practical knowledge and understanding. Not only does this approach enhance personal development, but it also offers new research possibilities for our profession, our colleagues, and our working climate. This chapter argues that mentoring need not be restricted to a one-to-one prescribed match, but can also be treated as a dynamic process that offers flexibility, accommodates diversity, and encourages creative development within a collaborative, caring context. The chapter also suggests that collaboration should be recognized as an important catalyst for the advancement of diverse opportunities for peers to work together in a stimulating and interactive professional setting.

Epilogue

It seems appropriate at this point to highlight the fact that Alice Schutz provided the initial idea for this chapter, as well as the majority of the data collection and research. As a result, the theoretical framework is heavily situated within the context of graduate courses that she teaches. Sharon Abbey agreed to edit an early draft of the chapter, and postponed another writing project in order to spend more time on the revisions. Alice, working overseas, trusted Sharon's judgment, and remained open and willing to consider the structural and conceptual changes that she suggested. Sharon was mindful of maintaining the central integrity of Alice's thesis, and Alice provided ongoing feedback from Germany. As an example of "collaborative mentoring," Sharon gained insight from Alice's ideas, while also adding her own personal experiences of mentorship and collaboration. She also became more conscious of her own implicit writing strategies as she struggled with the challenges that revision presents. The result: deepened and extended perspectives for both writers, and a chapter coauthored in true collaborative spirit!

REFERENCES

Abbey, S. (1999). Mentoring my daughter: Contradictions and possibilities. *Canadian Woman Studies Journal, 18*(2 & 3), 22–29.

Benard, B. (1992). *Mentoring programs for urban youth: Handle with care.* Portland, OR: Northwest Regional Center for Drug-Free Schools and Communities.

Bettelheim, B. (1975). *A home for the heart.* New York: Bantam Books.

Butler, E. (1989, March). *Empowering teachers through collaborative mentoring designs: An empirical assessment.* Paper presented at the annual meeting of the American Association of Colleges for Teacher Education, Anaheim, CA.

Castle, J., Drake, S., & Boak, T. (1995). Collaborative reflection as professional development. *Review of Higher Education, 18*(3), 243–263.

Castle, J., & Giblin, A. (1992). Reflection-for-action: A collaborative venture in preservice education. *Teaching Education, 4*(2), 21–34.

Castle, J., & Schutz, A. (1999, July). *Voices at the top: Perceptions of self as full professor.* Paper presented at the 9th Biennial ISAAT Conference, St. Patrick's College, Dublin, Ireland.

Clandinin, D. J. (1993). *Learning to teach, teaching to learn: Stories of collaboration in teacher education.* New York: Teachers College Press.

Clift, R., & Say, M. (1988). Teacher education: Collaboration of conflict? *Journal of Teacher Education, 39*(3), 2–7.

Coleman, J. (1987, August/September). Families and schools. *Education Researcher*, 32–38.

Colling, K., Grabo, T., Rowe, M., & Staneva, J. (1998). How to develop and sustain a peer-mentored research work group. *Journal of Professional Nursing, 14*(5), 298–304.

Cranton, P. (1996). *Professional development as transformative learning*. San Francisco: Jossey-Bass.

Dillon, J. T. (1982). Problem finding and solving. *Journal of Creative Behavior, 16*(2), 97–112.

Drake, S., & Woloshyn, V. (1994). Women as new professors: Exploring our gender consciousness. *Journal of Staff, Program and Organization Development, 12*(1), 31–40.

Edlind, E., & Haensly, A. (1985). Gifts of mentorship. *Gifted Child Quarterly, 29*(2), 55–60.

Elliott, A. E., & Woloshyn, V. E. (1997). Some female professors' experiences of collaboration; Mapping the collaborative process through rough terrain. *Alberta Journal of Educational Research, 43*(1), 23–36.

Field, B., & Field, T. (1994). *Teachers as mentors: A practical guide*. Washington, DC: The Falmer Press.

Flaxman, E., & Ascher, C. (1992). *Mentoring in action: The efforts of programs in New York City*. Unpublished paper, Institute for Urban and Minority Education, Teachers College, Columbia University.

Friend, M., & Cook, L. (2000). *Interactions: Collaboration skills for school professionals*. New York: Longman.

Frymier, R., Flynn, J., & Flynn, R. (1992). *School–university collaboration*. Bloomington, IN: Phi Delta Kappan Educational Foundation.

Fullan, M. (1993). Why teachers must become change agents. *Educational Leadership, 50*(6), 12–17.

Gaeddert, W., Kahn, A., Frevert, R., & Ralph, S. (1981). *Role model choice: Who do women say their models are?* (Unpublished report available from ERIC Reproduction Service, No. ED 206 986).

Gaston, J. & Jackson, J. F. L. (1998). *Mentoring and its implications*. (Unpublished report available from ERIC Reproduction Service, No. ED 426 990).

Gehrke, J. (1991). Toward a definition of mentoring. *Theory Into Practice, 27*(3), 190–194.

Gray, B. (1989) *Collaborating: Finding common ground for multiparty problems*. San Francisco: Jossey-Bass.

Hamilton, S., & Hamilton, M. (1992). Mentoring programs: Promise and paradox. *Phi Delta Kappan, 73*(7), 546–550.

Harnish, D., & Wild, L. (1994). Mentoring strategies for faculty development. *Studies in Higher Education, 19*(2), 191–201.

Hawkey, K (1997). Roles, responsibilities, and relationships in mentoring: A literature review and agenda for research. *Journal of Teacher Education, 48*(5), 325–335.

Hunsaker, L., & Johnson, M. (1992). Teacher under construction: A collaborative case study of teacher change. *American Educational Research Journal, 29*(2), 350–372.

Johnson, G. G. (1998). African American women as mentors: Significance and strategies. *Initiatives, 58*(3), 49–56.

Johnston, M. (1997). *Contradictions in collaboration: New thinking on school/ university partnerships.* New York: Teachers College Press.

Kealy, W. (1997). Full circle: Insights on mentoring from my mentor's heroes. In C. Mullen, M. Cox, C. Boettcher, & D. Adoue (Eds.), *Breaking the circle of one: Redefining mentorship in the lives and writings of educators* (pp. 175–188). New York: Peter Lang.

Lieberman, A. (1992). The meaning of scholarly activity and the building of community. *Educational Researcher, 21*(6), 5–12.

Little, W. J. (1989). The picture of success. In L. Shalaway (Ed.), *Learning to teach . . . not just for beginners* (p. 267). New York: Scholastic.

Mitchell, C., & Boak, T. (1997). Collaborative research: The power, the perils and the possibilities. *Brock Education, 7*(1), 1–13.

Moore, K. (1982). The role of mentors in developing leaders for the academic. *Educational Research, 63*(1), 23–28.

Mullen, C., Cox, M., Boettcher, C., & Adoue, D. (Eds.). (1997). *Breaking the circle of one: Redefining mentorship in the lives and writings of educators.* New York: Peter Lang.

Niles, J., McLaughlin, R., Magliaro, S., & Wildman, T. (1989, March). *The influence of collaboration on the thinking and practice of mentor teachers.* Paper presented at the annual meeting of the American Educational Research Association, San Francisco.

Noller, R., & Frey, B. (1983). *Mentoring: An annotated bibliography.* Buffalo, NY: Bearly.

Richards, M., & Schutz, A. (1997a). Reflections on the collaborative experience. The CCR in review. *Brock Education, 7*(1), 76–84.

Richards, M., & Schutz, A. (1997b, October). *Learner strategies and teacher responses in language learning.* Paper presented at the International Study Association on Teachers and Teaching Conference, Kiel, Germany.

Ross, J., Rolheiser, C., & Hogaboam-Gray, A. (1999). Effects of collaborative action research on the knowledge of five Canadian teacher-researchers. *Elementary School Journal, 99*(3), 255–274.

Sands, R., Parson, A., & Duane, J. (1991). Faculty mentoring faculty in a public university. *Journal of Higher Education, 62*(2), 174–191.

Schutz, A., Abbey, S., Drake, S., Reynolds, C., Elliott, A., Castle, J., Richards, M., & Woloshyn, B. (1992, November). *Collaborative reflection through story: The graduate educational experience.* Paper presented at the Annual Conference of Research on Women and Education, Special Interest Group of the American Educational Research Association, Penn State University, University Park.

Smith-Mohamed, K. (1998). Role models, mentors and native students: Some implications for educators. *Canadian Journal of Native Education, 22*(2), 238–259.

Stewart, H. (1997). Metaphors of interrelatedness: Principles of collaboration. In H. Christiansen, L. Goulet, C. Krentz, & M. Maeers (Eds.), *Recreating re-*

lationships: Collaboration and educational reform (pp. 27–54). New York: State University of New York Press.

Stewart, H., Woloshyn, V., Richards, M., Harris, B., Elliott, A., Scott, R., Abbey, S., Schutz, A., Castle, J., & Wells, J. (1995, June). *Issues in the collaborative process*. Paper presented at the Canadian Society for Studies in Education, University of Montreal.

Sydor, S., & Schutz, A. (1997, July). *Spreading excellence and thinking about collaboration in education*. Paper presented at the International Study Association on Teachers and Teaching Conference, Kiel, Germany.

Torrance, E. (1984). *Mentor relationships*. Buffalo, NY: Bearly.

Vaillant, G. (1977). *Adaptation to life*. Boston: Little, Brown.

Wildman, T. M., Magliaro, S. G., Niles, R. A., & Niles, J. A. (1992). Teacher mentoring: An analysis of roles, activities, and conditions. *Journal of Teacher Education, 43*(3), 205–213.

Yamamoto, K. (1988). To see life grow: The meaning of mentorship. *Theory Into Practice, 27*(3), 183–189.

Zimpher, N. L., & Reiger, S. R. (1988). Mentoring teachers: What are the issues? *Theory Into Practice, 27*(3), 177–182.

CHAPTER 10

Collaboration: A Vehicle for Professional Development

Anne Elliott and Vera Woloshyn

It is generally agreed that students need to possess a variety of academic and independent learning skills in order to be successful in the 21st century (Kennedy, 1993). As teachers are an important element in student learning (Tompkins, 1998), it is expected that they will continue to grow in professional competence throughout their careers if they are to effectively help students.

We are two university professors in a Faculty of Education who have long been committed to facilitating professional growth for teachers. We have both come to believe, however, that not only must we continue to promote life-long learning with teachers and students, but also that we must be active participants in this process ourselves.

In this chapter, we describe how we came together to establish a long-term professional development project in which we collaborated with six classroom teachers. The context of the project is described as background. The primary focus of the chapter, however, is the professional development that we, as well as the participating teachers, experienced as a result of this collaboration. Finally, we discuss how the processes of collaboration and professional development complement each other.

Vera is an Associate Professor in a Faculty of Education. Her formal training is not in education. Indeed, Vera's graduate training was in a discipline and department that, in many ways, differed from the one in which she accepted a position. For instance, Vera had no experience with qualitative research and little in teaching. In particular, she was not used to teaching mature students.

As a graduate student, I elected not to teach. There was an unstated sentiment that teaching was an inefficient use of time and that it would distract from the more important task of completing research. What really mattered was that students carried out solid quantitative research and that they published their findings. These were the factors that would determine whether you achieved an academic position.

These experiences led to unexpected teaching difficulties during Vera's first year in the department. Specifically, Vera's first course was to teach general research methods to adult learners, where the premise of the course was to place equal weighting on quantitative and qualitative methodologies.

The transition from graduate student to faculty was not easy. I was unaware of the needs of adult learners and tended to use a traditional, teacher-directed method of instruction. Furthermore, I found myself teaching about a research methodology in which I had never participated. I could only rely on my "textbook" knowledge.

Despite all this, I was genuinely surprised and discouraged when students expressed concerns

about my course. I questioned my abilities as an instructor. I realized I would have to change my general teaching approach and acquire some "hands-on" experiences using qualitative research methods. I realized that I would not be able to teach this method if I had not experienced it.

Confiding in a trusted colleague who was recognized as an expert in qualitative research methodology, Vera initiated a short qualitative study. She also joined the Centre on Collaborative Research (CCR) and became involved in other qualitative research projects. As a result of these efforts and by learning to consult with her students, Vera was able to positively resolve the issues associated with her first-year teaching.

In retrospect, my first-time teaching was an incredible learning experience. I learned to teach in a way that was different from the method in which I was taught. It forced me to get to know my students and familiarize myself with their learning styles. More importantly, I discovered that I had tremendous respect for these individuals, that I admired their decisions to continue in their professional development, and that I had a lot to learn from them.

Collectively, Vera views these incidents as the first professional development experiences where she made "a conscious decision to start my own professional development." She believes that these efforts reflect her orientation to "learning by doing" and her disposition to "learn from others" in a collaborative setting.

In contrast to Vera, Anne had already had a career as a classroom teacher prior to obtaining her doctorate and accepting a position at the university in the Faculty of Education.

I realize now that even after I had been at the university for a couple of years, I still saw myself primarily as a good teacher. I took great pride in the rapport I established with my students and in the positive feedback I received from them about the courses I was teaching.

Anne gradually began to realize, though, that teaching related to only one expectation of her new position and that the university reward system in terms of tenure and promotion was based on establishing a strong research and publication record. This expectation was daunting to her: "That part of the job was where I felt most vulnerable, least competent, and least confident." She did conduct several small research studies, but never with a great deal of confidence, and always through the lens of being a teacher. Anne realized that she had much to learn in order to be as successful in her role in the university as she had been in the elementary classroom.

I disliked feeling incompetent and wanted to be able to feel the same pride in my work at the university as I was accustomed to feeling. I was well adjusted to the university culture now and was ready to learn new skills.

PROFESSIONAL DEVELOPMENT

We agree with Kagan (1992) that professional growth requires changes over time in individuals' behavior, knowledge, images, beliefs, and perceptions. Initially, professional knowledge about teaching tends to be university based, with individuals gradually gaining the specific skills to practice proficiently (Martineau, 1998). Many of these skills are further honed in the classroom setting. Over time, however, most teachers come to recognize the need for additional study outside the classroom, which leads to a translation of additional theory into renewed classroom practice. Thus, by continually seeking new theory and reflecting on its applicability in the classroom, a cycle of professional development is created. Ideally, teachers develop increased competence in acquiring professional theory and translating it into practical classroom action. According to Darling-Hammond (1998), it is a professional expectation that teachers continually add to their theoretical knowledge base and reflect upon their practice. As a result of these activities, it is expected that classroom instruction will continually improve. Indeed, this expectation is so central that it is usually supported by salary increases according to years of experience and evidence of additional study. As a result of our experiences, however, we reject the notion that professional development can be effectively attained through one-time workshops, but believe that it can be effectively accomplished in ongoing collaborative groups.

COLLABORATION

As members of the Centre on Collaborative Research at Brock University, we have long been dedicated to working collaboratively with our school partners (Castle & Hunter, 1997; Elliott & Drake, 1995; Elliott & Woloshyn, 1997). While there is no clear agreement on a precise definition of collaboration, we use the term to mean colaboring or working equitably with at least one other person on the same project or task (Elliott & Woloshyn, 1997; Stewart, 1996). We have also come to understand that the collaborative process usually consists of several elements, including building rapport, establishing goals and rewards, negotiating tasks, and sustaining commitment and satisfaction (Elliott & Woloshyn, 1997). Briefly, building rapport refers to an interval of time in which partners establish professional and/or interpersonal relationships. Next, collaborators determine the goals and rewards associated with the completion of their project. While these goals and rewards do not need to be identical, they need to be clearly defined and seen as compatible. The allocation of tasks is usually based on agreed-upon areas of expertise. Commitment is typically sustained across three levels: to the goals of the project, to the partners, and finally to the ideology of collaboration. Overall project satisfaction is usually derived from the quality of relationships with partners.

Our belief that professional development can be effectively accomplished in ongoing collaborative groups led us to approach six teachers to participate in a long-term professional development project. Additionally, we accepted that we would also be learners. While there was a clear expectation that all partners would gain in their theoretical knowledge, the exact nature of the learning process was unclear. That is, there was an expectation that we would provide teachers with insights about how a particular theory was best translated into effective instruction. They, in turn, would provide us with information about how that theory could be best applied in the classroom. We were continually surprised, however, at the breadth, depth, and new directions that unfolded for us during this process. In this chapter we analyze these professional development experiences with respect to the elements of the collaborative process through three lenses: those of the teachers, Vera, and Anne.

BACKGROUND TO THE COLLABORATIVE
PROFESSIONAL DEVELOPMENT PROJECT

The project was designed to familiarize intermediate-grade teachers with the use of explicit strategy instruction. In turn, teachers were expected to use this knowledge to provide their students with information about effective reading, writing, and study strategies in order to help them become independent learners. Briefly, explicit strategy instructions involve having teachers frequently model learning strategies and provide students with specific information about the parameters associated with their use. Explicit instruction also entails providing students with opportunities to practice the strategies and to "discover" that the strategic approach to learning is superior to a nonstrategic one. Explicit strategy instructors often share personal learning experiences with their students, and continually prompt them to transfer and generalize relevant strategies across the curriculum. Finally, explicit instruction involves providing students with information about important factors that affect their learning (Duffy, 1993; Gaskins & Elliott, 1991).

Throughout this four-year project, we met monthly with the teachers to explore explicit strategy instruction and to share implementation experiences. Collectively, we read relevant literature to acquire knowledge about this teaching method. We also designed curriculum, appropriate for each classroom, that would translate the newly acquired theory into practice. Finally, we recorded, reflected, and shared our experiences as a group. In short, we needed to become risk-takers by experimenting with a new teaching method and sharing the results with one another. The outcome of this longitudinal study has been reported elsewhere (Woloshyn & Elliott, 1998; Woloshyn, Elliott, & Riordon, 1998).

We believe that the ultimate success of this project rested upon the assumptions that teachers learn best from other teachers, and that learning is a social activity. Specifically, the sharing of experiences, readings, and interpretations provided us with an impetus to try new approaches to teaching. During the monthly meetings, all participants deepened their respect for one another as teachers and learners. Simultaneously, solid friendships were established among all the partners. In this sense, the personal and the professional became intertwined.

THE TEACHERS' PROFESSIONAL DEVELOPMENT

All the teachers ultimately agreed that they grew professionally as explicit strategy instructors, although it took time for them to recognize and feel satisfied with their learning. The following comments were typical of early frustrations: "I found that at the beginning, I was kind of floundering. . . . I wasn't sure of what direction I was going." "When we started talking about modeling, I didn't have a clue what we were talking about." Eventually, though, all six teachers reported changes in their knowledge of explicit strategy instruction. "My comfort level is a lot better." "I feel a lot better about where I am right now."

They also acknowledged that they were now more familiar with the strategies that their students required to become independent readers and writers: "Sometimes I teach the process and model it outside the curriculum content. I think that is important because if it is a complex strategy, they need to focus on it." Another participant commented, "You have to personalize these strategies. You can give them a million strategies, but if you are not going to integrate them, then there is not going to be any transfer to other subjects."

Additionally, they focused on explicitly teaching their students how to study effectively, which many of them had only done implicitly in prior years. One teacher noted the changes in her planning:

In the past when implementing study strategies, I went through the stages rather unsure of where I was going when planning. But then, as time went on in this project, I became more aware of where strategies could be used or modeled for students. And students also began to show me where they needed strategies.

Another commented, "I always felt there was a need for study skills, but I never exactly focused on the thinking part of it."

All the teachers reported that they became more reflective or cognizant of their teaching practices as a result of providing explicit strategy instruction. One teacher summarized, "I think it has really improved my teaching. Now I know why I am teaching lessons." They also reported asking more "what" and "why" questions about academic content and process skills than they had in previous years. "Planning explicit lessons really makes you think about what you are teaching and the direction your lessons are going to go." Another teacher stated her new awareness of explicit instruction this way:

I know that I still have to work on being clearer with the students about the purpose of things. And I think that's something a lot of us in the profession have to work on. The students need to know why they are doing it. . . . What is the purpose and what is the value . . .

The regular meetings of the group established a dynamic environment that encouraged change in a number of ways. First, a sense of being in a community of learners was established. Here it was safe to be vulnerable, ask questions, and share both positive and negative experiences. Indeed, group rapport developed so that participation was seen as a desirable activity, and missed meetings were both few and regretted. Finally, the teachers grounded their learning solidly in the classroom (Renyi, 1998). Specifically, they tried new methods of teaching, and reported on their perceptions of the results in terms of students' response and learning.

VERA'S PROFESSIONAL DEVELOPMENT

In the second year of the explicit strategy project, Vera decided to complete the requirements for a teaching degree. She felt that this decision was the kind of professional development that would be appropriate, given her position in a Faculty of Education. Her primary responsibilities at that time were to teach educational psychology courses at the preservice and graduate levels. Her background was well suited to this assignment, as she had studied psychology and had been a psychologist in a school board and a hospital.

Throughout the explicit strategy project, much time was spent in schools interacting with teachers and their students. Vera quickly learned some aspects of school culture. For instance, she recalled that,

Anne was always very, very adamant that we could not come in as experts, that we could not tell the teachers what to do and that we would have to respect their ways of knowing and their prior experiences. They would control the agenda.

Throughout this time, Vera found herself gaining more and more respect for the teachers both in the project and in her preservice and graduate classes. "Every now and then, someone would point out to me that I wasn't from the culture—I wasn't a teacher." She began to see the possibility of taking her Bachelor of Education degree in the context of the project: "It was a moment to be seized." Additionally, there were some pragmatic reasons for her decision: "There is always the fear that the criteria for working in a Faculty of Education might change." But most importantly she says, "I did this because I wanted to."

In order to obtain a Bachelor of Education degree, Vera had to fulfill the course requirements and teaching assignments that were necessary for preservice teachers at Brock University. When doing her practice teaching, she "learned to respect the issues teachers face in their lives and the realities of daily teaching" in a new way. She also developed great respect for the teachers in the explicit strategy project, who had between 10 and 25 years of classroom experience. Their willingness to become vulnerable and to take risks in order to become better teachers continually impressed Vera.

I was struck that they would participate in the strategy project because they were all good teachers. They didn't need to do this and there was no reward for them. They came because they thought it would make them better teachers.

One of Vera's rewards from this professional development activity was the respect that she gained from the teachers in the explicit strategy group. "Maybe that's what it takes to learn collaboratively. You have to respect each other as learners."

During her time in classrooms, Vera had the opportunity to teach the kind of explicit lessons that the teachers in the project had been doing. A strong rapport developed between Vera and the teachers whose classrooms she entered as a "student." "They gave me a lot of leeway and trust. They also gave me time, and said, 'Do what you want.' " This trust gave her the freedom to find her own way to interact with children and their learning. The preservice coursework, which she took from her colleagues, also provided additional knowledge for her to translate into practice.

Vera believes that she owes much of her professional development to the fact that it was conducted in a collaborative setting. She worked with Anne as an advisor for her practice teaching, with her associate teachers for her classroom teaching, and with several of her university colleagues to accomplish her course work. Finally, Vera shared her ongoing learning with her partners in the explicit strategy project. She found these interactions exciting: "This is the stuff of growth and the growth is a result of interactions with others."

This professional development lessened Vera's former sense of vulnerability with faculty and students at the university, and began to replace it with a new sense of credibility. Additionally, she feels that she modeled the principle of life-long learning for both the teachers in the project and her university students.

I think in everything we do, we can't ask people to do things we are not prepared to do ourselves. I really do believe that. I believed it as a researcher and I never asked a student to do something I wouldn't do . . . I think the same can be said of teaching. When students find out that I'm also a student, they seem to appreciate it.

Vera also feels strongly that the experience of studying for her Bachelor of Education has enriched her other roles at the university. "What's really incredible now is that everything is connected. Research is connected with teaching, and teaching with research, outside-in, and inside-out."

It is not Vera's career path to teach in an elementary classroom in the near future. She sees herself predominantly as a university-based researcher. However, she has many teaching responsibilities, which she is enjoying more than ever as a result of her determination to become a good teacher. Having sat in classes, and having experienced the anxieties of practice teaching, she comments, "I can understand my students much better now and that will make me a better instructor."

Finally, Vera's own sense of satisfaction was strong. "I don't think I will ever again be afraid to say I'm a learner or that I'm learning this new skill." She feels strongly that "If we expect teachers to develop professionally, how can we not develop ourselves?"

ANNE'S PROFESSIONAL DEVELOPMENT

On reflection, in contrast to Vera, Anne realized that, at the onset of this project, she still saw herself "as a teacher first." At the same time, she recognized that the university reward system, in terms of tenure and promotion, was based primarily upon having a strong research and publication record. Anne remembers, "that [research] was the part of my job description where I felt most vulnerable, least competent, and where I had little confidence."

When Vera asked her to become involved in the explicit strategy project, Anne saw an opportunity for professional development with a partner who had excellent research skills. She felt comfortable because the project would be conducted with teachers in schools. A partnership was formed to which she brought school contacts and her familiarity with the school culture. She relied on Vera to provide the research design, the grant money, and the initial vision. "I wanted to become a proficient researcher and I thought this was an opportunity to learn by doing."

Anne understood clearly that this was a good method of professional development for the teachers and herself. Anne also was a member of the CCR and knew that she enjoyed working and learning with others in the social context of an interactive project.

I had been very involved with professional development with school boards over the years. I had often done "one shot" presentations or been a guest speaker on a professional development day. There was never any longitudinal follow-up or assurance that any learning or growth had occurred. The literature, in fact, told me that it probably hadn't. I really felt that we were just going through the motions with that kind of attempt at professional development, that it was rather superficial.

On the other hand, this project had a longitudinal aspect that seemed more likely to promote real change for the participants, and that appealed to Anne. She felt that at this stage of her career, "I really needed to participate in something more substantive than I had been involved in up to that point." She also recognized the potential of this project to enable her to become a better researcher.

Anne was well aware that she too learned best by doing. She knew that she would only learn to be a good researcher by getting involved in a project and actually doing it.

I'm a very concrete, visual kind of learner. I learn from doing, from my own experiences. Every skill I've ever learned in my life, I would say, I've learned in that way: by doing it, thinking about it, and changing my response and adapting on the basis of what I perceived to be successful or not.

As a result of working on the project, Anne believes that she learned a great deal about data collection and management. She observed and was amazed at Vera's dedication to detail regarding data collection. For instance, meetings were always taped, even when they seemed to be long and rambling. Anne observed that all data was transcribed and filed in a careful and orderly manner. She also learned that,

You had to get everything you needed, because you cannot go back. I saw that a very important rule of research was making sure that the full range of data that is available was collected; otherwise, you may have a hole later.

Anne also noted that data was collected for both qualitative and quantitative purposes. Much of Anne's past experience had been in the qualitative paradigm, so it was a revelation to her about how qualitative and quantitative data could be collected and integrated to deepen the understanding of results. She saw that, "qualitative and quantitative research really support each other, and the project is strengthened by having both lenses on the data." With projects that are longitudinal and multidimensional, Anne realized that there were many different approaches to data analysis: "Everything I had been involved in up to that point had been reported in one way, and that was that." She noted how this longitudinal project had the advantage of providing enough data so many questions could be asked.

I think the strength of a longitudinal project will stay with me for along time. I can't even see myself getting involved in something really short unless it is in the context of a larger question that has some depth and meaning.

Another aspect of the project that was unfamiliar for Anne was the use of graduate students as an integral part of data collection. Several students even used part of the data to obtain their Master's of Education degree. Graduate students were trained in the making of field notes and sent into each participant's classroom weekly to observe explicit strategy instruction. The collection, monitoring, and organization of their field notes was a labor-intensive part of the data collection that yielded many interesting results. "This experience enhanced the graduate experience for students, while also contributing to the project."

These types of research experiences had not been a part of Anne's own graduate experience, as she had been studying under the constraint of working full time and maintaining a family of lively teenagers.

I had all the balls in the air and kept on juggling. I had a full-time job plus trying to take my courses and finish my thesis. I often had so many balls in the air that I couldn't keep them up all the time. It didn't turn me into a really good researcher. I knew at the time I was cutting corners. It was a conscious choice.

Anne thus was able to see first-hand how graduate students could be useful to a project and how a project could provide valuable research experience for them.

As the project unfolded, there was a sense of accomplishment that was felt by the partners. Anne was no exception. She comments, "I felt absolutely confident that this did make a difference to all of us." While the teachers were pleased with the response and progress their students made toward becoming independent learners, Anne, "felt a lot more competent and confident about myself as a researcher." She now says that she feels excited about research, particularly the kind of research that has the potential to make the classroom a better place for students to learn. Anne believes that this research experience held the kind of authentic purpose and meaning that she recognizes is essential if she is to be fully engaged and learning herself.

DISCUSSION

Results indicate that this collaborative research project, where partners learned together from one another, produced individualized professional development for all. We agree with Clark and colleagues (1996) that an essential aspect of the collaborative relationship was respect for the work of each participant. We also note that as we came together, it was the shared dialogue facilitated by the use of the same language (Elliott & Drake, 1995) that played a role in individual professional development. A shared language emerged gradually, based on readings and experiences. We believe, however, that much more was involved than dialogue (John-Steiner, Weber, & Minnis, 1998).

Several additional components can be identified as being central to this outcome. The blending of school and university cultures served to overcome the limitations of any one participant. Institutional constraints on both sides create a culture that is not conducive to conducting one's own professional development. The cultures share a sense of isolation and competition, which was broken down or diluted by blending partners from the separate cultures. This outcome may have been aided by the fact that all of the teachers were from different schools, although they were from the same school board. Also, Anne and Vera were from different departments in the Faculty of Education: Anne was from the Preservice Education Department, and Vera from the Graduate Education Department. Hence, traditional constraints were less able to dominate or direct activities, and decisions were discussed and shared.

Each person came to the project possessing both strengths and weaknesses in terms of the project goals. All strengths and weaknesses were openly acknowledged over the first few months, and tasks were allocated on the basis of expertise. The teachers determined the diverse learning needs of their own students and selected appropriate strategies to teach. Anne and Vera brought resources related to the theory of explicit strategy instruction and facilitated the meetings. No one assumed the mantle of "expectations" in all areas. A school-based partner commented once that, "the ivory tower has been breached in this group." Throughout the project, theory and practice were united in such a way that they informed each other. We agree with Hunt (1987), who said, "There is nothing so theoretical as good practice" (p. 11). As the project continued over the four years, needs changed and partners continually adapted and adjusted to one another.

There was a relaxed and flexible approach to all goals and tasks that eventually created a true community of learners. Partners began to recognize that it was professionally stimulating to be together. Simultaneously, strong friendships developed based on mutual liking and respect and commitment to the project goals.

All participants in this project believed firmly in ongoing professional development and took pride in watching their expertise grow. The commitment made by experienced teachers to enhance their own classroom practice with explicit strategy instruction was shared with their students. This sharing provided a model of life-long learning for the students. Vera and Anne also shared the project with their university students, and agreed with Stallworth (1998), who said, "I build learning activities into my professional life so I can have more experiences to share with my students. I am trying to model for my students that teaching is also a learning process" (p. 77).

It is becoming the norm for teachers to work together (Anderson, Rolheiser, & Gordon, 1998). As the Centre of Collaborative Research at Brock University exemplifies, more university personnel are conducting research together. We believe that shared professional development in education occurs best when theory and practice unite and when universities and schools work together to model life-long learning.

REFERENCES

Anderson, S., Rolheiser, C., & Gordon, K. (1998). Preparing teachers to be leaders. *Educational Leadership, 55*(5), 59–61.

Castle, J. B., & Hunter, R. (1997). Exploring "front-line" views: Veterans' perceptions of one professional development school after four years. *Alberta Journal of Educational Research, 43*(4), 177–191.

Clark, C., Moss, P. A., Goering, S., Herter, R. J., Lamar, B., Leonard, D., Robbins, S., Russell, M., Templin, M., & Wascha, K. (1996). Collaboration as dialogue: Teachers and researcher engaged in conversation and professional development. *American Educational Research Journal, 33*(1), 193–231.

Darling-Hammond, L. (1998). Teachers learning that supports student learning. *Educational Leadership, 55*(5), 6–11.

Duffy, G. C. (1993). Teachers' progress toward becoming expert strategy teachers. *The Elementary School Journal, 94*, 109–120.

Elliott, A. E., & Drake, S. M. (1995). Moving from "two solitudes" towards a "blended" culture in school/university partnerships. *New Forums Press, 13*(2), 85–95.

Elliott, A. E., & Woloshyn, V. E. (1997). Some female professors' experiences of collaboration: Mapping the collaborative process through rough terrain. *Alberta Journal of Educational Research, 43*(1), 23–36.

Gaskins, I. W., & Elliot, T. T. (1991). *Implementing cogitive strategy instruction across the school: The Benchmark manual for teachers.* Cambridge, MA: Brookline Books.

Hunt, D. E. (1987). *Beginning with ourselves.* Toronto: Ontario Institute for Studies in Education Press.

John-Steiner, V., Weber, R. J., & Minnis, M. (1998). The challenge of studying collaboration. *American Educational Research Journal, 55*(4), 773–783.

Kagan, D. (1992). Professional growth among pre-service and beginning teachers. *Review of Educational Research, 62*(2), 129–170.

Kennedy, P. (1993). *Preparing for the twenty-first century.* New York: Random House.

Martineau, S. (1998, March). Moving towards professionalism. *Professionally Speaking*, 18–19.

Pressley, M., Woloshyn, V. E., & Associates. (1995). *Cognitive strategy instruction that really improves children's academic performance.* Cambridge, MA: Brookline Books.

Renyi, J. (1998). Building learning into the teaching job. *Educational Leadership, 55*(5), 70–74.

Stallworth, J. (1998). Practicing what we teach. *Educational Leadership, 55*(5), 77–79.

Stewart, H. J. (1996, Spring). Towards improved education practice. Lessons learned from Brock University's Centre of Collaborative Research. *Education Canada*, 20–25.

Tompkins, G. E., Pollard, M. J., Bright, R. M., & Winsor, P. J. T. (1999). *Language Arts: Content and teaching strategies.* Canadian edition. Scarborough, ON: Prentice Hall Allyn and Bacon Canada.

Woloshyn, V. E., & Elliott, A. E. (1998). Providing seventh and eighth grade students with reading, writing and study strategy instruction: Comparing explicit-strategy and implicit-strategy programs. *The Reading Professor, 20*(2), 59–79.

Woloshyn, V. E., Elliott, A. E., & Riordon, M. (1998). Seven teachers' experiences using explicit strategy instruction in the classroom. *Journal of Professional Studies, 5*(2), 18–28.

Wood, E., Woloshyn, V. E., & Willoughby, T. (1995). *Cognitive strategy instruction for middle and high schools.* Cambridge, MA: Brookline Books.

.

CHAPTER 11

Mentoring Graduate Students through Involvement in Faculty Research

Susan Gibson, Dianne Oberg, Rosemarie Pelz, and Doug Zook

> Graduate students learn about research from how it is shown to them. The opportunity that Dianne and Sue provided for us to be involved with them in research has brought all kinds of learning for Rosemarie and myself.

In this comment, Doug, a graduate research assistant, identifies the importance of mentoring graduate students through involvement in faculty research. In this chapter, we explore the experiences of two graduate students who were mentored through immersion in a faculty research program. Sue and Dianne, the professors, first establish the context by outlining the research program and explaining how the graduate students were involved, and then Rosemarie and Doug highlight the experiences that enhanced their growth as researchers and future faculty members. Throughout the chapter, individual voices and perspectives are identified. At the time of this writing, Dianne and Sue continue their research program, Rosemarie is writing her doctoral thesis, and Doug is in his first year of a tenure-track position at a Canadian university.

DIANNE AND SUE: WHY INVOLVE GRADUATE STUDENTS IN FACULTY RESEARCH?

Our approach to involving graduate students in our research grew out of a firm belief that mentoring meets the needs of both graduate students and faculty. Although graduate programs always include coursework in research methodologies, many students find it difficult to get first-hand experience of research other than their own thesis-related work and often express feelings of being unprepared for that research. As faculty members, we could not easily complete the kind of labor-intensive, school-based, qualitative research that we do without the contributions of skilled research assistants. The graduate students involved in our studies provided invaluable help by conducting interviews, observing in schools and classrooms, writing field notes, transcribing interview data, and doing preliminary data analysis.

We believe it is important to provide graduate students with the opportunity to work as junior colleagues in research, and we view developing graduate students' research skills as an important aspect of socializing them into academic culture. While mentoring is often seen as a relationship between two individuals, we typically work with a group of students in the context of a research team engaged in research as a collaborative endeavor. We want our graduate students to see that research involves not only working together as team members, but also calling on the advice of a whole network or community of researchers. As part of the team's work, students are oriented to the research projects on which they will be working and given preparation for their participation in research. As important as learning the process of research is reflecting on issues that arise in research. Regular opportunities for debriefing, reporting progress, and collaborative problem solving are provided as the research work progresses.

THE MENTORING LITERATURE

The existing literature on mentoring in academic institutions comes primarily from an examination of the relationships between graduate students and their supervisors and the relationships between junior and senior faculty (Brown-Wright, Dubick, & Newman, 1997; Knox & McGovern, 1988). Mentoring extends beyond a supervisory role or a senior faculty member's providing "survival tips," involving mutual support between a mentor and a "mentee." "The human dimension [in any mentoring relationship] is the key to success" (Knox & McGovern, 1988, p. 40). Mentees benefit from advice and support in learning a new life role and understanding the workings of the academic culture (Kram, 1983). Mentors can experience both generativity and revitalization through mentoring relationships (Otto, 1994; Wunsch, 1994). Mentoring brings advantages not only to the mentor and the mentee but also to the institution: "Mentorship is more than just a relationship between two individuals; it's a growth process that also involves the institution within which both are working" (Wunsch, 1994, p. 11). Since academics who are mentored are likely to become mentors of future generations, this adds to the capacity of institutions to nurture the development of researchers and scholars.

In a study examining graduate students' and faculty perceptions of mentoring relationships, Blankenmeyer and Webber (1996) found that both faculty and graduate students perceived mentoring relationships in terms of four factors: mutual support, professional development, research, and comprehensiveness. Mutual support, which involved valuing an individual and sustaining his or her progress in graduate school, was characterized thus: "the mentor enjoys working with the mentee, the mentor fosters the mentee's career in a variety of ways, and the mentor supervises and critiques the work of the mentee" (p. 34). Professional development activities referred to the guidance given to students in developing career goals and guiding them along the path to their first academic position. The research factor involved learning about research design, data collection and analysis, the dissemination of results, and grantsmanship. Comprehensiveness referred to broader-based interactions between mentor and mentee in settings beyond the academic environment but related to professional issues. These interactions frequently included discussion of personal dilemmas and problems. Waldeck, Orrego, Plax, and Kearney (1997) identified this factor, which they termed psychosocial support, as the factor most valued by graduate students in mentoring relationships.

Mentoring, as a four-fold endeavor, is a model that is particularly informative for our work with graduate students involved in our research. We address each of the four factors in mentoring relationships later in this chapter. We have chosen to use the term "psychosocial support" for the fourth factor because it more clearly captures our understanding of this factor.

DIANNE AND SUE: THE CONTEXT FOR MENTORING

Over a two-year period, our team of researchers conducted three school-based studies of Internet use by teachers in Alberta schools. Altogether, 10 research assistants worked with us over the two years; some were involved in only one study while others were involved in all of them. Rosemarie worked on all three studies; Doug worked on the second and third studies.

The first school-based study, conducted in winter 1997, involved case studies of Internet use in six school sites from the K–12 sector. Principals, teachers, parents, and technical support people in each school were interviewed by graduate research assistants. Data were collected about how teachers were using the Internet, about how they learned to use it, and about their perceptions of its value as an educational tool.

In fall 1997 and fall 1998, collaborative research partnerships in those same schools examined how teachers who were novice and experienced

Internet users utilized the Internet as an instructional tool, and what factors supported and hindered that use. For these studies, one teacher in each school was partnered with a graduate research assistant trained in the use of search engines and search strategies. Then the teacher and the graduate student formed a research partnership in which they spent about 30 hours together over a four-month period, creating projects aimed at integrating the Internet into specific subject area curricula, and discussing issues related to learning about and using the Internet. Data were collected through interviews, field notes, and online reflective journals.

EXPLORING THE MENTORING EXPERIENCE

The four factors in a mentoring relationship are explored here by Sue and Dianne as they pertain to the program of research described above. These four factors are mutual support, professional development, research, and psychosocial support. Rosemarie and Doug provide their perspectives on each of the four factors as they related to their research experiences.

Mutual Support

Blankenmeyer and Webber (1996) defined mutual support as valuing an individual, working with the individual, and generally supporting his or her progress in graduate school. From our experience, we see mutual support more in terms of a reciprocal relationship where both faculty members and graduate students benefit from working together. For example, the students' different perspectives and special knowledge and skills can enhance the faculty members' research project. We were fortunate to be able to select graduate students who were practicing classroom teachers and therefore familiar with the culture and rhythms of school life. That meant that these students could easily move into the school setting and establish rapport with the teacher participants. We supported the students by introducing them to the theoretical framework of the research, and helped them to begin to refine their research skills through orientation sessions and regular team meetings. Orientation sessions were provided for the graduate students on the nature of the research process and on Internet search strategies they would need in order to work with the research participants in the schools.

Mutual support was characteristic of these orientation sessions and regular team meetings. For example, the graduate research assistants helped us to refine the interview questions for the initial study. As the fieldwork progressed, members of the team met to share progress and to address dilemmas. We also stayed in contact electronically at least once a week to

ensure that students knew we were available to assist with any unanticipated problems or concerns.

Rosemarie on Mutual Support

Collaborative relationships permeated every aspect of our research
experience. Those relationships included the research investigators, the research assistants, and the classroom teachers who were our research partners. From the beginning Sue and Dianne established a supportive and
scholarly atmosphere. They provided the model for collaborative research.
This was apparent in their interactions with each other and with the research assistants. The entire project was structured around a team
approach. Throughout the three studies, we (research assistants and co-
investigators) often met to update our progress. We were encouraged to
share our successes and our dilemmas. This was part of the collaborative
research process. Dianne and Sue were always available through e-mail,
telephone, or in person to discuss various aspects of the project or to answer questions. They respected us as research partners. Throughout the
project, I think we all felt that our contribution was valued, and this
strengthened our commitment to the project. The meetings provided a forum to share experiences and receive support.

Doug on Mutual Support

Dianne and Sue carefully laid the necessary groundwork for the studies
through the orientations and in-services they provided for the research team
and for our teacher research participants from the school sites. Dianne and
Sue joined us in the in-services, and we learned together. During the orientations to each of the studies, Sue and Dianne set the context, explained
the purposes and the process of the study, and provided an opportunity
for each of us to get to know the others in the group. Talking with others
in the research team during our meetings provided a forum to share experiences and receive support.

Research

Blankenmeyer and Webber (1996) defined the research factor in mentoring in terms of learning about research design, data collection and analysis, dissemination of results, and grantsmanship. This definition is
generally appropriate to our experience, but we also include the work of
preparing proposals for conference papers and planning conference presentations. Through involvement in our research, the graduate students
learned about interviewing, taking field notes, and setting timelines as part
of the data collection process. They also benefited from being involved in

data analysis, writing summary reports, helping to identify themes emerging from the research data, and presenting at conferences.

Rosemarie on Research

During the first study, I was in the Master's program and had very little formal interviewing experience. Sue and Dianne introduced us to formal interviewing by sharing anecdotes from their repertoire of field experiences and encouraging the more experienced among us to do the same. In the first study, I was not completely relaxed when I was conducting my first interviews. Fearing I might reveal my lack of Internet and computer knowledge, I was reluctant to stray from the suggested list of questions. During one tape-recorded interview with a teacher, I was so focused on asking the questions that I was not being attentive to the tape recorder I had borrowed for the interview work. Later, when I decided to check the recording, I made the big discovery: a blank tape. Fortunately for me, the person I was interviewing had a great sense of humor. Unfortunately for me, she promptly shared the incident with everyone within hearing distance. My image of myself as a scholarly researcher evaporated. The following week I interviewed another teacher. This time I tested the recording twice at the beginning of the interview. Three days later when I played the tape, I discovered it was blank. It was then that I decided to purchase my own tape recorder. It was fortunate that in both instances I had field notes (thanks to Sue's insistence) to rely on. Sue and Dianne were very gracious about these mishaps, and they helped me to recognize that making mistakes is an inevitable part of the research experience. Again, I was learning much more than just the skills of interviewing.

In the second study, I found it was impossible to take field notes while working with the children. On Sue's advice, I jotted down key words when a rare free moment became available and later fleshed out the data in my weekly summaries. I quickly learned to make the notes as soon as possible after I left the school. While this may seem extremely basic to seasoned researchers, the novice researcher, regardless of age and other life experiences, appreciates the mentoring from experienced investigators.

Another important area of learning was how to analyze data. At the end of the first study, I was invited to participate in the data analysis with Sue and Dianne. We began by reading the data collected from all six schools and identifying themes that emerged. Up to this point, I had only looked at the data collected from my school research site. The quantity before me was a bit overwhelming. I was just beginning to realize what it meant to "do research." Reading about data analysis in a research methods course and actually engaging in data analysis are very different experiences. The latter raises the level of understanding considerably. True to the collaborative process, Sue and Dianne arranged for us to meet so that we could compare notes and discuss findings. I learned two very efficient ways of organizing information that later proved helpful for my own research. My final role in this process was to pull quotes that essentially captured the essence of the themes we had identified. The collaborative relationship established by Sue and Dianne allowed me the opportunity to learn about process in a meaningful context. The entire experience of data analysis enabled me to risk becoming involved in a project of my own for a course taken in another department.

Sue and Dianne opened up the entire process of their research project to all of us, from the proposal application to the literature review that supported this study. We were privy to all the little details in between that are the composite pieces of a research venture. They provided a supportive research atmosphere that allowed us to flourish as new researchers.

Doug on Research

During research for my Master's thesis, I had interviewed seven individuals, so I felt quite comfortable interviewing the teachers involved in this study. However, the interview with my teacher research participant in the third study proved most interesting. I learned the importance of continual clarification about the research process with those involved. Toward the end of the initial interview with my teacher research participant, I realized that he thought he was helping me with my doctoral research on the use of films in secondary social studies (which we had discussed at our first meeting), rather than research about teachers' use of the Internet. He even had a list of films for me! I corrected his misunderstanding and reemphasized the purpose of the study and our expected roles in it. We both left the interview with a clearer understanding of the research task before us and the realization of the importance of open dialogue between us.

I found that scheduling and timelines are an important part of successful data collection. The best-laid plans can easily go awry, so it is necessary to have an optimistic spirit of adventure. When two busy people are brought together to participate in research, the scheduling can become a nightmare. My teacher research participant and I found that e-mailing and phone calls were incredibly helpful, as often it did not work for us to meet at the school or face-to-face at another location. This reality was especially true for my work in the third study. Dianne and Sue were gracious to the research assistants in terms of timelines, which alleviated any deadline pressure. Their understandings of the busyness and numerous responsibilities of graduate student life were much appreciated.

I also learned that often how things begin is not how they may end. The time the teacher in the third study was allotted by his principal to participate in the study was significant, but due to numerous factors, about halfway through the study he began questioning whether he could continue or not. After talking with Sue and Dianne and the teacher, we agreed to renegotiate our work, but in doing so, aspects of our original plans for collaboration were lost. I learned that research often becomes complex and that there is a definite need for flexibility and renegotiation as the research progresses.

We were required to submit summary reports for each study. I prepared a document describing the research site, explaining my work with my research partner, and tracing our learning about the Internet. These reports were useful in synthesizing our learnings of the research process and our findings with our research partners. Again, Dianne and Sue were sensitive to our individual situations as graduate students and to the individual situations of our research sites and made accommodations in terms of the details and deadlines for these reports.

Professional Development

Blankenmeyer and Webber (1996) defined professional development as the guidance given to develop career goals, to secure grants, and to guide students through a path to their first academic position. From our experience, we see professional development in somewhat broader terms, perhaps because our graduate research assistants were already practicing teachers, experienced professionals accustomed to examining and enhancing their professional practice.

Involvement in the Internet studies gave our graduate research assistants the opportunity to develop skills important for furthering their professional practice. In particular, their involvement in the research gave them opportunities to enhance their technological and informational skills. It also helped them to rethink their visions for using the technology in their own teaching.

Rosemarie on Professional Development

This study has provided me with a tremendous opportunity for growth in a variety of ways. Aside from the important work of learning about research practices in general, my familiarity with the Internet has reached a level that allows me to conduct searches within the framework of my own study. I am far more comfortable accessing not only my own university library from my computer at home, but also those across the country. Understanding how the Internet works has also provided me with the opportunity to connect with other people who are doing similar work.

My work in this research study also has led me to rethink some of my enthusiasm for using the Internet. From what I have seen in classrooms, the claims that are made and the incredible sums of money that are involved do not translate into immediately effective teaching strategies. I continue to mull over several of the questions I raised in my journal responses about Internet utility: Does the use of the computer, and the Internet specifically, create an eventual disinterest, impatience, and dependency in students?

What are the long-term benefits to using the Internet besides accessing the most current educational strategy? How can teachers stimulate critical and creative thinking when using the Internet with their students? How can teachers manage the amount of information that is available to them? To what extent is the Internet creating a new class of have-nots? Does the expense involved translate into significant student learning? Does the implementation of virtual schools deprive schooling of its most important relationship, that of the dialogical?

Some of us had limited experience with either the computer or the Internet when we first began the project. Because of the nature of the project and the nature of the research process, our skills with both improved measurably. Not only were we becoming a part of the research community and improving our writing and research skills through many collaborative relationships, but also we became much more familiar with search engines and search strategies. These skills are definite assets in our other lives as graduate students.

Doug on Professional Development

My computer technology skills were significantly expanded through involvement in these studies. I became much more fluent in the use of the Internet and e-mail communication. Conducting the research has reaffirmed for me that, while the Internet can be a useful tool in data retrieval, it is rarely effectively used in an interactive way that develops students' critical or creative skills. The exception to this statement occurred in the Grade 11 computer class, but the tasks here were designed by the teacher, and then the students were required to complete these tasks, as far as I could tell, as closely as possible to what the teacher had designed. The potential for student creativity and Internet capabilities were not being realized through such assignments. It is also important to note that the teachers I was working with are certainly doing the best that they can, given the limitations of full-time teaching. I know how hard it is to try to live the life of a high school teacher. The myriad of tasks involved with the job and the priority of relating to students do not always leave a great deal of time for working with new learning tools, especially in this era of educational cutbacks. I gained significant learning from working with the research participants, in terms of my understanding of teaching practice and the implications of Internet use for my own pedagogy.

Psychosocial Support

For this factor, we drew on the work of Waldeck, Orrego, Plax, and Kearney (1997) as well as that of Blankenmeyer and Webber (1996). Waldeck and colleagues found that psychosocial support was the factor most valued by graduate students in mentoring relationships. The latter used the term "comprehensiveness" for this factor. Psychosocial support involved a broad range of personal interactions between mentors and mentees, often in settings outside of the institution. For us, psychosocial support included those interactions both inside and outside the context of the research, interactions that were not directly required by the research itself but that were nevertheless important to the lives of graduate students and faculty members. Some examples of these interactions included discussions about the students' preparations for candidacy examinations, the progress of their own research projects, their relationships with their supervisory committee, and their preparation for job interviews. Many of these interactions helped students feel more confident and capable in meeting the new demands of their academic lives.

Rosemarie on Psychosocial Support

Entering the research community is similar to entering a new country. Upon arrival you are not familiar with the language, the norms and values, and codes of behavior. Initially, the community is somewhat disorienting as you begin the journey of navigating your way through the new territory. Sue and Dianne, through their invitation to participate in the project, allowed us the "lived experience" component of what it means to be a part of the research community. They introduced us to the research process and helped us to negotiate our way. We learned the language and codes of behavior in our small research community that allowed us to interact in a more meaningful way with the larger community of researchers at the university. As research assistants, we were invited to participate in research symposiums, graduate student orientations, and conferences, all of which served to make us feel a part of the academic community.

People often assume that because you have been teaching for a number of years, you are very comfortable speaking in front of any group. Alternatively, those who have always felt quite at ease with public speaking may hold little understanding or compassion for those of us who do not. Sue and Dianne were very sensitive to presentation fears, and introduced us to this aspect of the research community in incremental steps. Our first presentations were to each other, in the form of summaries of our work at the schools. Next, we had an opportunity to do an informal presentation at the school research site, a community we knew well. Following this, some of us were invited to present at the graduate student orientation and at a research symposium in our department at the university. And last, there was an invitation to copresent at conferences. Copresenting is a supportive and informative way of introducing the graduate student to conferences. Both Dianne and Sue took the time to carefully walk us through the process, never once making us feel as if our many concerns and questions were wasting their time.

Learning something new can be a lonely and intimidating process. With-

out the benefit of support, the temptation to abandon the learning altogether can be overwhelming, especially when an individual already has a
plateful of responsibilities. I think that dialogue is a crucial part of any
learning, whether it be learning to navigate the Internet or learning to navigate your way through the culture of graduate school. Talking about the
process with others enables us not only to reflect on our thinking, but also
to shift the direction of our thinking. The talking generates new ideas and
understanding, and often provides direction for the next step in the process
that you are trying to learn or illuminates what was previously hidden from
view. Sometimes we are not quite aware of the importance of discourse in
new learning until we actually engage in verbal and written communication. The opportunity to discuss the process at all levels of new learning
needs to be built in. The complexities of the research process, the lived
experiences of the researcher, and the messiness of everyday lives were understood and validated by Sue and Dianne's approach to working with us
as coresearchers.

Doug on Psychosocial Support

Moving from high school teaching to pursuing a Ph.D. has been an ar-
duous journey. I entered the research study conducted by Sue and Dianne
with a sense of where I was going, but a lack of clarity on how I would
get there. It was through their mentoring that I discovered a greater sense
of clarity.

Sue and Dianne, the lead researchers, invited those of us on the research
team to be co-investigators with them in the study. They also provided
opportunities to write about the research and present the research findings
at scholarly conferences. Their positive, flexible, and helpful attitudes provided a comfortable and affirming working relationship extending beyond
the confines of the research study. Through numerous conversations,
Dianne and Sue offered much appreciated knowledge about academic life.
They provided a necessary perspective that I as a graduate student had
found lacking in my other contacts at the university. What others seemed
to assume was common knowledge, but was not commonly known by
graduate students aspiring to enter the academy as professors, Sue and
Dianne were willing to share. They were optimistic about life at the university, but they were also honest about how to survive in such an environment.

In particular, Sue and I, probably because of our common interest in
social studies, engaged in numerous conversations. I was anxious for someone to provide some guidance; Sue willingly listened to my questions and
observations, and provided useful suggestions and possible directions for
me to pursue. Sue provided a mentoring role for me beyond that of developing research skills. I gained a greater sense of confidence and perspective
on what to expect in the life of the academy from her. She has been in-

volved with my candidacy and encouraged me in the writing of my dissertation, as well as being an invaluable resource for securing a position at
the university where I am currently employed. Sue's willingness to hear and
respond to my queries and concerns has provided a much-needed perspective for me as I begin my career at the university. Her encouragement and
honest conversations have been important parts of my emerging sense of
being an academic.

It has been through the desire to mentor graduate students that Dianne
and Sue have consciously and effectively enabled me and others to become
engaged in the highly demanding, yet rewarding, pursuit of working in the
university. Their practice underscores Galileo's comment that "You cannot
teach anyone anything. You can only help them to discover it within themselves."

DIANNE AND SUE: CONCLUSION

In this chapter we have described the mentoring relationships that we
have tried to build with our graduate students through their involvement
in our program of research. These mentoring relationships have been examined using a four-fold model based on the work of Blankenmeyer and
Webber (1996) and Waldeck and colleagues (1997). This four-fold model
of mentoring relationships included mutual support, professional development, research, and psychosocial support.

The graduate research assistants who worked with us really worked with
us as junior colleagues in research. Mentoring has been a reciprocal relationship in which both our graduate research assistants and we as faculty
members benefited from working together. Our graduate students learned
much about research, and their involvement in our research also gave them
the opportunity to develop skills important for furthering their professional
practice. They will be able to use the knowledge gained through working
with us to inform their own work in schools and in the teacher education
programs here in the university. Psychosocial support helped our graduate
research assistants to feel more confident and capable in meeting the new
demands of their academic and professional lives. Several of them have told
us how valuable this support has been for them in completing their own
doctoral research and in preparing for their first academic position.

The contributions of graduate research assistants like Doug and Rosemarie have enabled and enhanced our research work. We have also gained
much pleasure and satisfaction from our work with them. Based on our
personal experiences and on those of Doug, Rosemarie, and other research
assistants, we highly recommend the involvement of graduate students in
faculty members' research projects. Working together on research projects
provides rich opportunities for mutually supportive mentoring relationships
among faculty and graduate students. These relationships enhance the qual-

ity of academic life and contribute to the capacity of institutions to nurture the development of researchers and scholars.

NOTE

This chapter had its roots in a presentation at the Canadian Society for the Study of Education Conference in Sherbrooke, Quebec, in 1999. Coral Mitchell was interested in the graduate students' perspective on their involvement in the research and encouraged Sue and Dianne to revisit the experiences of the research team as a mentoring relationship. Rosemarie and Doug agreed that it would be interesting to embark on such an endeavor.

REFERENCES

Blankenmeyer, M., & Webber, M. (1996). Mentoring; The socialization of graduate students for the 21st century. *Journal of Family and Consumer Sciences, 88*(3), 32–36.

Brown-Wright, D., Dubick, R., & Newman, I. (1997). Graduate assistant expectation and faculty perception: Implications for mentoring and training. *Journal of College Student Development, 38*(4), 410–416.

Knox, P., & McGovern, T. (1988). Mentoring women in academia. *Teaching of Psychology, 15*(1), 39–41.

Kram, K. (1983). Phases of the mentor relationship. *Academy of Management Journal, 26*, 608–625.

Otto, M. (1994). Mentoring: An adult developmental perspective. In M. Wunsch (Ed.), *Mentoring revisited: Making an impact on individuals and institutions* (pp. 15–24). San Francisco: Jossey-Bass.

Waldeck, J., Orrego, V., Plax, T., & Kearney, P. (1997, November). *Graduate student/faculty mentoring relationships: Who gets mentored, how it happens, and to what end?* Paper presented at the annual meeting of the National Communication Association, Chicago.

Wunsch, M. (Ed.). (1994). *Mentoring revisited: Making an impact on individuals and institutions.* San Francisco: Jossey-Bass.

CHAPTER 12

University Researchers' Collaborative Experiences: A Gender Analysis

Merle Richards and Nancy Murray

As collaboration becomes increasingly common in a research culture of limited resources and highly specialized researchers, it is critical to seek increased understanding of collaborative practice. As members of the Centre on Collaborative Research (CCR), we were encouraged by extensive work done on collaboration, and wished to know whether findings from previous studies within our own disciplines were valid across other academic disciplines. Although authors in several fields have written about collaboration, we found little information on the relationship of academic content to the collaborative process as described by researchers. Moreover, since no men have responded to invitations to join the CCR, we questioned whether collaboration was a female, perhaps feminist, style of partnering and if, when men do collaborate, they do it differently and for different reasons. Our experience appeared to support the assumption of a connection between collaboration and gender, a position supported by previous studies such as that of Drake, Elliott, and Castle (1993), in which the authors reported that one outcome of their collaborative project was an increased sense of feminist values. Several CCR members have stated their belief that "collaboration is a women's way of working," but we remained dubious about this view because multiauthored reports in the research literature of many disciplines suggest that collaborative research may be discipline rather than gender directed.

Therefore, this study was designed to investigate the nature of collaborative research conducted by university professors, both men and women, who described their work as collaborative, but who worked in diverse academic fields. Specifically, the focus was upon the processes and products of collaborative pursuits, with an analysis of gender differences should they exist.

We therefore questioned researchers' perceptions regarding the nature of their collaboration, how they engage in it, and why they choose to work in particular ways. The study, we believe, adds to the understanding of collaborative processes, relates them to various academic disciplines, and raises questions about the interrelationships among the nature of work, gendered perceptions, and perceived tensions involved in different kinds of collaboration.

The study illuminated the major issues of collaboration as addressed by four male and seven female professors from various university departments (Graduate Studies in Education, Environmental Policy, Health Studies, Math, Preservice Education), who were interviewed about their collaborative experiences. Semi-structured interviews were conducted with each participant and the tapes transcribed. We listened to narratives of researchers in Africa struggling to educate local women about safe water use, mathematicians creating theorems via e-mail, and teachers using creative drama to address behavioral problems. The academic contexts of the professors whom we interviewed ranged from mathematical research, where the data were theoretical and created through "pure" calculation, to an empirical investigation of medical-social issues involving diverse areas of expertise, to social activism through community consciousness-raising. Amid this diversity of research questions, methods, and personal experiences, we found both familiar patterns in the narratives of researchers in our own disciplines, and new information about the influence on research practice of subject areas and their accompanying politics, and how the ensuing political tensions may, perhaps, be confronted in a gendered fashion.

FORMS OF COLLABORATION

It was clear from the narratives that the relationship of the discipline to the research process is important, particularly as it affects procedures for gathering collaborating partners and collecting data. Our interviewees described essentially three types of collaborative projects, which we illustrate through musical metaphors. These forms of collaboration are important to note as they appear to be shaped not only by the professor's academic discipline, but also by a gendered orientation to relationships, which will be addressed later in the chapter.

Linear Projects: The Symphony Orchestra

A symphony orchestra is characterized by a conductor who guides many musicians, each of whom serves a highly specific function in the creation of a particular predetermined goal. The music has been selected by the conductor, the musical score indicates the notes for each individual musician to follow, and the final product is very likely a group performance.

Some collaborative projects are constructed in a similar way: The idea or research question is initially well defined, participants' roles are clearly delineated, and experts are recruited to fill those roles. The process and products are explicit and clear to all. This is the "tidiest" forum for goal and role definition, as each person has such a specialized area that little discussion is needed regarding who will perform specific tasks. The outcome is a publication of work that no individual or small group could have accomplished alone. In this kind of work, the principals often come together as a result of familiarity with and respect for one another's work, and select other coresearchers with a view to pooling knowledge from different fields to permit large studies beyond the expertise of any one researcher.

These projects tend to be relatively short term, with clear goals and expectations about the products to be created. In such projects, one may not choose everyone with whom one works; however, this may be of little consequence, as each person contributes a different expertise and there is little blending of contributions. Fraser, a researcher in the health sciences, illustrates, "It's like we're putting a hockey team together; if we need a goalie, then we go and get one. We don't give the job to someone who has to learn how to be a goalie."

Such projects are common in fields such as the medical sciences, where large empirical studies require many specialized skills. Nurses, physicians, technologists, statisticians, software specialists, biochemists, psychologists, and others may be recruited for a single team, with one or more principals directing all phases of the project. The research questions must be precise, so that data interpretation can be orderly. Although both quantitative and qualitative analysis may be part of such a study, the emphasis is on the former, especially as large masses of data must be handled with sophisticated statistical methods capable of combining clusters of data from different sources.

The collaborative elements are mainly in the transdisciplinary (Krug, Chapter 6, this volume) brainstorming sessions held at various stages to ensure that many possibilities are entertained, and that the group contributes to the best possible decisions about the research structure, procedures, and interpretation of findings. Otherwise, the research might be characterized as "cooperative" (Toepell, Chapter 4, this volume). As the goals of the project are clarified, participants' roles must be decided. For Julia, a Physical Education professor, this phase is the essential ingredient of successful collaboration, and the issue is often one of structure and time management:

I need to create a framework for the piece that will subdivide into areas and then people will be responsible for those subdivisions. . . . So if I have a very vigorous sense of timeline, structure, and framework that I am working with, and I am working with you and you don't, [if] your approach is entirely different, then we're going to have difficulty.

Problems in the collaborative process are few, arising chiefly if one individual does not fulfill his or her obligations, when communication is not maintained, or when the principal investigator is not effective in the leadership role.

Interweaving Projects: The Vocal Quartet

A vocal quartet is characterized by four singers each singing a specific line, but at various times anyone may take the lead. Sometimes one may diverge from the written score, exchange notes with another, or sing the same line. There is no leader; all listen carefully to one another to maintain the balance of the music. Anyone may suggest ideas about how to play or interpret a particular part. While roles are fairly clear and the final product mostly predetermined, there is room for discussion and divergence from what may have been anticipated from the onset.

This is perhaps the most common model for collaborative research, operating when colleagues create an idea and the research proposal together, then work as a team to carry it out. The symbolism of the quartet is apt, because such research is practical only for a group small enough to meet frequently and ensure that all members are cognizant of every member's progress. Often, the process begins with only a general agreement on a question or method, so that much initial discussion is needed to develop the proposal. The partners work collectively to refine the research question, the shape of the project, and participants' roles, although each person usually embraces the role most congruent with his or her strengths. For example, Bailey, a mathematician collaborating with another expert in his field, explains why fruitful discussion is critical to the formulation of the research question:

When we get together, it may not be clear in advance what we are going to work on. He'll probably have some projects that he's interested in and I'll have some. What we actually wind up working on will depend on the relative levels of conviction.

In this type of collaboration, as in the first, brainstorming sessions are used to generate ideas and group decisions. Here, however, discussion can revolve around goals, methods, role clarification, or all three. Jean, collaborating on a book for educators, comments on the necessity for extended focusing: "We spent the first week saying, 'What's our basic statement and our definition? What we are about?', [defining] the five important principles that we used throughout to guide us, to ask, 'Are we doing it?' "

Philosophical issues, intentions, and purposes must be addressed and made explicit to ensure that the partners understand their positions in the same way. The loose structure of such projects places special responsibilities on every participant. Mitchell and Boak (1997) remark that "collaborative research requires authentic involvement and active participation from all partners" (p. 8); that is, that the partners understand and are involved in all aspects of the project. Purpose, activities, and role definitions are articulated and rearticulated through reflective discussion and feedback from the various perspectives. Hence, this type of project demands an unusually high commitment of time and patience.

Role clarification, simple in some projects, can become quite complex in others. For Martine, an expert in international development, it is essential to continue discussions until all decisions have been arrived at equitably and to everyone's satisfaction. She comments:

We were very explicit about what our rules were. . . . I wouldn't like to be part of a collaboration where we haven't discussed the roles that people have. But then it's not a collaboration if you haven't done that. . . . I'm not afraid of conflicts in this type of context because my experience is that they do get resolved.

Mitchell and Boak (1997) comment that "early and ongoing communication with all partners is essential to keep everyone 'reading from the same page' " (p. 9). Martine's work provides an example from transdisciplinary projects, where role boundaries can be an issue:

Right at the beginning, we had a little bit of jostling about this territory. . . . It takes a few days for your perspectives to evolve . . . which starts to make a difference and then different issues come up. I remember one particularly tense dinner, when we sort of [argued]: "This is what I'm doing. What are you doing?" But [being] . . . the kind of people we were, we could talk and figure this out . . . that was definitely a phase.

If the initial meetings have been successful, the goals, tasks, and roles are clear, although they remain open to renegotiation and change. At this stage, researchers feel confident that their work will be able to proceed successfully. During the implementation phase, the participants each carry out their own roles, meeting as necessary to keep one another informed about their progress, and perhaps assisting one another when time constraints or other pressures on individual participants interfere with the research process. Problems can arise at this stage if communication breaks down or transparency has not been sustained: Zoe was disappointed by a colleague who did not share information or admit to his inexperience in research: "We also discovered . . . that he really didn't know anything about research, or questionnaire design, or even data analysis . . . [Had it been me,] I'd have had a hard time sleeping at night."

Mari experienced a "sour" collaboration that was painful in its failure to communicate openly or to discuss the outcomes desired by each participant within the project. The coworker's refusal to speak frankly led to serious misunderstandings about the goals and activities of the project, and aroused much anxiety in the researcher, who was unable to keep the team working toward the project's stated goals. Without mutual trust, each partner tried to take control. There was no sense of exchange or openness about strengths and needs, no "Here's what I can do, and here's what I need help with."

Most collaborative projects culminate in a report written in some collaborative fashion. Again at this phase, there is a danger of loss of commitment and energy; interest flags after the data have been gathered and analyzed. Jean found that, "It helps working with another person. The exciting part is even more exciting, the interesting part should be more interesting, and the mundane part should be at least less mundane because it's being shared with somebody else."

Emergent Projects: The Improvisational Jazz Band

Jazz music may be characterized as dynamic, responsive, and energizing. When a group of jazz musicians gather, their intent is to spontaneously blend various instruments to create a new sound with a strong rhythm. "Jamming" is done with passion; it is emergent, flexible, full of surprises. Each musician may play one or more instruments; flexibility is key as the music emerges from the moment.

The analogous form of collaborative work, especially in action research, is the emergent design, where the purpose of the research is known, but the roles, methods, and outcomes are not. Much depends on the collaborators' mutual understanding and shared philosophy as well as on their skills. Martine comments on her approach to this form: "The best of academic collaboration for me is a longer-term collaboration, where from the beginning you start by discussing your values and principles and you come from there toward the focus and come up with a research proposal."

Moreover, for some researchers, the motivation for collaboration is not simply instrumental; Mitchell and Boak (1997) show that for some, it is "more a philosophy of interaction and personal lifestyle than a structure of interaction designed to facilitate the accomplishment of a goal" (p 12). Carla holds such a philosophy:

The whole is far greater than the sum of the parts . . . in the end we can all leave saying, "We agree." This common thread in all the collaborative [work] I find successful is that what motivates us is the desire to see positive social change . . . I have this sense that I'm grounded in collaboration, that I grew up in this paradigm, that these things are second nature to me.

Drakenburg (1999) examines the concept of collaboration in a different context, but her remarks apply to problems researchers encounter in open-ended projects:

. . . collaboration is given an idealistic approach. In reality, collaboration often means bringing together . . . [participants] having diverse experiences and ideologies, as well as unclarified expectations regarding each other. Often these issues are left in the private realm, and thus they can undermine the foundation of collaborative efforts. (p. 5)

Drakenburg's comments apply especially to the problem of role definition in open-ended projects. Clarity of role or function within the collaborative process was critical to everyone we interviewed. Each individual within a project requires specificity regarding what must be done and who will do it, but this is especially problematic in the third type of collaboration. Usually, roles are related to the purpose and structure of the desired outcome, but in an emergent design, all three must be continually redefined and re-negotiated. This is an important issue even when minds are flexible and the collaborators readily adjust, because the need to communicate intensely is demanding of both time and mental energy. In these projects, moreover, it appears that the skills and knowledge of the participants may be ambiguous and vaguely defined. Clark (1996) comments that "people who have a vision need to understand what the others want and need" (p. 8), but the others may not realize that they must make their needs explicit, and not merely assume that they are understood. Carla's community-based environmental project provides an illustration:

We agree on the general direction that we're going, but in the detail, I'm not sure if we do agree about what's important, and how important is information as opposed to participation in processes that are seen to be radical or progressive.

GENDER AND COLLABORATION

These forms of collaboration, which range in the extent of malleability of the research process, also range in the degree of professional and personal intimacy appropriate for the researchers. Our colleagues in the sciences and social sciences, who in this study were mostly male, seem to work most often in the linear "symphony" and the interweaving "choral" models, in which members of the collaborative group may or may not know one another. If the project is well organized, the degree of interaction is well calculated to preserve time and energy in the production of a predictable research product. The relationships do not seem to affect the quality of the study, as long as each carries out his or her tasks effectively. In this case, the "hockey team," to use Fraser's metaphor, is determined by areas of expertise rather than relationships previously established. Generally, the research precedes the relationship.

The different forms of collaboration illustrate the effect of both academic discipline and a gendered orientation to professional relationships. Most of the females and only one male whom we interviewed preferred research projects that began in friendships, or at least acquaintances. These researchers, in social sciences and education, all spoke at length on the quality of their collaborative relationships and their importance to the researchers' personal and professional lives. They chose to work with others with whom they could share a friendship or bond. Their attitudes are not based on female exclusivity; but rather reflects an attitude that "if there is work to be done, let's do it with friends and make it fun." Julia illustrates, "I have to feel comfortable with the individual first, before I'm willing to work collaboratively. I am currently in a research project with two brand-new faculty and I'm excited about that because I will get to know them."

Zoe notes, moreover, that working with friends can heighten commitment to the task, and for women with many distractions in life, this may be the way to sustain the effort to complete research projects. "I'm more motivated with this collaborative research to get things accomplished. . . . I feel I have more of a responsibility to other people than where I'm the sole researcher."

Gendered Approaches to Collaborative Relationships

It was clear that all of the professors were deliberate about their professional collaborative relationships. When asked how they chose collaborative partners, all the researchers replied, "It has to be someone I can respect." This implied a person whose work was thorough, who was reliable as a partner, and knowledgeable in his or her field. Hord (1998) observes that collaboration also makes demands such as

personal and professional characteristics. Among these are the kind of respect and trust among colleagues that promotes collegial relationships, a willingness to accept feedback and to work to establish norms of continuous critical inquiry and improvement, and the development of positive and caring relationships. (p. 5, original emphasis)

In comments about their colleagues' contribution to the research process, and the benefits or tensions that resulted, our participants showed attention to the processes of collaboration. Each could readily articulate why a colleague was involved in the research and the characteristics of the relationship. Jean illustrates:

[I had to say] "I'm not a doctoral student, I'm your collaborator. We're working together as colleagues on that." . . . I wanted to get that very clear. . . . That was a critical moment . . . in terms of establishing the proper relationship that we needed to have if we were to work together.

Our interviews revealed a forthright attitude about the relationships, which convinced us that relationships are focal for all, both male and female. Every colleague expressed a caring attitude toward partners. Bailey, for example, describes three different colleagues, each with much affection:

He is the most down-to-earth, generous human being you could imagine.

He gets very depressed, and over the years I have, on occasion, had to sort of build him up.

I don't imagine that we could be really close friends . . . [but] the point is, we trust each other completely.

While all the researchers demonstrate an attitude of care, the degree of involvement with colleagues differed. It was here that the interplay of academic discipline and gendered orientation to relationships was observed.

In our sample, all of the researchers hoped that publication would be an outcome of successful research, but for the men, development and publication of new knowledge constituted the prime goal of collaboration. Paul states:

I contacted the rehabilitation center in Ottawa, and we began to interact, and it was quite clear to me that she was someone from whom I could learn a lot. She also had a lot of patients I could learn a lot from.

Such a relationship begins with the research question, and the recognition that each can contribute to it, but ongoing collaborative work often leads to rich friendships that go beyond the research. Paul talks about the complementarity between the personal and the professional: "We started as professional colleagues and became personal friends."

However, for many women, particularly those who have reflected at length on the nature of collaboration, the collaborative relationship itself is one of the goals. For them, collaboration goes beyond "just working together" or cooperating on a task. The difference lies in the relationship, which empowers and nurtures through shared decision making, holding power equally, and maintaining collegial support as the project progresses.

For some women, collaborative work can become exhilarating. Julia states with much enthusiasm:

It was an incredibly productive two hours that was very energizing, so I came out of the room feeling uplifted, physically as well as socially, having felt I'd made a connection with people I wouldn't otherwise have known. . . . I love connecting with women. . . . If I work with someone on a research project, I think we develop a sense of trust and a relationship, a friendship, and I like that.

Another reason why our female participants consider collaboration to be a women's issue is that it can become one of their main sources of social support and personal networks. Many professional women with families have little time or energy for socializing, and yet they crave friends. For both men and women, small, harmonious partnerships often deepen into friendships, but for women, this goal is more likely to shape the design and outcomes of a study. Several commented that collaboration provides a shelter from the isolation felt by women surrounded by male researchers who do not share their interests, and that the encouragement and motivation conferred by working with others made them seek out collaborative projects. For some, collaboration becomes the main source of social life; their research partners and colleagues become their friends, and therefore it is extremely important to develop working partnerships with people who are personally compatible. Naomi shares her stories of textbook writing with a coauthor:

We have stories we laugh about. . . . We had this woman from Gage and they had flown in somebody from Winnipeg—a reviewer—and the woman from Gage always wore these wonderful ultra-suede suits, and here I was with a baby in the bath water and nursing her at some point . . . we have a good sense of humor and we remember times like that.

Carla, Julia, and Martine go further, viewing collaboration as an issue of social action and a way of advancing women's power. Although their position is stronger than that of the others in our study, they do represent a feminist attitude to collaboration as an instrument of both social reform and personal growth. Hence, they believe that for women, the social aspects of collaboration are as important as the research product, because they can contribute to the quality of the research. As Martine comments,

[Friendship] makes it both tougher and easier. It's tough because you won't let each other off the hook that easy. If she came up with a value that I didn't agree with, or I did, we would probably challenge each other. It makes it easier that the challenge takes place in a very secure kind of context.

Friends expect one to make allowances for them, however, and this can hinder progress, especially when the project is not fully defined. One may be more forgiving with friends, and sometimes that causes problems. Of course, the greater the investment in the degree of collaboration and collegiality in the relationship, the greater the potential loss if the symbiosis that characterizes effective teamwork is also lacking. Members may hesitate to confront problematic issues. Zoe states:

We had a meeting this week, and it was supposed to start at 5:30. Sheri and I were here with the agenda, but Sarah didn't show up until 6:00, and then Anita until 6:15. Sarah was late because she was teaching a class, and I thought, "At least tell us you'll be late, or reschedule."

Sometimes, friendship developed in one area may leave one unsure of the partner's interests or abilities in another. Carla talks of her work with a friend whose company she enjoys. They each have a toddler and meet occasionally for both social and professional reasons. Carla finds tension in these "dual purpose" meetings, as she is disappointed in the lack of research productivity: "I'm surprised because I'm thinking, as an activist, she would be really skilled at organizing meetings, planning and having the agenda, and yet it is not happening."

Gender and Altruism

In our sample, the women were more likely to name altruistic goals as a reason for engaging in collaboration, but that may have been partly a function of the participants' areas of specialization. For example, Carla's work as an ethicist implies social goals:

It's the big enterprise that you share commonly with the other person . . . in our cases, we're motivated by social justice in our research . . . so we weren't doing the project to be successful researchers so much as to make a difference in the world through our work.

Mentoring is both an altruistic and a professional goal. Many senior faculty see it as a service to their research community, as well as to junior colleagues, to assist beginners along their career path. One reason for collaboration, therefore, is to mentor younger colleagues or students; several of our researchers viewed collaboration as a way of helping others to develop research skills and earn publications. Bailey, for example, spoke proudly of a mentoring relationship: "Two of my collaborators have been my university students . . . perhaps the major part of my motivation was to give them their first publication."

In this respect, the men mostly mentioned students, while the women mentioned both students and younger colleagues. For instance, Julia considered the possibility of mentoring to be one of the criteria for deciding on a research project: "I ask, can I help them, now that I'm a bit senior in the department and in a position to mentor younger faculty?" Many participants, but especially the women, emphasized their mentoring strategy with respect to publications, commenting that those most in need of "points" for status or accomplishment are given first authorship. The men also used this way of assisting young researchers, but the women tended to speak of it in an ironic tone that revealed a certain skepticism, or even cynicism, regarding the academic "game" and the need to "beat the system," or at least, exploit it for the benefit of one's female colleagues.

Cynicism and Time Management

For women in particular, time pressures are overwhelming. All of the men and women interviewed commented on the stress of deadlines and the necessity of maintaining the energy to complete research projects on time. But only the women mentioned the interference of work in their personal lives and vice versa. Those with young families, especially, expressed anxiety about neglecting either. They also felt the need to continue their research even during maternity leaves, in order to stay in the queue for tenure and promotion. A certain resentment was expressed toward those men who seem to feel that only when obviously working is one truly "professional." The women, on the other hand, both feared appearing unprofessional and felt selfish when putting their work before personal obligations.

The value that the university reward system places on publications was thus viewed more cynically by the women. Some felt that the need to appear productive could compromise their true purpose in doing research. Carla, for example, found that "genuine authentic human research conflicts with the agenda of the academy. . . . You lose your sense of purpose, because it's 'What's going to go on your CV next?' All these things that might make a huge difference, they don't matter." This is especially troublesome in applied disciplines, where professional ethics must meet "academic" standards. For example, professors may work with practitioners in their fields, both to enrich practice and develop theory, but if they publish in trade or professional magazines, they do not gain the academic credit accorded to little-read, but prestigious refereed journals. Therefore, if they wish to write for practitioners, the academy demands that this writing be in addition to "scholarly" publications. Because the kind of work published in "reputable" journals may not also support values of field-based professional practice and communication with practitioners, conflict arises between these two aspects of the researcher's professional life. Where successful, collaboration with practitioners can help to overcome the tension between the two sets of values by allowing the researcher to participate in both the applied and the scholarly aspects of research. But to be productive as academics, perhaps even more productive than their male colleagues, the women struggle with the conflict between social outcomes and getting a publication for their CV.

Whatever their attitude to university values, all the researchers accepted that publication is a necessity. It was acknowledged that collaborative work is less honored by the university; and therefore, most of the participants also worked on solo projects, partly because aspects of their work did not coincide with colleagues' interests, but also from academic necessity. This increased the time pressures even more. Carla expressed strong feelings about the conflicting elements in her life:

But the other dimension, a huge dimension, is that my role as an academic doesn't value that kind of work [community environmental projects], and so when I'm thinking about the time investment in it, I'm not as motivated. If I want to stay in academia, this [productivity] is what is required. . . . So the time tension is really a huge factor—I'm wasting all this time just visiting her as a friend and not progressing on the task we are trying to do.

The time constraints that women feel are resolved to some degree by the notion that every activity must be multipurposed. Research must support teaching, publishing, social life, and personal well-being. The concentrated efforts required to do this contribute to the skeptical outlook of these women. Some female academics believe that male colleagues are promoted and tenured even with fewer publications or productivity than they have, as though they have some mysterious way not only of "buying into the system," but of knowing what the system is.

Julia's view of collaboration emphasized her belief that collaboration has a different meaning for women, a different purpose, and different methods:

Men are in a different position of power and authority, and as such, I think their collaboration is different. It's no longer survival. . . . I still see women as oppressed; as a result, I see collaborative research as a survival technique. Women in academic life are now collaborating in order to survive. But in one respect, collaboration seems to have served the institution, the patriarchal institution, quite well, in the sense that a number of academics have used it to garner a lot of publications. On the other hand, there's the survival that I think it gives a lot of women. I think collaboration and collaborative research is our life-ring in the sense that it allows us to survive. So I'm intrigued about the whole idea of collaboration, not only my own process in it, but how it serves. Collaboration builds community, it builds reinforcement, and bolstering that energy, bolsters you for the fight, the next round.

Thus, we see that despite the cynicism and weariness expressed by some of our female colleagues, close collaboration appeared to give them hope, energy, and a sense of community that the men did not even mention as a lack in their lives. The excitement of shared discovery is always a spur to the next step. Carla says whole-heartedly, "Yet I find each time I engage in collaboration there are things that are new, that take me by surprise when I realize that this is a whole new dimension of collaboration."

REFERENCES

Clark, K. L. (1996). *Human Systems Engineering: A leadership model for collaboration and change.* Paper presented at the National Conference of the Association for Global Business, Dallas, TX.

Drake, S. M., Elliott, A. E., & Castle, J. (1993). Collaborative reflection through story: Towards a deeper understanding of ourselves as women researchers. *Qualitative Studies in Education, 6*(4), 291–302.

Drakenburg, M. (1999). Problems facing the professional teacher: Curriculum texts and their metaphors in the Scandinavian countries. *Journal of the International Society for Teacher Education 3*(2), 1–8.

Hord, S. M. (1998). Creating a professional learning community: Cottonwood Creek School. *Issues About Change, 6*(2), 1–8.

Mitchell, C., & Boak, T. (1997). Collaborative research: The power, the perils, and the possibilities. *Brock Education, 7*(1), 1–14.

CHAPTER 13

Not Just Smooth Sailing: Issues in Collaboration

Alice Schutz, Nancy Murray, Vera Woloshyn, Anne Elliott, Norah Morgan, and Bev Haskins

We are a group of university professors and school-based teachers who share an interest in the collaborative process. In 1991, we formed the Centre on Collaborative Research (CCR), with the primary purpose of establishing school and/or university partnerships and exploring the collaborative process that most effectively sustains them. Because we had been researching the collaborative process in the CCR for several years (Castle, 1997; Elliott & Drake, 1995; Stewart, 1996, 1997), we were eager to present what we had learned about collaboration in a fresh, captivating manner at a national educational conference being held at our "home" university. We determined that we wanted a medium that was not only creative, motivational, and academic, but would also provoke lively discussion among academics and classroom teachers. Agreeing that presentation form profoundly affects content acquisition (Coger & White, 1973), we sought an alternative to the traditional forms of conference presentations, and readily embraced our drama educator's suggestion that the medium be a modified Readers' Theatre.

The purpose of this chapter, therefore, is three-fold: (1) to present the script as an instructional instrument, (2) to describe the process that created the script, and (3) to present insights about collaboration that emanated from this process.

THE PROCESS

The creation of the Readers' Theatre, titled "Not Just Smooth Sailing: Issues in Collaboration," unfolded over the course of 12 months. In the germinative stage of this project, we sought a metaphor that would characterize the breadth and depth of collaborative work. Eventually, we adopted the metaphor of a sailing adventure, with its various stages and challenges.

Writing

Approximately 12 out of 20 CCR members gathered to begin the writing process. Our first task was to review our own writings (Castle, Drake, & Boak, 1995; Drake & Basaraba, 1997; Haskins, 1996), and other literature (Fullan, 1993a, 1993b; Miller, 1990; Nias, 1987; Senge, 1990) for quotations that represented the sailing metaphor. Returning with pages of seemingly unrelated quotes, it became obvious that we needed to identify categories (Marshall & Rossman, 1995; Miles & Huberman, 1984). We divided the sailing metaphor into parts: "charting the course," "launching," "plain sailing," "becalmed," "storming," and finally, "recharting." We formed smaller groups, with each group taking one or two sections of the sailing metaphor, and resumed our search for relevant quotes.

As time passed and other agendas intervened, 7 of the original 12 people declared they were able and eager to continue to participate in the presentation. Three members of the group were then entrusted to transform the quoted passages into one coherent script. Eventually, they developed a script consisting of six voices and a narrator, and having completed their task, the writers passed the responsibility of shaping the script into a dramatic presentation to a new group of three.

Rehearsals

The first task of the production team was to create plausible characters for the script. Six personalities were created: "The Believer," "The Academic," "The Skeptic," "The Peacemaker," "The Keener," and "The Stressed." Each character's lines represented a distinctive response to collaboration.

Scripts in hand, we ventured forth to rehearse our performance. For some, expressing themselves on the stage felt natural, whereas others felt timid, and some even terrified. We agreed that the ambiance we desired could best be created in a "black box" classroom theater. Agreeing that a few key props would enrich the narrative, we chose sailing hats to represent group membership, a rope for slack and tension, a sail for progress, a map for direction, and a wheel for revolving leadership.

Because of time restrictions, each member of the production team assumed a specific responsibility for the rehearsals. One person took on the lengthy responsibility of scheduling, preparing the space, and interpreting the dialogue. Another created the soundtrack, located the props, and directed choreography, while the third assumed the role of narrator and became the stage director.

Once each person became familiar with her lines, we began to stage the production. This required a shift in the way we viewed the project, as the rehearsals required more artistic and less "academic" skills. Furthermore, the production team made it quite clear that this was a professional undertaking.

The Performance

By the time of the conference, we were well rehearsed and generally confident that not only did we have important information to share about the collaborative process, but that we were also breaking the traditional pattern for academic presentations. Our concerns now focused on how the performance would be received. Would this kind of presentation be taken seriously by our academic colleagues? Would the performance generate relevant discussion?

Our presentation began. The audience reacted; they laughed, applauded, frowned, and smiled. They responded emotionally and intellectually and each individual, on- or off-stage, was fully engaged.

The Post-Presentation Discussion

Throughout our rehearsals, we envisioned a lively post-presentation discussion. We hoped for equity among an audience composed of both school and university instructors, and rejected the notion that school teachers would address only practical issues while university professors would address only theoretical ones (Cornbleth & Ellsworth, 1994; Cuban, 1992; Lieberman, 1992a, 1992b; Miller, 1992). Thus, our narrator, a school-based teacher, facilitated a lively discussion in which both performers and audience participated. Positive comments were made regarding both the form and content of the performance.

Most surprising and rewarding, a number of individuals suggested that we should take the production "on the road" to perform at other conferences and schools. Thus, at the end, our energy was high, our confidence buttressed, and our friendships deepened.

The Aftermath

As is typical of our collaborative group, we gathered at a member's home to celebrate and to share a simple meal. We knew that repeating the performance was not a realistic option, given our busy professional and personal lives. We became convinced, however, that the script could be published in an academic forum and thus be made available to other educators.

INSIGHTS ABOUT COLLABORATION

As we reflected on and discussed the collaborative process that produced the performance, we realized that we had deepened our understanding of collaboration through connecting our own experiences with the literature (Gitlin et al., 1992; Olds, 1992). We believed that by grounding the literature in the process of producing this performance, collaboration had been illuminated in a new way, highlighting the themes of accommodation, inclusion, situational leadership, authorship, synergy, and breaking boundaries.

Accommodation

The above process occurred over a particularly harried year for educators. We were constantly required "to do more, do it better, and do it with less." At various times, individuals were unable to complete tasks. The project, however, proceeded, because at each stage accommodation occurred. We define accommodation as the ability to shift personal ways of working to achieve group goals. There was at least one person involved at each stage who was willing to assume extra responsibilities to ensure the completion of the task. For example, when one of the members of the writing team became ill, another member assumed her responsibilities. Little acrimony was voiced because there was group sympathy with work circumstances and a strong belief in the worthiness of this project.

We think that this accommodative process may be a central element of many successful collaborative relationships. Although some people tend to work in the same pattern regardless of the type of the task, others are able to adopt a more flexible way of working (Cornbleth & Ellsworth, 1994; Fullan, 1993a, 1993b). We have come to believe that the successful completion of a project may partially depend upon the accommodative ability of at least some of the collaborators.

Inclusion

As CCR members, we share the belief that everyone should feel welcome to participate in any group project, and that those present are the ones who are meant to be involved. This project challenged this belief, forcing us to look at the strengths and limitations of our "inclusive" pattern.

In the initial planning stages, we followed our usual policy, and people came and went from the project. However, once decisions related to writing, directing, and performing were made, inclusiveness was no longer possible. This modification of our former inclusive principle may have been related to the need to be as efficient as possible.

Fortunately, group identification was so strong that all members of the CCR felt successful regardless of whether they had participated in the production or not. This shared sense of pride grew from the sense that the production represented a compilation of the group's collaborative experiences (Hargreaves, Earl, & Ryan, 1996; Senge, 1990).

Situational Leadership

True collaborative relationships are not hierarchical in structure (Bickel & Hattrup, 1995; Helgesen, 1995); rather, partners are seen as equals with diverse areas of expertise. Yet, at times, a leader is necessary in order to accomplish specific tasks (Elliott & Woloshyn, 1996; Harris, 1994). This kind of revolving leadership we call "situational leadership."

Given that our production required various kinds of expertise, the emergence of knowledgeable leaders at various stages facilitated our success. For instance, when the three writers completed their task, the script was handed to three others who had experience with theater. They then assumed leadership for the project until the presentation. Another example of situational leadership occurred when the writers were challenged to find an appropriate dialogue for the storm scene. Another member, who was an expert in movement education, solved this problem by choreographing the storm through actions rather than words.

The respect we accord to the expertise of our partners is an important component of situational leadership (Helgesen, 1995; Wheatley, 1992). This was particularly evident with our director, who also served as script narrator. As she was a newer member of the CCR, we had not had occasion to view her as an "expert." "Being respected and followed," she said, "was a milestone, as I felt important to the group for the first time."

Our experience suggests that if situational leadership is to be successful, specific characteristics must be present in the collaborative relationship. First, it is essential to know the others' strengths and weaknesses. Second, respect and trust must be shared among the partners. And third, negotiation of tasks must be clear (Elliott & Woloshyn, 1997). Most important, if situational leadership is to strengthen a collaborative partnership, members must be willing to assume the leadership position when their particular strengths are required. Equally important, individuals must have the insight to step down when others' expertise is needed. We believe the ability to move in and out of a leadership position is a central tenet of genuine collaboration. The inability to do so may cause some collaborative projects to flounder or become hierarchical in nature.

Authorship

One dilemma emerging from this process was the order in which to place collaborators' names on the conference proceedings. A flat, equitable writing structure is not valued in academia (Boice, 1990; Moxley, 1992). Rather, conventional structure deems that the individual who contributes the most becomes the "first author," and the one who contributes the least becomes the "last author," with the former usually being more highly regarded. Our collaborative way of working made it impossible to determine who had worked hardest or who had made the most significant contribution. What was obvious was that some members had made minimal contributions. It was suggested that we could author using the name, "Centre on Collaborative Research," but this was an unacceptable solution to some. As a compromise, we placed all participants' names in reversed alphabetical order, although we realized that this solution was not totally satisfactory either. This issue remains an ongoing dilemma for the CCR, and we continue to experiment with different ways of addressing it.

Synergy

Synergy may be defined as a momentum or energy that is greater than the sum of its parts and that is far more conducive to feeling than to words. In this project, our commitment to shared beliefs, to each other, and to the performance created a synergy that none of us could have experienced alone. Individuals sustained one another. Everyone who was a part of the project appeared energized and connected. We knew that this endeavor was innovative and that it pushed professional boundaries. The effect of combining all of these elements was an invigorating synergy.

BREAKING BOUNDARIES

We believe that the value of working collaboratively is found in the new territory into which it leads. By participating in an untraditional academic format, members risked criticism. One member's vulnerability showed when she peeked out into the darkened theater to see a large audience expectantly waiting. She whispered to her colleague. "What am I doing here? How did this happen? I can't do this!" Her colleague responded, "This is collaboration—it takes you into new territory where you would never go on your own." This comment has remained with the group as a cornerstone for how collaboration can extend boundaries.

As we learned about sailing terminology, acting, and staging, we realized that we were also extending our understanding of the collaborative process. What began as a method of disseminating information became a method of gaining new knowledge.

Conclusion

In summary, we have presented here not only the collaborative process that created the script, but also the insights we gained as a result of this process. We, like others (Hollingsworth, 1992, Van Manen, 1990), have long believed that research has two layers: first, the content of the research project and second, reflections about the process. Additionally, we believe that the attached script may serve to stimulate lively discussion among other educators who are interested in finding more collaborative ways of working together. Such discussions are especially important given the mandate for schools and universities to form genuine collaborative relationships.

THEATER PRESENTATION: "NOT JUST SMOOTH SAILING" (A Metaphor for Collaboration)

CHARACTERS

Narrator

Teachers:	University Professors:
Skeptic	Believer
Peacemaker	Stressed
Keener	Academic

Black stage boxes are set out on opposite sides of the stage—three each in triangle formations. A black bench is placed on its side at the front of the stage. Props are hidden behind it. Teachers and university professors enter from opposite sides of the stage, one at a time, and take a seat on the boxes doing various activities related to their professions. All are wearing sweatshirts with university names. When all are in place, narrator rises at stage right. When not speaking, Narrator sits on a chair off-stage at the right front.

INTRODUCTION

NAR: Once upon a time, teachers and researchers were like ships that passed in the night . . . they did not dialogue. . . . But one day, they began to talk . . . let's see what happens.

University professors freeze.
Teachers talking to each other:

SKEPTIC: The Common Curriculum, outcomes-based planning, new assessment strategies, integrated learning . . . and now collaborative action research . . . these changes create a lot of stress . . . I don't understand them . . . I can't do it alone.

PEACEMAKER: I've worked with others on small projects. It's a comfort to know you don't have to come up with all the ideas yourself.

KEENER: We're in this for the students, right? How can we make learning better for them? We need to see the value of learning together. By working with other teachers and other researchers, we would be modeling the process for them.

PEACE: The changes we are being asked to make are huge. We have to rely on our collective strength to get through.

SKEPTIC: It's going to take a lot of time to work as a group, because we are very different people.

PEACE: But if we are committed . . .

KEENER: If we trust each other in the process . . . we will get there.

Teachers freeze.
University professors talking to each other:

BELIEVER: Traditionally, we have used a theory-into-practice model of research that has generated a knowledge base for teachers.

STRESSED: There is always pressure on us to publish our research.

ACADEMIC: I have always prided myself on my pursuit of absolutely context-free theory.

BELIEVER: Maybe it's time we challenged the narrow standards on which our expertise is based.

STRESSED: Perhaps one of the agents of change is the practitioner?

BELIEVER: Yes, research on teacher development that does not have direct relevance or benefit to classroom practice, and that doesn't take into account the complexities of teaching and classroom life is of limited value.

On the word "teachers," the teachers react and look at the professors.

ACADEMIC: Perhaps Patti Lather [1991] was right when she claimed that teachers have a moral right to participate in decisions about themselves.

BELIEVER: If we are to effectively collaborate with teachers in order to generate knowledge from action, then we are going to have to break out of our traditional roles and relationships.

ACADEMIC: We must learn to remain open about our research designs and procedures, and be willing to participate with teachers as they try to make meaning of what they do in order to close the gap between theory and practice.

STRESSED: Yes, I agree, we must be careful that the agenda includes the teachers.

BELIEVER: Collaboration with teachers represents an important opportunity to connect with the world of practice in a more extensive and intensive way.

As the next few lines are said, the speakers stand and address each other and then move their boxes into place to create the ship, basically a "V" shape around the stage.

KEENER: Who will lead?

ACADEMIC: We need a shared dialogue.

PEACE: Who's agenda will we follow?

STRESSED: We will have multiple perspectives.

SKEPTIC: What do we have to offer one another?

BELIEVER: We may be surprised.

Sweatshirts come off, revealing striped or colorful t-shirts underneath, ready for work.

NAR: Our crew is in place now, but they will certainly need to make a lot of decisions. Where will they go? Who will do what?

Narrator walks on stage and collects shirts, except from the Skeptic, who ties hers around her waist. All crew go to the front of the stage where they collect their "Tilley" hats and put them on.

THEME ONE: SETTING GOALS

PEACE: Many believe that a partnership between a school and a university will benefit both institutions.

KEENER: We may have slightly different objectives, but they are complementary in nature.

BELIEVER: Collaboration takes time . . . it's really hard to rechart a course when the ship is sailing. The time to chart is when you can put the boat in the harbor and get all your sailors together.

NAR: Really, it is a coming together of minds . . . to get a sense of where each of them is coming from . . . where they want to go . . . and how they get to a better place.

Narrator walks to center stage, picks up a coiled rope from behind a bench, and hands it to Believer. Crew all undo the rope and help place it across the front of the stage.

KEENER: We just knew that if we kept plotting, somehow the best course would emerge.

THEME TWO: NEGOTIATING THE TASKS

NAR: The decision to sail together can force a great deal of negotiation.

ACADEMIC: The relationship between classroom teachers and university researchers must be multifaceted and not powerfully hierarchical.

PEACE: Effective collaboration requires breaking out of traditional roles and relationships.

BELIEVER: Greater possibilities seem to emerge when the responsibility is shared.

KEENER: To work together toward the goal is essential.

SKEPTIC: How can you provide holistic experiences if everybody isn't on board and if everybody isn't part of the team?

PEACE: Everybody should have a part in the planning and in the delivery.

ACADEMIC: The dilemma of equity in participation is a persistent one. Given the differences in our day-to-day professional lives, roles, and responsibilities, is it reasonable to expect equal involvement in all aspects of partnership?

PEACE: As long as responsibilities and tasks are negotiated and mutually agreed upon, doesn't it make sense that time, opportunity, and personal preference are key factors in the decision about who does what?

All crew now begin various tasks. Keener and Academic go to the map at the front of the ship . . . Believer gets the wheel in place. Stressed and Peacemaker put the sail in place, but not up yet. Skeptic watches all with dismay.

NAR: (*when all crew are actively engaged, narrator steps into place; crew freeze*) Now that the ship is ready, someone needs to be at the helm. In days gone by the captain commanded a subservient and dependent crew as they sailed off into dangers and uncharted waters. In collaboration, how will the leadership issue be resolved? Who captains the ship? Who guides, charts, inspires, sustains, and forges ahead? Who steers today? And who tomorrow? How many at a time? What happens when there is no one at the helm?

PEACE: A crew without a leader is not necessarily a crew without leadership.

BELIEVER: Leadership involves tension between stepping in and knowing when to let go.

ACADEMIC: This tension is a problem of balance between freedom and responsibility . . .

PEACE: . . . between personal initiative and the respect for a group process.

KEENER: Leadership has to be inviting rather than enforcing.

ACADEMIC: The leader in one context may be the follower in another. There is the potential for leadership in all people.

SKEPTIC: I am new to the process, and I am afraid to act lest I appear to take over the group. I wonder, when is it leadership and when is it power? (*stands as these lines are said and moves one foot up onto box at front of stage*)

STRESSED: Oh, the guilt. If I assume too much power in my leadership, I'm destroying the process; if I hold back, I'm not giving my best.

PEACE: A leader has to hear the different voices in order to assess critically what the group does.

NAR: A different understanding of leadership has emerged. Leadership is *always* dependent on the context, but the context is established by the *relationships* we value.

BELIEVER: In genuine collaboration, leadership revolves, is emergent and shared.

ACADEMIC: The art of leadership involves sizing up the players, assessing the needs, and crafting suitable strategies.

CHARTING

The map is placed on the floor in the center of the ship. All look at it, move away, cast glances off in different directions, and return to the map to look again. Freeze in a position with all pointing in different directions.

NAR: Before any journey starts, a course must be charted, but the initial path is rarely definitive (*pointing at crew*). The crew must rechart their course several times throughout its journey.

BELIEVER: For research to be truly collaborative, it needs to be a process of ongoing negotiation.

ACADEMIC: Collaboration is a paradox that can be a stalemate or a catalyst for negotiation and renegotiation.

KEENER: The paradox is creative, vital, and powerful.

PEACE: No one knows where we are going, but everyone knows explicitly that there is movement toward a destination, and everyone shares a vision of both the goal and the process of achieving it. The route, however, is not rigidly defined, but constantly negotiated.

BELIEVER: One of the most persistent myths about collaboration is that it requires consensus. This is emphatically not so. Collaborators constantly bicker and argue. For the most part, these arguments are not personal, but focus on genuine areas of disagreement.

NAR: (*from a seated position, look toward crew*) Then who charts the course?

ALL: We all do.

RECHARTING

Everyone takes a new job. It is important that everyone have a turn at the helm. Indications are given that the ship is about to move forward. The sail is put up. Throughout this next scene, people keep exchanging jobs and moving about the ship. A sound effects tape of moving through the water begins.

NAR: To keep the process afloat, collaboration may need to leave some behind, bring some on board, attend to those who are having difficulty, and continue to challenge those who are too comfortable.

ACADEMIC: The negotiation and renegotiation in the collaborative process can bridge the gap between the efficient and the humane.

PEACE: Those who wish to modify professional knowledge must recognize that the unlearning of established ways of perceiving, and the learning and practice of new ways, is a lengthy, hard, and potentially painful process, in which the challenge and support of others play a crucial role.

KEENER: A minor spark can change the group. Not just the powerful have influence.

BELIEVER: We live in changing times; the waters and winds eddy and swirl in new ways and are fraught with new dangers and new possibilities. All hands who come aboard are valuable and the right ones for the journey . . .

STRESSED: . . . Each one has a vision that will be further developed by working with others.

SKEPTIC: I don't understand how this working with others creates the context for leadership roles.

PEACE: Our research together creates the spaces in which we find the support and encouragement to speak . . .

STRESSED: . . . to voice our concerns and our hesitations about the limits and possibilities of our collaboration . . .

KEENER: . . . and its extensions into our daily educational lives.

BELIEVER: Our collaboration also enables us to hear how our voices are constantly emerging, subsiding, and reemerging, creating a revolving sense of leadership.

BECALMED

All sit, not looking at one another . . . each speech is slow and deliberate . . . there are long pauses . . . voices are somewhat flat and uninteresting.

NAR: Our crew is on track now, they know where they are going, they have addressed the issue of leadership. Everyone knows what to do. However, as we all know, sometimes, on a ship, the wind dies, and the ship stops moving forward for a time.

SKEPTIC: We have a lot of trouble finding the time to meet face-to-face. It takes so much time to consult with everyone and meet everybody's needs. And personalities can often be excessive (*looking directly at Keener*) and inefficient (*looking directly at Stressed*).

STRESSED: I feel very guilty through most of this because I don't give it enough of my time and attention.

KEENER: Emerging visions can die because people get overwhelmed and lose their focus.

PEACE: Visions can also die because people become discouraged by the apparent difficulty in bringing the vision into reality.

BELIEVER: People become disheartened . . .

SKEPTIC: . . . uncertain . . .

ACADEMIC: . . . even cynical . . .

BELIEVER: leading to a decline in enthusiasm.

KEENER: There is no energy here. Sometimes it feels like you work and work in a vacuum, against the current.

NAR: It is in this period of silence that people can contemplate themselves and their fellow crew members. From these contemplations, dark clouds can develop, threatening a storm.

   Sounds of rain begin. As this scene progresses, the crew become more and more agitated. They begin to stand and move about, not looking at one another and disagreeing with what each speaker says.

PEACE: On some occasions, the actions of my partners surprise me, disappoint me, and provoke me.

SKEPTIC: I have to ask myself some hard questions about collaboration.

ACADEMIC: To what extent is our collaborative research self-serving or even not collaborative?

KEENER: Perhaps we have romanticized the concept, or been too idealistic, and are content to merely pay lip service to it?

STRESSED: Maybe I expect too much of collaboration, or have intentions that are unrealistic.

SKEPTIC: (*moving away from the others*) I need space . . . and time alone.

ACADEMIC: How willing am I to address the times when personal gain, reputation, security, or promotion lure me back to conventional structures and competitive power struggles?

PEACE: Part of having a strong sense of self is to be accountable for one's actions. No matter how we explore motives or lack of motives, we are what we do (*looking directly at Skeptic*).

BELIEVER: Collaborating includes listening . . . really listening to others, and trying to find something in what they say or believe that is the same as our own beliefs. It can be a soul-searching, heart-rending exercise.

THE STORM

As the wind and low rumbling sound begin to pick up, the crew move from their seats and look fore and aft, starboard and port side in a concerned manner. They freeze in those positions as the narrator speaks.

NAR: Storms are inevitable. Every crew needs to develop the skills and strategies so that the ship and crew members survive the storms and the voyage can continue. A storm is a crisis that can have a variety of causes:

Do they trust one another enough to address the times when collaboration doesn't feel like collaboration?

Are they tired of waiting around for everyone to be convinced that this will work?

Are they just plain fed up with one another?

Is there so little time that they become completely frustrated with aborted efforts?

Let's see how our crew fares when the storm hits.

Sounds heighten. There are two cracks of thunder that send the crew reeling from side to side of the ship. From this point until the storm sounds subside, the crew frantically work together in a rhythmic pattern to do various jobs like bailing the ship and manning the wheel. When the sounds end they look skyward and stop their frantic motion. Freeze.

PLAIN SAILING AGAIN

NAR: The reality of lack of funds, lack of time, altered agendas, and disagreements could have sunk this ship, but they didn't . . . Why not? (*asking the crew*)

BELIEVER: It was the process of genuine collaboration that provided the support we needed to survive.

KEENER: We have learned to interact constructively and appreciate one another.

SKEPTIC: I am beginning to understand how involvement becomes commitment and collaboration becomes very important on a personal level.

ACADEMIC: Now that we are aligned, a common direction has emerged and individual energies have harmonized.

STRESSED: I have a strong desire to avoid letting the others down.

All begin moving together now, close to the wheel.

ACADEMIC: There has to be a commitment to the goals of the voyage . . .

PEACE: . . . to the crew . . .

BELIEVER: . . . and to the idea of collaboration itself.

NAR: (*moving toward center stage behind the bench*) A finely tuned collaborative group is not just a "think tank." It is a flexible, interdependent team in which each member has been a . . . (*Narrator is interrupted as the crew speak for her, she turns and looks directly at them*)

BELIEVER: a leader . . .

STRESSED: a follower . . .

SKEPTIC: a dissenter . . .

KEENER: a promoter . . .

PEACE: an insider . . .

ACADEMIC: and an outsider.

NAR: This results in a connection where each member is valued and in which the whole is greater than the sum of its parts. But I wonder, how will this affect learning in the classroom?

The performance ends with an open discussion and question-and-answer period with the audience.

REFERENCES

Bickel, W. E., & Hattrup, R. A. (1995). Teachers and researchers in collaboration: Reflections on the process. *American Educational Research Journal, 32*(1), 35–62.

Boice, R. (1990). *Professors as writers: A self-help guide to productive writing.* Stillwater, OK: New Forums Press.

Castle, J. (1997). Rethinking mutual goals in school–university collaboration. In H. Christiansen, L. Goulet, C. Krentz, & M. Maeers (Eds.), *Recreating relationships: Collaboration and educational reform* (pp. 59–67). Albany: State University of New York Press.

Castle, J., Drake, S., & Boak, T. (1995). Collaborative reflection as professional development. *Review of Higher Education, 18*(3), 242–262.

Coger, L. I., & White, M. R. (1973). *Readers' theatre handbook: A dramatic approach to literature.* Chicago: Scott, Foresman and Company.

Cornbleth, C., & Ellsworth, J. (1994). Teachers in teacher education: Clinical faculty roles and relationships. *American Educational Research Journal, 31*(1), 49–70.

Cuban, L. (1992). Managing dilemmas while building professional communities. *Educational Researcher, 21*(1), 4–11.

Drake, S., & Basaraba, J. (1997). School–university research partnership: In search of the essence. In H. Chistiansen, L. Goulet, C. Krentz, & M. Maeers (Eds.), *Recreating relationships: Collaboration and educational reform* (pp. 209–218). Albany: State University of New York Press.

Elliott A. E., & Drake, S. M. (1995). Moving from "two solitudes" towards a "blended" culture in school/university partnerships. *Journal of Staff, Program and Organizational Development, 13*(2), 85–95.

Elliott, A., & Woloshyn, V. (1996). Adopting collaborative learning strategies in the classroom. *The Canadian School Executive, 15*(9), 3–9.

Elliott, A., & Woloshyn, V. (1997). Some female professors' perceptions of collaboration: Mapping the collaborative process through rough terrain. *Alberta Journal of Educational Research, 43*(1), 23–36.

Fullan, M. (1993a). *Change forces: Probing the depths of educational reform.* Bristol, PA: Falmer Press.

Fullan, M. (1993b). Why teachers must become change agents. *Educational Leadership, 50*(6), 12–17.

Gitlin, A., Bringhurst, K., Burns, M., Cooley, V., Myers, B., Price, K., Russell, R., & Tiess, P. (1992). *Teachers' voices for school change.* New York: Teachers' College Press.

Hargreaves, A., Earl, L., & Ryan, J. (1996). *Schooling for change.* Washington, DC: Falmer Press.

Harris, C. (1994). Discovering educational leadership in connections: Dr. Elizabeth Murray of Tatamagouche. *Canadian Journal of Education, 19*(4), 368–385.

Haskins, B. (1996). *Collaborative action research for teachers: A qualitative report on a specific project.* Unpublished masters' project, Brock University, St. Catharines, Ontario, Canada.

Helgesen, S. (1995). *The female advantage: Women's ways of leadership.* New York: Currency Doubleday.

Hollingsworth, S. (1992). Learning to teach through collaborative conversation. *American Educational Research Journal, 29*(2), 373–404.

Lather, P. (1991). *Getting smart: Feminist research and pedagogy with/in the postmodern.* New York: Routledge.

Lieberman, A. (1992a). The meaning of scholarly activity and the building of community. *Educational Researcher, 21*(6), 5–12.

Lieberman, A. (1992b, October). School/university collaboration: A view from the inside. *Phi Delta Kappan,* 147–156.

Marshall, C., & Rossman, G. B. (1995). *Designing qualitative research* (2nd ed.). London: Sage.

Miles, M. B., & Huberman, A. M. (1984). *Qualitative data analysis.* London: Sage.

Miller, J. (1990). *Creating spaces and finding voices: Teachers collaborating for empowerment.* Albany: State University of New York Press.

Miller, J. (1992). Exploring power and authority issues in a collaborative research project. *Theory and Practice, 31*(2), 165–172.

Moxley, J. (1992). *Writing and publishing for academic authors.* Lanham, MD: University Press of America.

Nias, J. (1987). Learning from difference: A collegial approach to change. In J. Smyth (Ed.), *Educating teachers: Changing the nature of pedagogical knowledge* (pp. 137–154). London: Falmer Press.

Olds, L. (1992). *Metaphors of interrelatedness.* Albany: State University of New York Press.

Senge, P. (1990). *The fifth discipline: The art and practice of the learning organization.* New York: Currency/Doubleday.

Stewart, H. J. (1996, Spring). Collaboration: Towards improved education practice: Lessons learned from Brock University's Centre of Collaborative Research. *Education Canada, 36*(1) 20–25.

Stewart, H. J. (1997). Metaphors of interrelatedness: Principles of collaboration. In H. Christiansen, L. Goulet, C. Krentz, & M. Maeers (Eds.), *Recreating re-*

lationships: Collaboration and educational reform (pp. 27–53). Albany: State University of New York Press.

Van Manen, M. (1990). *Researching lived experience*. London: The Althouse Press.

Wheatley, M. J. (1992). *Leadership and the new science*. San Francisco: Berrett-Koehler.

Index

About the Contributors

SHARON ABBEY is a professor in the Faculty of Education, Brock University, St. Catharines, Ontario, where she teaches courses in Language Arts, Holistic Education, and Women's Studies and supervises teacher candidates in their practicum placements. She is a founding member of the Centre of Collaborative Research at Brock University, president of the Canadian Association for Studies on Women in Education, and co-editor of two books on changing images and identities of motherhood. Dr. Abbey's experiences as an educator include twenty years as an elementary school principal, curriculum consultant, and classroom teacher. She looks forward to continuing her collaboration with faculty colleagues on narrative inquiry and personal storytelling.

JOYCE B. CASTLE is an associate professor in the Faculty of Education at Brock University where she teaches curriculum courses in language arts at the pre-service and in-service levels and also works with beginning and veteran teachers to promote professional growth. Prior to completing her doctorate she was a classroom teacher and also a special education consultant at the elementary school level. Her research interests and publications focus on literacy development, professional development, school–university collaboration, and gender issues within these contexts.

SUSAN M. DRAKE teaches in the graduate department at Brock University. Her research interests revolve around holistic education and interdisciplinarity. She worked in school systems in a number of different roles including facilitator, researcher, and teacher. She found that implementation of such approaches involved collaborative efforts among educators (and often a wider community). These experiences focused her attention on collaborative processes. Dr. Drake was a founding member of the Brock Faculty of Education Centre on Collaborative Research.

ANNE ELLIOTT is an associate professor in Brock University's Faculty of Education in St. Catharines, Ontario, where her primary focus is teaching pre-service and beginning teachers. She teaches courses in Language, Children's Literature, Teaching Methods, and Motivation. Dr. Elliott's research interests, conference presentations, and publications focus on topics related to narrative as a way of knowing, literacy, professional growth, collaboration, teacher education, and the nature of strategy instruction in classrooms.

SUSAN GIBSON has always enjoyed taking a collaborative approach to whatever she is involved in. She is currently an associate professor in the Department of Elementary Education at the University of Alberta. Dr. Gibson's area of specialization is social studies curriculum and instruction. Her research interests include the integration of technology in social studies and the role of technology in teacher education.

BEV HASKINS has been an elementary school educator for many years. At present she is a principal with the District School Board of Niagara. Her passions in life are swimming, drama in education, and promoting action research as a viable means of teacher supervision and growth. At present she is involved in several pilot projects in this area.

KAREN KRUG trained in ethics and teaches in an environment program. Her interest in collaborative learning arises from her commitments to social justice. Participating in informal educational experiences such as international exposure trips and service projects provided her with a passion for creative, learner-centered education. Dr. Krug is still finding ways to harness the energy of students to enrich their learning in more formal settings. She especially enjoys teaching when students are clear about how their passions might shape their educational endeavours.

LINDA L. LANG is an assistant professor of Drama Education in the Arts Education Program, Faculty of Education, University of Regina. Her doctoral research used collaborative action research within the context of a school–university partnership to support and encourage classroom teachers to become innovative risk takers.

JESSIE LEES is a freelance researcher and independent scholar. Her academic interest in beginning teacher induction programs began when she worked with Florence Samson on an Atlantic study. She has worked in the areas of school computer use, narrative inquiry, and women and power. At present, she is part of a project of the Canadian School Boards Association that looks at ways in which schools can and are attempting to alleviate the effects of child poverty. This phase of the project is about mobilizing the community, and collaboration is a major theme. She is deeply impressed by the work that is being done by principals, teachers, students, and parents acting together, as well as by interagency partnerships. In the face of budgetary restrictions and overwhelming work loads, collaboration has enabled action.

CORAL MITCHELL is an associate professor in the Faculty of Education at Brock University, St. Catharines, Ontario. Her primary teaching and research interests are in the area of educational change and school renewal. From that foundation, she has considered issues related to educational leadership, professional development, and organizational learning. One of the elements that has been central to Dr. Mitchell's work is the profound influence of reflexive reflective practice, at both the individual and the group level and by educators at all levels of the institution, on professional practice and school development.

NORAH MORGAN became an adjunct professor of Drama and Theatre in Education at Brock University in St. Catharines, Ontario, from which she has retired five times. Like the operatic Soprano, she keeps giving a final "performance." Dr. Morgan is co-author, with J. Saxton, of two books, *Teaching Drama* and *Asking Better Questions*. As a member of the International Drama in Education Research Institute (I.D.I.E.R.I), a scholarship was created in her name for Research in Collaboration between Teachers in the Classroom and University Professors. She is currently writing a third book on the value of intuition as a form of knowing in drama and education.

NANCY MURRAY teaches movement education in the Department of Physical Education at Brock University. With a passion for progressive curricula and sensitive pedagogy, she is constantly seeking collaborative ventures to enhance her understanding of the phenomenon. She engages in a varied array of projects that require collaboration: co-authoring a textbook (*Children and Movement: Physical Education in the Elementary School*), teaching and researching with university colleagues, developing curriculum with school physical education teachers, and assisting students of all ages to collaborate in the choreography of their movement sequences. Dr. Murray choreographed the movement of her colleagues for the performance of "Not Just Smooth Sailing: Issues in Collaboration." This experience, coupled with her participation in the Centre on Collaborative Research, precipitated her interest in exploring, with Dr. Merle Richards, how the academic content situated within various contexts influences the collaborative process for both men and women.

DIANNE OBERG has benefited from the wisdom of mentors in schools as well as in academia. Her work in mentoring graduate students is one way she says thanks to her mentors. Currently she is professor and chair of the Department of Elementary Education at the University of Alberta. Dr. Oberg's area of specialization is school librarianship. Her research interests include inquiry-based learning and the role of the principal in program implementation.

ROSEMARIE PELZ has worked on a number of research projects in elementary education at the University of Alberta. Dr. Susan Gibson's and Dr. Dianne Oberg's Internet project provided her with a meaningful introduction to the research community and the research process. She is nearing completion of her doctoral work in curriculum and instruction. Her work focuses on print media and the shaping of public understanding of educational issues, particularly those related to curriculum.

MERLE RICHARDS is an associate professor in the Faculty of Education at Brock University. She has conducted research and taught in teacher education programs for aboriginal communities as well as in regular university programs. Specializing in language teaching, Dr. Richards has collaborated in research on strategies and perceptions of language, learners, and teachers.

ALICE SCHUTZ teaches Curriculum and Adult Education in the Graduate Department of the Faculty of Education. She has been with the Brock Centre on Collaborative Research since its beginning. Dr. Schutz's focus on collaborative mentoring grew out of her research on creativity and role modeling.

SUSAN SYDOR is an assistant professor in the Faculty of Education at Brock University, St. Catharines, Ontario, where she teaches undergraduate and graduate courses; her primary assignment is teaching in the pre-service program. Her research interests, conference presentations, and publications focus on topics related to education law, leadership, and teacher education. Prior to her appointment to the Faculty of Education, Dr. Sydor worked as a teacher educator at the Faculty of Education, University of Toronto, and as an elementary school teacher. Her interest in collaboration stems from her commitment to educational reform. Currently, she is working on a project to integrate technology into pre-service education.

VIANNE TIMMONS, the dean of Education at the University of Prince Edward Island, has a strong commitment to collaboration and to the teaching profession. Dr. Timmons engages in numerous research partnerships and community partnerships and is well aware of the benefits and challenges of working collaboratively.

ANDREA TOEPELL, is an assistant professor in the Department of Community Health Science at Brock University in Ontario, Canada. Dr. Toepell's research and teaching interests include population health, health promotion, gender and health, aging women and sport, health among marginalized populations, and teaching and learning in higher education.

VERA WOLOSHYN is an associate professor in the Faculty of Education at Brock University where she is also a member of the Centre on Collaborative Research. Her research interests are varied and include the investigation of effective learning strategies and teaching techniques. She has been the recipient of several national research grants including SSHRC (also the Community University Research Alliance [CURA]), Trillium, the Government of Ontario, and the Office of Learning Technology. Dr. Woloshyn has edited several books and published numerous papers pertaining to her research and role as a faculty member at Brock University.

DOUG ZOOK has experienced the value of collaboration through school experiences and graduate work. Exploring collaborative efforts with his colleagues is important to him. At the time of writing he was a doctoral student in the Faculty of Education at the University of Alberta. He is currently an assistant professor in the Department of Teacher Education at Goshen College. His area of specialization is social studies curriculum and instruction. His research interests include citizenship education as related to popular culture, psychoanalysis, and critical pedagogy.